HOUSING FOR THE ELDERLY
THE DEVELOPMENT AND DESIGN PROCESS

HOUSING FOR THE ELDERLY
THE DEVELOPMENT AND DESIGN PROCESS

Isaac Green

Bernard E. Fedewa · Charles A. Johnston

William M. Jackson · Howard L. Deardorff

VNR **VAN NOSTRAND REINHOLD COMPANY**
NEW YORK   CINCINNATI   ATLANTA   DALLAS   SAN FRANCISCO
LONDON   TORONTO   MELBOURNE

Van Nostrand Reinhold Company Regional Offices:
New York   Cincinnati   Chicago   Milbrae   Dallas

Van Nostrand Reinhold Company International Offices:
London   Toronto   Melbourne

Copyright © 1975 by The Michigan State Housing Development Authority, Lansing, Michigan

Library of Congress Catalog Card Number: **75-11630**
ISBN : 0-442-22833-3

All rights reserved. Certain portions of this work copyright © 1974 by the Michigan State Housing Development Authority, Lansing, Michigan. No part of this work covered by the copyright hereon may be reproduced or used in any form or by any means—graphic, electronic, or mechanical, including photocopying, recording, taping, or information storage and retrieval systems—without permission of the Michigan State Housing Development Authority and the publisher.

Manufactured in the United States of America

Published by Van Nostrand Reinhold Company
135 West 50th Street, New York, N.Y. 10020

Published simultaneously in Canada by Van Nostrand Reinhold Ltd.

15 14 13 12 11 10 9 8 7 6 5 4 3

Library of Congress Cataloging in Publication Data

Main entry under title:

Housing for the elderly.

   Published in 1974 under title: Housing for the elderly: development process
  Bibliography: p.
  Includes index.
  1. Aged—Dwellings. I. Green, Isaac.
HD7287.9.H69   301.5'4   75-11630
ISBN 0-442-22833-3

foreword

Serious attention has been given to the housing of older Americans for only the last two decades. During this brief period, however, much has been learned about the subject through both research and experience. In any new field such as housing the elderly, there is a need for the facts, principles, and conclusions that accumulate bit by bit to be systematized periodically in order to provide a measure of progress and give direction to their applications. The authors of *Housing for the Elderly: The Development and Design Process* have achieved this task with notable success.

Beginning with a careful study of the literature, the authors have made current what is known about the characteristics of older people, particularly as related to their special needs and preferences in living arrangements. They have also identified the principles of design and environment which satisfy these needs and wishes. By casting their exposition in the framework of the developmental process, the authors have provided a step-by-step guide which is equally useful to professional planners, architects, designers, developers, and sponsoring laymen who must share a common set of concepts and vocabulary if they are to communicate effectively among themselves in bringing their efforts to a successful conclusion.

The authors have made a clear distinction between housing for the elderly and nursing homes or other care institutions. Wisely, they have left the latter to the initiatives of the providers of medical care facilities and have confined the guide to those types of shelter, environments, and services required to support independent lifestyles of tenants. Independence is treated in the book as including two levels: (1) that which requires ability to cope fully with demands of everyday living, and (2) that which is possible only if a special setting of congregate housing complete with a program of personal, social, and health services, short of full medical care, is made available. In *Housing for the Elderly: The Development and Design Process,* these two groups are discussed separately and guidance in site selection, design, standards, and programs are offered for both levels of independent living. The book is especially timely because currently many sponsors of elderly housing are concerned about the growing number of elderly tenants in their developments who need some level of aided living which cannot be provided satisfactorily in projects designed for fully independent elderly tenants. Sponsors who are seeking aid in planning this new type of facility will find this book a tremendously helpful guide.

The current emphasis on state and local planning inherent in the new federalism and revenue sharing, and the inclusion of consumers in the planning process adds to the importance of this book. It is a handbook which local development teams can use in presenting the needs of the elderly and in securing support for well-conceived projects. The book also constitutes a much needed addition to the instructional resources required in the training of architects and planners and in the preparation of managers of elderly housing. Community service organizations seeking to understand how they can best serve the elderly in housing developments will find that the handbook is essential to their planning. In short, the book raises the housing of the elderly to a new level of professionalism.

Wilma T. Donahue, Ph.D.
Director
International Center for Social Gerontology

Director Emeritus
Institute of Gerontology
The University of Michigan
Ann Arbor, Michigan

preface

This book is an outgrowth of the formulation of a development and design process for elderly housing prepared by the authors for the Michigan State Housing Development Authority.

Most often, this form of housing consists of medium- and high-rise structures. As a result, this book tends to reflect this trend toward higher density housing for the elderly. Nevertheless, other building types, such as low-rise apartments, townhouses, and single family houses are also appropriate and sometimes even preferable for the elderly. In an earlier book, *Townhouse Development Process,* published by the Michigan State Housing Development Authority in 1970, we established guidelines for the development and design of townhouses and apartments. Therefore, where we felt it would be repetitious to enumerate design principles for low density housing, we have referred to this earlier work.

While the original orientation of this book was concerned with housing for elderly persons with low and moderate incomes, much of the background information and conclusions about elderly needs and lifestyles as well as the analysis and recommendations about dwelling unit design and broad functional organization of the development is applicable to elderly persons of all income levels.

We are hopeful that the development and design process which we have defined will help to discourage disfunctional thinking by designers and developers. We are also hopeful that, because of this publication, the work of the development team will be characterized by knowledge, creativity, and sensitivity, culminating in quality housing for the elderly.

While this book is meant to be used as a reference and guide, it can also serve as a comprehensive overview when read from cover to cover. It is not the ultimate or, for that matter, the only process for creating successful housing for the elderly, but is rather intended to be a good beginning.

Isaac Green, A.I.A.
Deputy Executive Director
Michigan State Housing Development Authority
Lansing, Michigan

Bernard E. Fedewa
Manager, New Development
Michigan State Housing Development Authority
Lansing, Michigan

Charles A. Johnston, A.I.A.
O'Dell, Hewlett & Luckenbach, Inc.
Architects, Engineers, and Planners
Birmingham, Michigan

William M. Jackson
Beckett Jackson Raeder Inc
Land Planning, Landscape Architecture and Applied Research
Ann Arbor, Michigan

Howard L. Deardorff, A.S.L.A.
Beckett Jackson Raeder Inc
Land Planning, Landscape Architecture and Applied Research
Ann Arbor, Michigan

special acknowledgements

The authors acknowledge the special contributions obtained from the following resources:

Central Mortgage and Housing Corporation
Ottawa, Canada

Environmental Research and Aging, May 13-15, 1973, St. Louis, Mo. Conference sponsored by the Gerontological Society, Washington, D.C.

Guide Criteria for the Design and Evaluation of Operation Breakthrough Housing Systems, vol. 2, "Multifamily Low Rise." Washington, D.C.: U.S. Department of Commerce, National Bureau of Standards, September 1970.

"Housing Design Criteria." New York, N.Y.: New York State Urban Development Corporation.

International Symposium on Housing and Environmental Design for Older Adults, December 11-14, 1973, Washington, D.C. Conference sponsored by the International Center for Social Gerontology, Washington, D.C.

Institute of Gerontology
University of Michigan—Wayne State University
Ann Arbor, Michigan

Kaplan, Stephen. "The Challenge of Environmental Psychology: A Proposal for a New Functionalism." *American Psychologist,* vol. 27: 140-143, 1972; and "Cognitive Maps in Perception and Thought." In R. M. Downs and D. Stea, eds., *Images and Environment.* Chicago: Aldine, 1973, pages 63-78.

Locational Criteria for Housing for the Elderly. Philadelphia: City Planning Commission, December 1968.

Pastalan, Leon A., and Carson, Daniel H., eds. *Spatial Behavior of Older People.* Ann Arbor: The University of Michigan Press, 1970.

Townhouse Development Process. Lansing, Mich.: Michigan State Housing Development Authority, 1970.

The authors also wish to acknowledge the following persons:

Nancy Leiserowitz, for her photographs which enhance this publication.

Frances Garelick, for her invaluable editorial contribution.

contents

Foreword

Preface

Introduction   1
   The Development Team   2
   Organization   3

Programming   5
   Intent and Organization   5
   Elderly Needs and Lifestyles   10
   Development Size and Dwelling Unit Mix   14
   Overall Site Spatial Requirements   15
   Development Density   15
   Dwelling Unit Sizes, Related Ancillary, and Common Spaces   18
   Major Activity Components and Floor Areas   21
      Dwelling Unit Activity Floor Areas   21
      Ancillary Activities and Facilities   23
      Common Activities and Facilities   24
   Amenities   27
   Conclusion   27

Site Selection   29
   Intent and Organization   29
   Elderly Needs   29
   The Community/Region   31
   The Neighborhood   33
      Urban Neighborhood Sites   34
      Suburban Neighborhood Sites   36
      Small Town Neighborhood Sites   37
      Proximity to Services and Opportunities for Community/Social Involvement   38
   The Site   42
      Site Size, Frontage and Configuration, and Topography   42
      Density   43
      Adjacent Land Use Compatibility   44
   Conclusion   44

Design   45
   Intent and Organization   45
   Human Needs and the Aging Process   46
   Development Activity Components   50
      Site Activities   50
      Building Activities   56
      Dwelling Unit Activities   70
      Functional Organization of Activities   91
   Development Design   109
      Design Determinants   110
      Design Expression   116

Building Efficiency Guidelines   127
5 Technical Standards   129
    Intent   129
    Site Grading   130
    Paving   131
    Planting   132
    Lighting   133
    Recreation Facilities   133
    Outdoor Furniture   133
    Trash Removal and Service   134
    Signing   135
        Outdoor Signs   136
        Indoor Signs   137
    Circulation   138
        Corridors   138
        Stairs   140
        Ramps   140
        Elevators   141
        Doors and Access Openings   141
    Natural Light and Ventilation   143
    Acoustic Control   144
        Design and Construction   **144**
    Ceiling Heights   146
    Surfaces   147
        Floors and Flooring   147
        Walls and Ceilings   147
    Food Preparation Equipment   148
        Minimum Standards   **148**
        Optimum Standards   150
    Personal Hygiene Equipment   151
    Mail Equipment   153
    Emergency Systems   154
    Mechanical Systems   155
        Plumbing   155
        Fire Protection   156
        Heating   156
        Ventilation   157
        Air Conditioning   158
    Electrical Systems   160
        Electrical   160
        Lighting Outlets   160
        Exit Signs and Emergency Lighting   161
        Receptacles   161
        Branch Circuits   162
        Door Entrance Intercom System   162
        Electric Provisions for Air Conditioning   162
        Fire Alarm Systems   162
    Structural Systems   163
        Selection of Systems   164
6 Resources   167
    Bibliography   167
    Relevant Organizations and Educational Centers   170
        National Organization   170
        Education Centers   170
    Index   171

introduction

During the past few years the field of aging has witnessed various efforts directed at theory development. Much of this work is relevant to a discussion of housing for the elderly. While this book does not espouse one or another theory, it is based on some of the relevant theoretical treatments within the broader issues of aging and the elderly. At the same time, it is virtually impossible to define or even to identify all concepts within the field of gerontology which are germane to housing. We have, therefore, selectively addressed only such factors that are particularly relevant to housing.

Some approaches have centered around the disengagement process of aging, while others have emphasized continuing interaction throughout the aging process. Disengagement of the elderly from certain roles within society is inevitable while aging. However, there is also increasing recognition of reengagement and social interaction based on newly evolving roles for the elderly. The concept of retirement itself defies a universally acceptable definition and has grown to include aspects previously not envisioned as a part of the aging process. For instance, trends toward earlier retirement have created the need for developing new forms of involvement as the aging period lengthens.

We are witnessing the formation of special interest groups among the elderly in order to encourage recognition of the needs and lifestyles of elderly people. More people are living longer and maintaining activity-supporting health levels. These issues must also be taken into account when dealing with housing and addressed appropriately.

It became apparent early in our work that within the field of housing itself, a large body of research information, data, and conclusions exists concerning residential environments for elderly persons. Nevertheless, the magnitude and diffuse nature of this information generally make it virtually unusable to the development team. While there is high quality housing for the elderly which has benefited from available research, much of this type of housing has suffered from a lack of access to needed knowledge. Development team members rarely have the time or resources when faced with a specific development problem to read or synthesize even small parts of available knowledge. Therefore, instead of doing more basic research, we have attempted a synthesis of available experience and information which we have organized to track with the development process.

The development of appropriate and applicable development and design guidelines involves a direct response to the physical, social, and perceptual needs of the elderly resident. The basic human needs of the elderly are identical to those of any other age group. However, aging processes add and influence specific need requirements. The central core of this book deals with the relationship between those universal and age-related needs and the designed housing environment.

It is our hope that the organization and orientation of this book will facilitate its use at key decision points and that it will remain on the desk top while the work is occurring.

THE DEVELOPMENT TEAM

The authors recommend that a development team approach be used to successfully carry out the development of housing for the elderly. The preparation and implementation of the housing proposal, the design and production of the units, and the marketing and management of the completed development are all equally important stages of the housing delivery process. Thus, by definition, several areas of expertise are required; the development team, working as a whole, can most meaningfully organize all of these necessary housing delivery components. The development team consists of the following participants:

- The sponsor/developer
- The financing source
- The architect/site planner
- The builder
- The attorney
- The management/marketing agent
- Special consultants

These participants are normally a part of any housing development endeavor. It is useful, however, to explicitly identify and recognize the role of all of the members of the team rather than to implicitly assume their presence and input.

The development of housing for the elderly demands special duties on the part of the development team members. For instance, the sponsor/developer must be aware of the locational requirements for elderly housing sites. He must evaluate market need and demand, community attitudes toward such items as tax relief, zoning variances, and site plan approvals. The attorney is most certainly involved in all of the legal aspects of these as well as other matters. The architect/site planner must react to design requirements. Management/marketing agents must recognize the special arrangements that must be made to carry out effective management of housing for the elderly. They must be apprised of community elderly social programming and coordinate the provision of on-going services and benefits for elderly residents. Putting together a housing development can often suffer from the predominance of any one member and his particular set of perceptions and motivations. This is especially a danger to be avoided in the development of housing for the elderly, given that this is an area prone to preconceptions. The development team, both collectively and individually, must be able and willing to formulate appropriate solutions to each particular elderly housing proposal. They must seek out available information and combine this information into satisfactory solutions. The ease of carrying out the development of housing for the elderly and the quality of the resultant product depend upon the meaningful participation and successful coordination of all team members.

ORGANIZATION

We have organized this book to achieve an optimum balance between overall cohesiveness and an easy-to-use manual. It can be used both to obtain an overview of the process of providing quality housing for the elderly and also as a source of information for specific technical questions. The following organization has been developed to achieve these purposes:

Programming: the criteria and process needed to define the magnitude and scope of a specific housing development. Against a background of understanding human values and needs of the elderly, a process of definition is initiated, including the type of development, the number, type, and magnitude of dwellings, ancillary spaces, and common spaces.

Site Selection: the criteria and process needed to make alternative and final site location decisions. Within a background of understanding the special needs of elderly people regarding location of housing, the procedure and criteria for site selection are developd and enumerated on the basis of the community/region, the neighborhood, and the site.

Design: the criteria and process of formulating design through a recognition of human living functions, how people perceive the environment, and the factors to be used in evaluating design solutions. Human needs and the aging process, development activity components, and development design are analyzed within the context of functional and perceptual requirements of the elderly.

Standards: the provision of required technical specifications regarding the physical components of dwelling units, the development, and the site. Specifics are given to dimensions and performance standards as related to site and building details. This section is intended to be used as a reference during the design process.

Resources: suggested sources for further information and bibliography.

programming

INTENT AND ORGANIZATION

The process of housing development logically begins with the creation of a housing development program. The dictionary definition of the word program is to create a plan to be followed. This procedure, set against the background of the human needs and values of the elderly, must define the type and scope of development intended. The following questions must be answered:

1. How many dwelling units, of what type and what floor area, will be provided?
2. What size site will be required?
3. How much defined outdoor area will be required?
4. How much parking will be required?
5. What type, number, and magnitude of ancillary services and facilities will be required?
6. What type, number, and magnitude of common services and facilities will be required?
7. What amenity level shall be provided in the development?

This section on programming is subdivided into seven parts which closely parallel the several levels of concern which must be traversed in the creation of a viable program. These are:

1. ELDERLY NEEDS AND LIFESTYLES
2. DEVELOPMENT SIZE AND DWELLING UNIT MIX
3. OVERALL SITE SPATIAL REQUIREMENTS
4. DEVELOPMENT DENSITY
5. DWELLING UNIT SIZES AND RELATED ANCILLARY AND COMMON SPACES
6. MAJOR ACTIVITY COMPONENTS AND FLOOR AREAS
7. AMENITIES

The first subsection is intended to provide insight into the nature of the housing user by specifically emphasizing concerns which affect programming. The remaining subsections address the particular issues which answer the questions listed above.

The program guidelines presented here are the product of careful analysis of the economic parameters of available housing for the elderly financing programs and the special needs of the elderly. They are predicated on the premise that successful housing for the elderly can only be achieved if great attention is given to maximizing the effectiveness of available construction dollars from the very beginning of the development process.

Before a development program can be judged viable it must have achieved an acceptable balance between amenity level and the construction and operating cost which a particular amenity level will generate.

These guidelines are not intended as inflexible prescriptions to be applied universally. Rather, they are to be used by the development team as the basis for creating a desirable and feasible development program. It is expected that some modifications will from time to time occur in response to specific circumstances. However, the guidelines represent an effectively synthesized response to the general factors affecting elderly housing development.

During development planning and design, these guidelines and the resultant development program should be used by the development team to evaluate and substantiate the effectiveness of potential design solutions.

The terms listed below are specially defined in order to establish a commonality of program language and evaluation procedure among the members of the development team. Unless noted below, the definition of terms and the methods of measurement will be used throughout this book as they are commonly understood in architectural and construction practice.

Density Ratio: The number of dwelling units per acre of total development site will be defined as the Density Ratio.

Building Coverage: The amount of the total development site covered by the building(s) including overhangs, canopies, etc., and stated as a percentage of the total site area will be defined as Building Coverage.

Gross Open Space: The amount of the total development site not covered by buildings or parking and stated as a percentage of the total site area will be defined as Gross Open Space.

Outdoor Common Area: A defined outdoor space that is separated from the neighborhood and adjacent, abutting properties will be defined as the Outdoor Common Area.

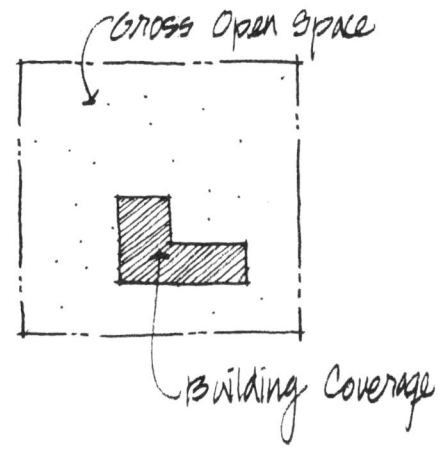

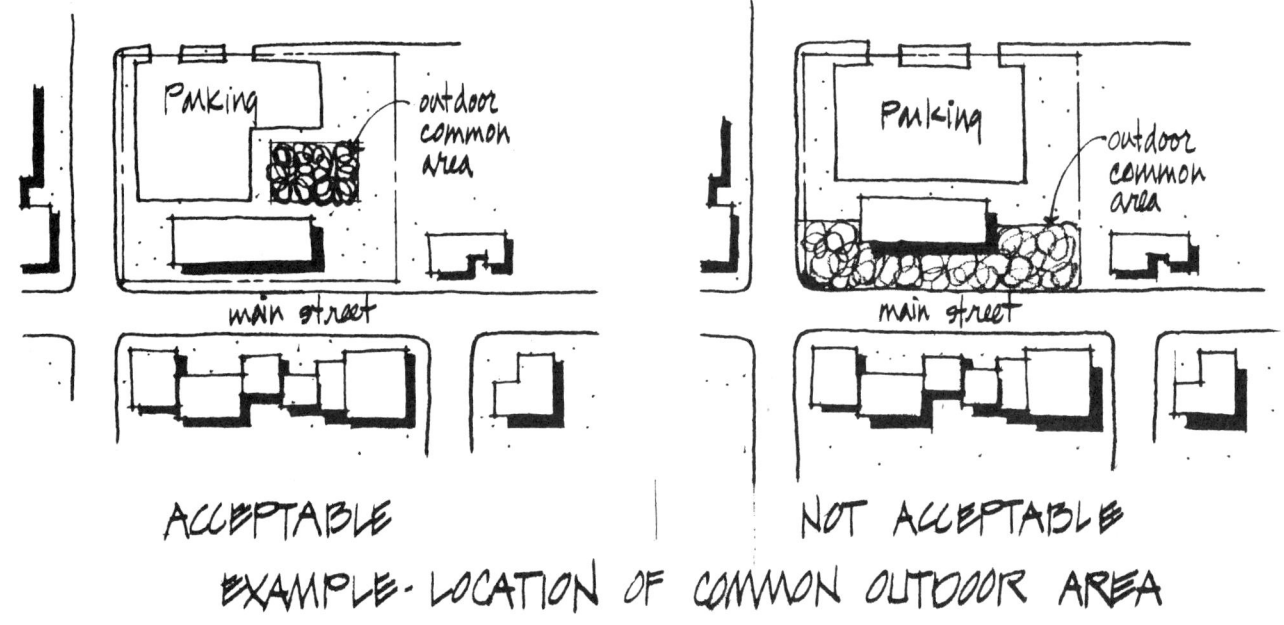

EXAMPLE - LOCATION OF COMMON OUTDOOR AREA

Building Gross Area (B.G.A.): All of the floor area (including construction and shaft spaces within the building) measured from the outside of rough exterior walls will be defined as Building Gross Area. Spaces that are only partially enclosed (such as balconies, entrance canopies, etc.) should not be included in Building Gross Area, but shall be listed as a separate gross area.

Dwelling Unit Area (D.U.A.): All of the floor area (including that occupied by walls, pipe spaces, built-in cabinets, etc.) within the dwelling unit measured from the outside of rough exterior walls, the center line of party walls, and the outside of public corridor walls will be defined as the Dwelling Unit Area. In a townhouse configuration private basements associated with a dwelling unit should not be included in this calculation. Required laundry and general tenant storage spaces which have been provided within the unit should not be counted. Balconies should not be counted in this area.

Activity Area or Room Area (A.A.): Unless otherwise noted, Activity Areas include all of the floor area inside the finish wall surfaces of a room except the areas occupied by offset room entrances, columns, pipe chases, closets, and stairs. The area of an alcove, offset, or recess directly off of a room may be included in the calculation of the Activity Area if its opening to the space is equal to or greater than the minimum required dimension of the space, or if it can be demonstrated that the alcove, offset, or recess substantially enhances the furnishability of the room. In dwelling units one-half of the floor area of the balcony may be included in the calculation of the floor area of the activity area (room) through which balcony access is gained and to which it is attached.

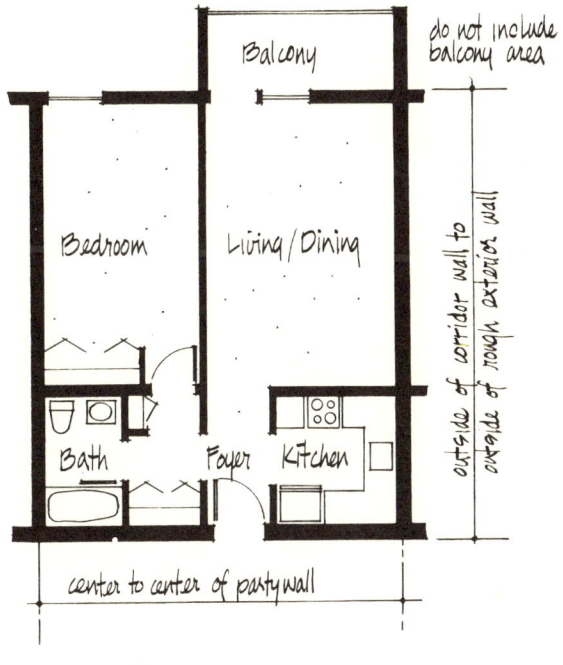

DWELLING UNIT AREA

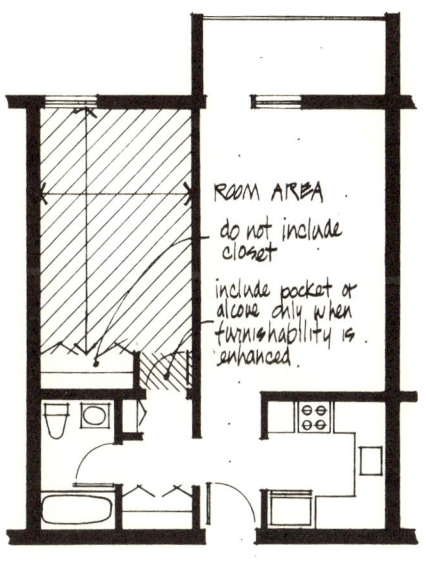

ROOM OR ACTIVITY AREA

Residential Gross Area (R.G.A.): The sum of all Dwelling Unit Areas within a residential building will be defined as the Residential Gross Area.

Ancillary Space Gross Area (A.S.G.A.): Ancillary spaces are those spaces which, although not included in the dwelling unit, are within the building or development and are essential to the residential function. These spaces include but are not limited to public lobbies and associated lounges and corridors, elevators and stairs, mechanical/electrical spaces, management office (not including social work or consultation spaces), manager's apartment, mail and receiving rooms, and congregate facilities such as the central dining room, medical/dental clinics, etc., where some or all D.U.'s are specifically designated as congregate housing units. Areas should be measured to include enclosing walls except where they are partially or totally included in the Residential Gross Area. Required laundry and general tenant storage area, whether centralized or contained within the dwelling unit, should be included in Ancillary Space Gross Area.

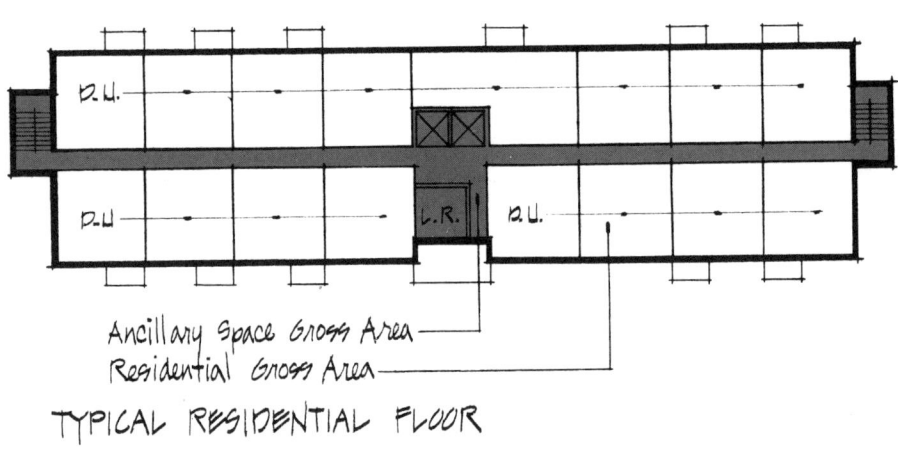

TYPICAL RESIDENTIAL FLOOR

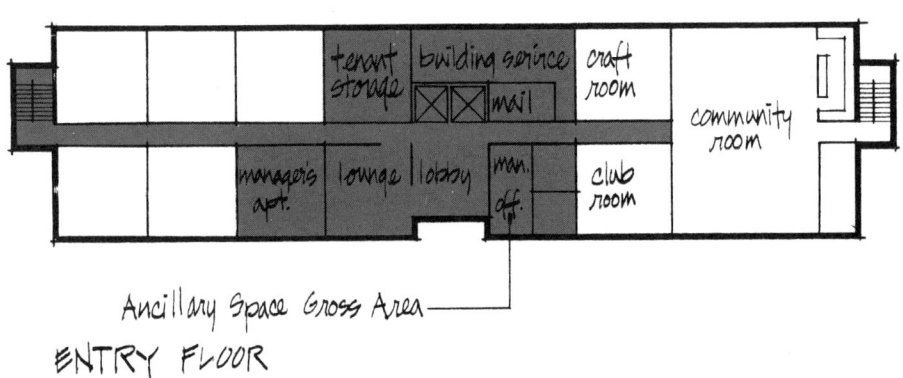

ENTRY FLOOR

Circulation Gross Area (C.G.A.): All floor area occupied by public (not inside of dwelling unit) circulation, such as, but not limited to, stairs, halls, corridors, lobbies, foyers, elevators, etc., should be included in the Circulation Gross Area. Floor area should be measured from the inside finish face of interior enclosing partitions and from the outside rough face of exterior walls.

Common Facilities Gross Area (C.F.G.A.): Community facility spaces within the building or development can be broadly defined as spaces provided for the convenience of residents but which are not essential to the residential function. These spaces include, but are not limited to, social work and consultation spaces, meeting rooms, handicraft areas, barber and beauty shops, party kitchens, etc., but they do not in-include congregate facilities. Measurement of the Common Facilities Gross Area should be conducted as described for Ancillary Space above.

Dwelling Unit Gross Area (D.U.G.A.): The Dwelling Unit Area together with its proportionate share of the Ancillary Gross Area will be defined as the Dwelling Unit Gross Area.

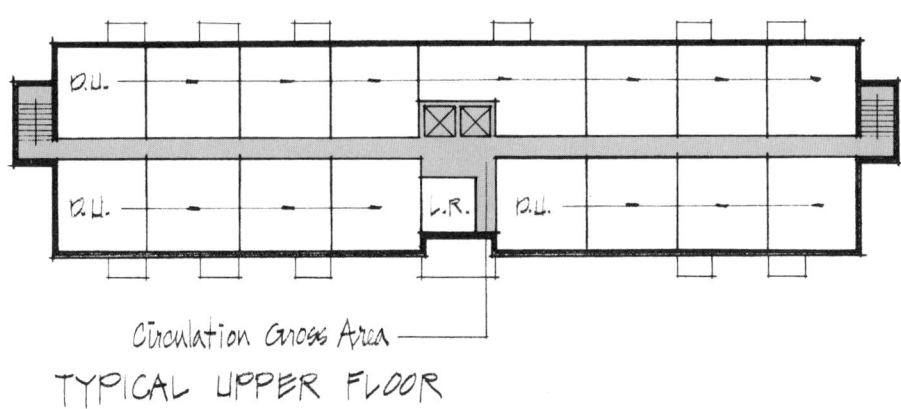

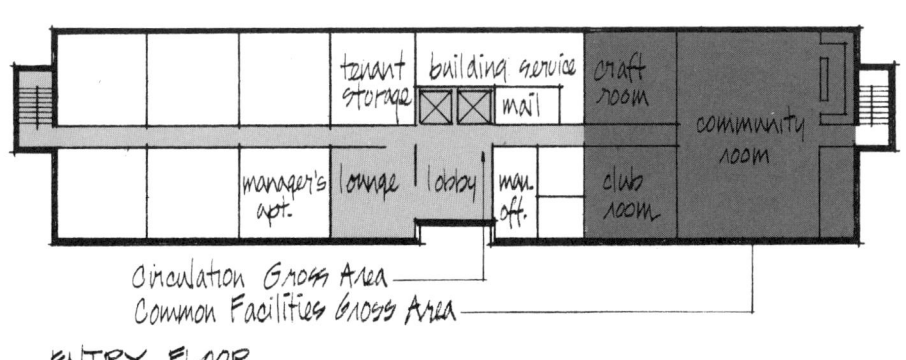

ELDERLY NEEDS AND LIFESTYLES

The development of housing for the elderly should begin with some understanding of what it means to grow older in our society. Aging is universal and normal, a process that begins at birth. To all persons, growing older means adaptation to changes in the structure and functions of the human body and changes in the social environment. Oftentimes, at the stage of retirement, an aged person is viewed as being obsolete and contributing little of value to a society enamored of youth. However, a large percentage of elderly people can lead active, productive lives and want to continue doing so as long as possible.

The elderly population is reputed to be one of the nation's most distressed minorities. Loss of income is an ever-present problem for the elderly. Social Security, private and public retirement plans, and personal savings have not been sufficient to decrease poverty among the elderly population. Approximately two-thirds of the elderly people in this country have annual incomes of $5,000 or less.[1] Currently, approximately 14.1 percent of the nation's population is composed of people aged 60 and over, and this segment of the population is increasing.[2]

Aging means changing functional roles for the individual and changes in the social environment. The role of the worker with its accompanying role status is lost for the great majority of employed aging men and women at retirement. Many persons who have been active socially and in civic and professional organizations often find that they are given positions of less importance as they grow older. Our society is one which, for the most part, refuses to honor the intrinsic values of old age.

Psychologically speaking, the results of this forced lessening of activity and retirement create in many individuals a passive, dependent manner. This is a result of the lack of opportunities

[1] U.S. Department of Commerce, Bureau of the Census, *Consumer Income,* Series P-60, No. 83, July, 1972.

[2] U.S. Department of Commerce, Bureau of the Census, *General Population Characteristics*, Final Report PC(1)-B1, 1972.

birth

infancy

childhood

adolescence

courting

parenthood

middle age

independent old age

partially dependent old age

dependent old age

provided for older individuals to establish their relevance in a society which prides itself on being young and independent. Negative attitudes and stereotypes about aging have created and perpetuated opinions damaging to elderly people. This generally accepted view of the aging process results in a forced segregation and alienation of the older person.

There is a tendency to make hasty and erroneous generalizations about meeting the housing needs of the elderly population. It is true that housing for the elderly must respond to the special needs of the elderly because of the physical and social changes accompanying the aging process. It is erroneous, however, to conclude from these shared characteristics that the housing needs of the elderly are totally different from what the concept of housing means for any age group. For all age groups "...housing is invested with the emotions of family living and independence of spirit and action. It encompasses friendship patterns and all of the dimensions of community life. It is an environment in which one can take pride and find the resources needed to mold a meaningful way of life."[3]

Moreover, recognition must be made of the diversity of this age group and the variety of ages, capabilities, needs, and desires that occur in people over time and with different lifestyles. The designer's responsibility rests in providing opportunities for elderly residents to adapt more comfortably and with more dignity to the aging and retirement process. Design can improve upon sociability, ease of adjustment to a new environment, safety and comfort, or it can effectively defeat these concepts. The physical and social housing environment must be designed to support normal human activity without lessening independence or causing isolation of the elderly person.

Housing the elderly is not only a physical undertaking. It is a social process, and those involved must have a sense of social inquiry. The physical design of the dwelling units, the overall housing development, and its relationship to the surrounding neighborhood or community must all be planned as a response to the facts and realities of aging.

[3] 1971 White House Conference on Aging, *Section Recommendations on Housing,* page 12.

Special concerns of the elderly and factors affecting the elderly should be considered in programming. A summary of the more significant factors follows:

1. Elderly people are less mobile than younger age groups. In fact, 90 percent of them don't move after they reach age 65. The dwelling unit should be conceived of as a home, not as transient housing.[4]

2. The elderly are generally less mobile in terms of their ability to reach community recreational and social services and facilities, and thus should be provided with at least the basic services and facilities within their immediate living environment (the housing development or contiguous thereto).

3. The elderly desire choice in living situations. Hopefully, a given community will have available a range of housing types for the elderly, and within a given development a range of unit types will be provided.

4. The elderly desire a sense of autonomy and need an environment which extends and enhances the time span of independent living.

5. Contrary to conventional wisdom, the elderly require as much, or more, floor area to carry on their activities as would a young person carrying on the same activities. Elderly people do require special design adaptation of spaces to account for possible physical limitations, but the market success of unusually small dwelling units is most likely a product of demand created by a housing shortage, and not by user desire.

6. The definition of the activity pattern for an elderly person should not be based on the assumption that his or her basic living activities by type are different from that of a young person. Activities differ only in the way the elderly wish to or are able to conduct them.

7. The elderly are no more willing to accept the inconvenient or undesirable superimposition of one living activity upon another than are younger age groups, such as exemplified in designs where bedrooms, bathrooms, and kitchens are fully visible from general living areas.

There is another factor not directly related to the elderly which must be considered. At the present time, this country is experiencing an increased response to a growing elderly housing demand. Housing for the elderly is by definition specifically designed to satisfy the needs of the elderly. Market analyses made for each development are directed at avoiding the possibililty of building more elderly units than are needed. Because mortgage terms generally run a considerable length of time, the development team must make sure that developments will remain economically viable for the full mortgage term. Therefore, dwelling units must be conceived and designed so that, in the unexpected event that the elderly market needs are met and some surplus remains, the units would be sufficiently flexible to successfully serve the general housing market.

In order to more clearly define housing facilities that represent a broad range of lifestyles, the following housing categories are defined.

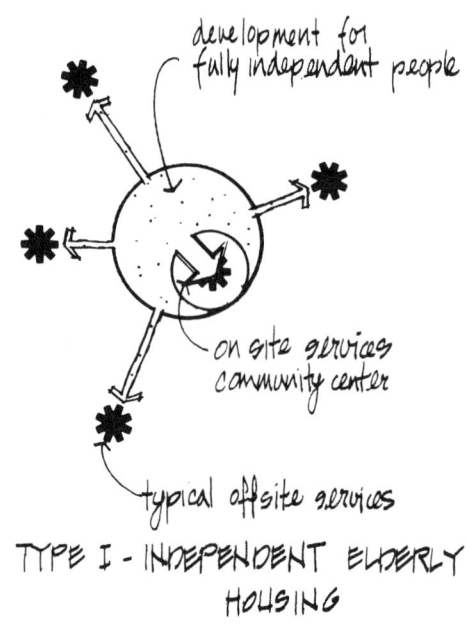

TYPE I – INDEPENDENT ELDERLY HOUSING

Type I–Independent Elderly Housing: This category would provide conventional housing facilities for self-sufficient residents who are completely independent. There would be no central dining room or other provision for special facilities or services. However, a community center would be provided encompassing social functions as well as some minimal independent living supportive services.

Type II–Independent Elderly/Family Mixed Housing: In this type of housing, facilities would be provided for independent elderly persons, designed so as to blend in with family

---

[4] U.S. Department of Health, Education and Welfare, *Patterns of Living and Housing of Middle-Aged and Older People,* Frances M. Carp, ed. (Washington, D.C.: Government Printing Office, 1965), pages 65-81.

housing and yet intended to function separately. The elderly residents living in this type of development could comprise the segment of the elderly population who has the means to own a car and the ability to drive it and who desires a high level of age integration.

quire some measure of assistance in their everyday living activities. At a minimum, supportive services would include common dining facilities and can also include housekeeping aid, personal health services, and other services as programming and finances allow.

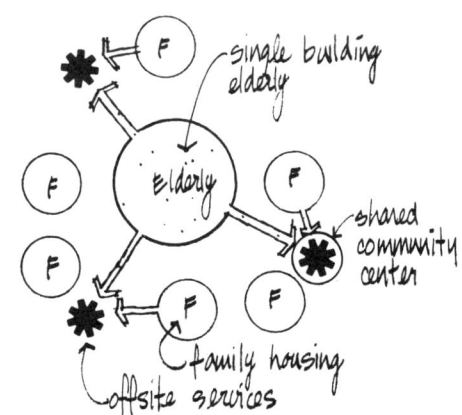

TYPE II (option a) - INDEPENDENT ELDERLY/FAMILY MIXED HOUSING

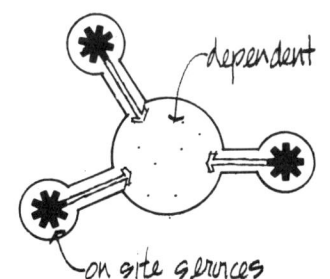

TYPE III DEPENDENT ELDERLY HOUSING

Type IV–Independent/Dependent Elderly Mixed Housing: One portion of the housing would serve elderly people needing some congregate services, and the other portion would house self-sufficient elderly people.

Each of these categories has special implications for housing development programming, both in terms of the types and magnitudes of the facilities provided and in terms of the type or types of structures used. The body of this section on programming (activities and concomitant floor areas) is presented in terms of these categories, primarily emphasizing the difference between independent and dependent housing.

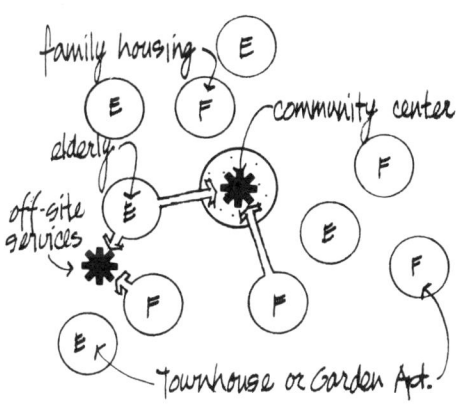

TYPE II (option b) - INDEPENDENT ELDERLY/FAMILY MIXED HOUSING

Type III–Dependent Elderly Housing: This is housing for occupants who are more or less dependent upon congregate facilities. Congregate housing is neither a nursing home facility nor an institution. It should be defined and conceptualized as a housing development with supportive services being provided for persons who desire residential accommodations, but who re-

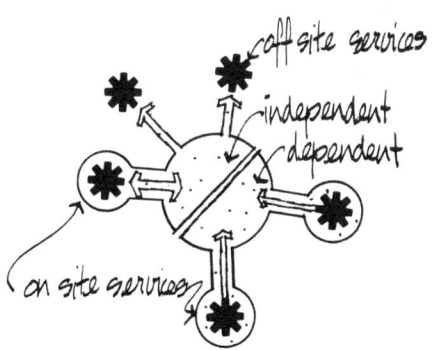

TYPE IV - INDEPENDENT/DEPENDENT MIXED HOUSING

DEVELOPMENT SIZE AND DWELLING UNIT MIX

As a general rule, developments solely for the elderly should not be smaller than 100 to 150 dwelling units or larger than 300 units. A minimum of at least 100 units is necessary to economically justify the development effort and the needed management, social, and recreational services and facilities. The maximum size is based upon the assumption that concentrations of elderly people beyond a certain size tend to encourage isolation from community life as well as cause abnormal neighborhood development. In developments of mixed independent elderly and families, the minimum number of elderly units may be reduced to fewer than 100 units because the cost of both development and services can be shared between the two types of housing. The number of elderly units in this case should be determined for each specific development with the decision taking into account total development size, elderly population to be housed, available off-site service, etc.

Each housing for the elderly development should offer a range of dwelling unit types (number of bedrooms) and sizes to insure the accommodation of the widest range of housing needs and lifestyles.

While the precise mix for each elderly housing development must be determined for each specific development and based upon its specific context, experience indicates the following general guidelines:

1. Up to 10 percent of the development should consist of two-bedroom units.

2. Up to 10 percent of the one-bedroom units should be sized for two-person occupancy or as larger than standard units.

3. In each development the aggregate of all larger than standard one-bedroom units should total from 10 to 20 percent of the total number of units. The focus of these larger units should be on one-bedroom units as opposed to two-bedroom units.

The desirable levels of mix between independent and dependent elderly housing will be determined individually for each development. Reference should be made to page 18 for dwelling unit sizes.

OVERALL SITE SPATIAL REQUIREMENTS

The development of specific dimensions which define physical relationships on a site are based on three categories of criteria:

1. The amount of outdoor space needed to accommodate certain activities or functions such as parking, recreation, and socializing

2. The number of residents being accommodated on the site and the type of housing to be provided

3. The location of the site and the site's design determinants, such as size, shape, topography, vegetative cover, etc.

To determine the total amount of space needed for parking and the outdoor common area, the following ratios have been developed:

1. 65 square feet of outdoor common area for every dwelling unit

2. Parking spaces to dwelling unit ratio:

a. .5 spaces for every dwelling unit on urban sites which have a full range of services (as outlined in the section on site selection, page 40) within 1,500 feet of the subject site

b. .75 spaces for every dwelling unit on urban-suburban and suburban sites

c. 1.0 spaces for every dwelling unit on small town sites

DEVELOPMENT DENSITY

One of the most elusive terms used by designers and planners today is livability. In many instances, livability is directly related to density, resulting in the establishment of a maximum number of dwelling units per acre which will be permitted. A maximum density ratio like this can limit creative approaches to the development of housing environments. Both the development program and the site itself should be included in the final determination of an optimum site density.

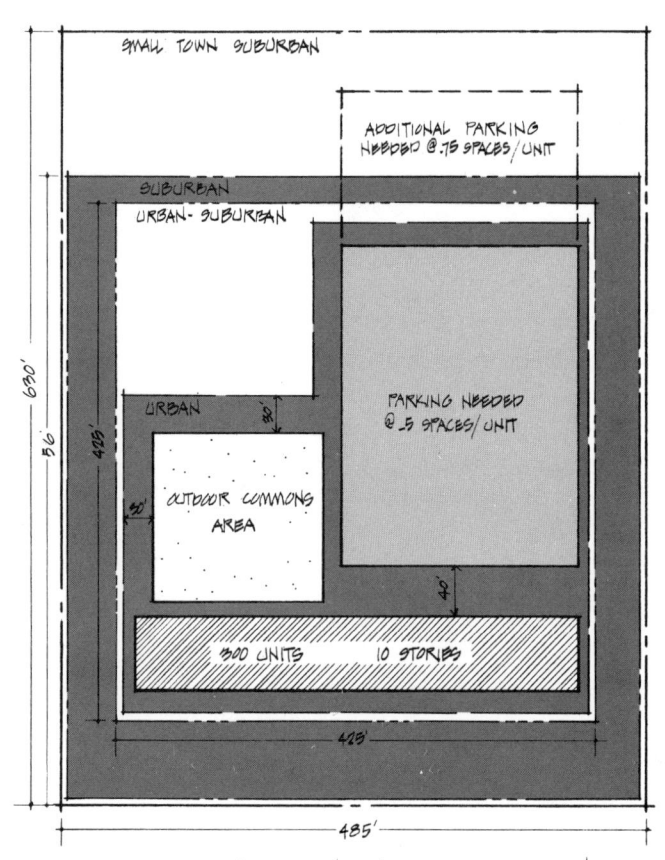

GRAPHIC OPEN SPACE/DENSITY COMPARISON

NUMERICAL OPEN SPACE/DENSITY COMPARISON

Determining site density should be considered as a process rather than as a set of preconceived density requirements. The first step of this process involves simple size comparisons between the site in question, the number of units being considered, the amount of outdoor common area, and the amount of parking and gross open space to be provided. An example of three such comparisons is illustrated by Table A.

TABLE A — OPEN SPACE/DENSITY TABLES

	SMALL TOWN		SUBURBAN		URBAN-SUBURBAN		URBAN	
100 UNITS	4 Stories	8 Stories	4 Stories	8 Stories	4 Stories	8 Stories	4 Stories	8 Stories
Site size (acres)	7	7	5.7	5.7	4	4	2	2
Density (units/acre)	14	14	18	18	25	25	50	50
Building coverage	6%	3%	8%	4%	11%	6%	22%	12%
Open space	83%	86%	81%	85%	74%	79%	58%	69%
Parking coverage	11%*	11%*	11%†	11%†	15%†	15%†	20%††	20%††
200 UNITS	6 Stories	10 Stories	6 Stories	10 Stories	6 Stories	10 Stories	6 Stories	10 Stories
Site size (acres)	7	7	5.7	5.7	4	4	3	3
Density (units/acre)	29	29	35	35	50	50	67	67
Building coverage	9%	5%	11%	6%	15%	9%	20%	12%
Open space	68%	72%	68%	73%	55%	61%	53%	61%
Parking coverage	23%*	23%*	21%†	21%†	30%†	30%†	27%††	27%††
300 UNITS	8 Stories	12 Stories	8 Stories	12 Stories	8 Stories	12 Stories	8 Stories	12 Stories
Site size (acres)	7	7	5.7	5.7	4	4	3.5	3.5
Density (units/acre)	43	43	53	53	75	75	86	86
Building coverage	10%	6%	12%	8%	17%	11%	19%	13%
Open space	56%	60%	56%	60%	38%	44%	47%	53%
Parking coverage	34%*	34%*	32%†	32%†	45%†	45%†	34%††	34%††

*1.0 spaces/unit   † .75 spaces/unit   †† .50 spaces/unit

Through the development of these area comparisons it becomes possible to determine how many units can be placed on a particular site. This kind of comparison, however, because it only considers location and space and not characteristics of the site, is not adequate to determine what the optimum density should be. Its main value is to begin to narrow the range of possible sites and to permit the sponsor to avoid unreasonable sites.

The second step of the density determination process is a site investigation to determine development potential such as site shape and topography and vegetation. These kinds of characteristics, in some cases, can cause a large site to shrink in regard to actual buildable space.

By combining these two steps, a realistic optimum density ratio of dwelling units per site can be determined. In some cases, local setback and parking requirements will take precedence over this method of determining the maximum density for a development.

As sites become smaller, as is usually the case for urban sites, the amount of gross open space and parking space required decreases. This usually implies more innovative architectural solutions in regard to creating a usable outdoor common area and in solving the problems of privacy normally overcome by landscaped setbacks.

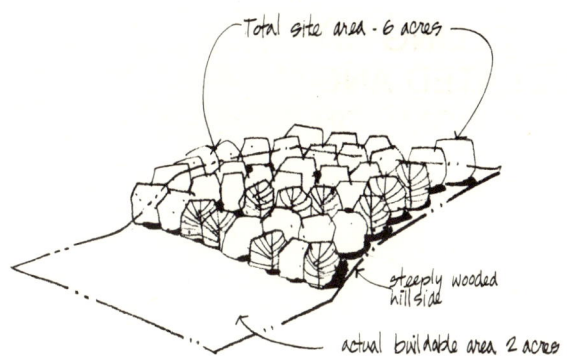

TOPOGRAPHY and VEGETATION EFFECT DENSITY

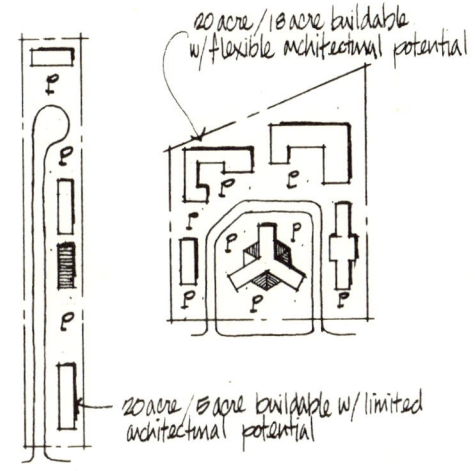

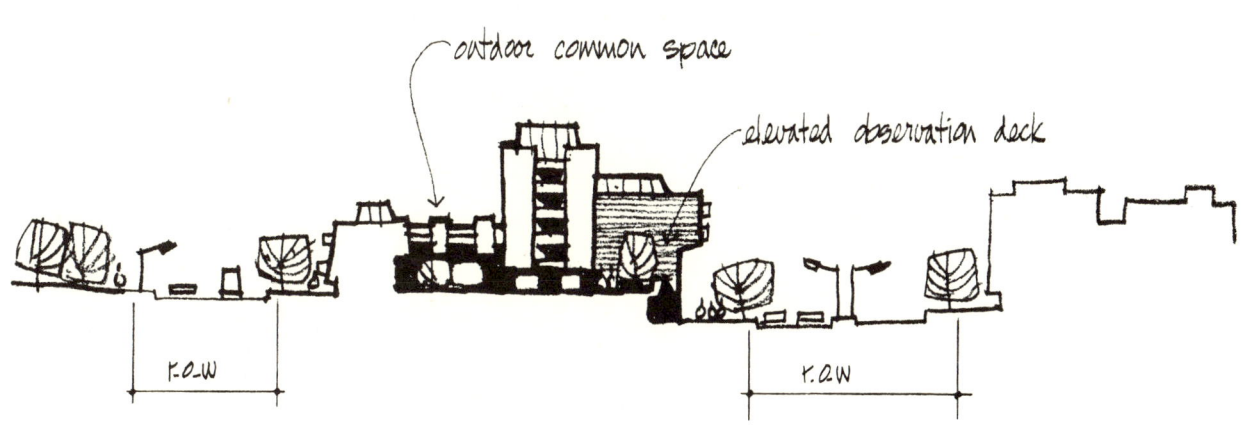

SMALL URBAN SITES IMPLY MORE INNOVATIVE ARCHITECTURAL SOLUTIONS

DWELLING UNIT SIZES, RELATED ANCILLARY, AND COMMON SPACES

Tables B and C contain ranges of Dwelling Unit Gross Area (residential plus ancillary space but not including common facilities space) for various types of dwelling units intended for the elderly. Dwelling units smaller than the sizes indicated are usually environmentally deficient and are, therefore, considered unacceptable. Units larger than the sizes indicated, while desirable, may be economically unfeasible under available elderly housing programs and should, therefore, be carefully studied and be utilized only when justified by the specific development situation.

Each table includes two Dwelling Unit Gross Area ranges. The first applies to housing for the independent elderly and to housing for the dependent elderly where space for congregate facilities is provided by taking space away from dwelling units (such as the partial elimination of kitchens and dining spaces). The second applies to housing for the dependent elderly where congregate space is added while all of the dwelling unit space normally provided for the independent elderly is maintained.

It is desirable that all housing for elderly developments include a substantial percentage of units of somewhat larger size than listed in Table B to provide both a range of choice and an opportunity for alternate lifestyles. These units would be specifically appropriate for elderly couples, single elderly people who wish to maintain a high level of family oriented activity, or for other situations requiring more than minimum space. The larger than standard units should be primarily

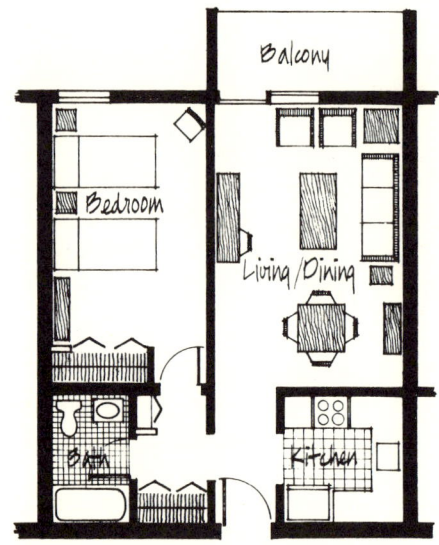

EXAMPLE - STANDARD ONE BEDROOM

TABLE B — STANDARD UNITS/STANDARD RENTS

TYPE	MAXIMUM OCCUPANCY	D.U.G.A. RANGE INDEPENDENT*	DEPENDENT (congregate)*
Apartment Structures			
1 Bedroom	1	665–690 sq. ft.	685–710 sq. ft.
1 Bedroom	2	715–740 sq. ft.	725–760 sq. ft.
2 Bedroom	2	865–890 sq. ft.	885–910 sq. ft.
Townhouse Structures:			
1 Bedroom	1	Not applicable	Not applicable
1 Bedroom	2	675–700 sq. ft.	Not applicable
2 Bedroom	2	925–975 sq. ft.	Not applicable

* These D.U.G.A.'s do not include an allocation for common space.

one-bedroom units because two-bedroom units are generally not as economically viable. The larger than standard units would be available at slightly higher rents and would generally not exceed 20 percent of the total number of units. The exact number of such units will, of course, be determined individually for each development. The size ranges for this kind of unit are shown in Table C.

Townhouses are generally not usable in congregate living situations. It is emphasized that these ranges are intended as guidelines and that efficient utilization of materials and construction systems in some situations may make larger units economically feasible. This form of optimization should be the goal of the development team. All of the above limits have been thoroughly tested and found not to inordinately inhibit design flexi-

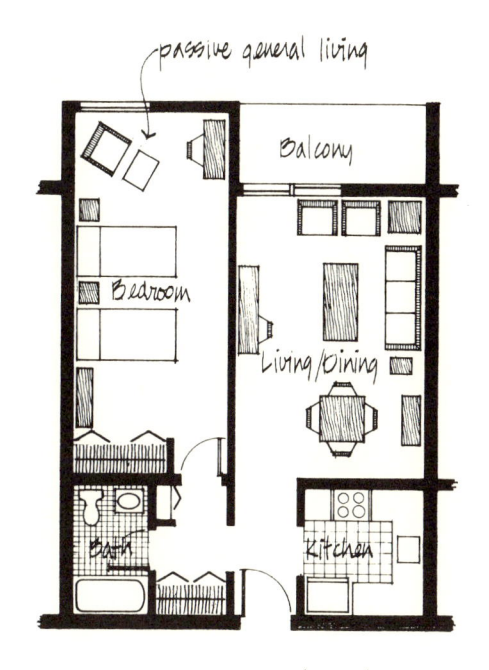

EXAMPLE - LARGER THAN STANDARD ONE BEDROOM

EXAMPLE - LARGER THAN STANDARD ONE BEDROOM

TABLE C — LARGER THAN STANDARD UNITS

TYPE	MAXIMUM OCCUPANCY	D.U.G.A. RANGE INDEPENDENT*	DEPENDENT (congregate)*
Apartment Structures			
1 Bedroom	1	715–740 sq. ft.	725–760 sq. ft.
1 Bedroom	2	790–815 sq. ft.	810–835 sq. ft.
2 Bedroom	2	900–950 sq. ft.	920–970 sq. ft.
Townhouse Structures			
1 Bedroom	2	725–750 sq. ft.	Not applicable
2 Bedroom	2	975–1025 sq. ft.	Not applicable

* These D.U.G.A.'s do not include an allocation for common space.

bility or the achievement of commodious and effective housing.

It should be noted that the relationship between residential space and ancillary space is very crucial (see efficiency ratios on page 127 in the section on design). Great care should be exercised in building design to make sure that circulation is efficient to insure maximum floor area in dwelling units. As a general guide, ancillary space should not exceed 135 square feet per dwelling unit for housing for the independent elderly or in housing where congregate facilities have been added to fully independent housing and are combined with same. However, in low density housing such as townhouses the ancillary space portion of the dwelling unit gross area is a very small part of the total; that is, as little as 20 square feet in most developments.

The Dwelling Unit Gross Area ranges do not include either common facilities space or private balconies. For purposes of programming, approximately two-thirds of all units should be assumed to have balconies with minimum sizes of from 50 to 60 square feet each in a climate where balconies are usable during at least 50 percent of the year.

The provision of common facilities within elderly developments will vary from project to project, depending on location and availability of services. The types, magnitudes, and design of such facilities are discussed on page 24. As a general guideline for programming and planning, however, each development should include approximately 35 square feet per dwelling unit for such facilities. In developments with 200 or more dwelling units, this provision may be reasonably reduced to 30 square feet. The calculation of space for common facilities should not include congregate facilities spaces, although under some circumstances the amount of common facilities space may be reduced where extensive congregate facilities are provided that can also be used for common activities (such as a dining room that can be converted to a meeting room).

MAJOR ACTIVITY COMPONENTS AND FLOOR AREAS

This subsection establishes the basic major activities which must be accommodated in housing developments for the elderly and, where appropriate, defines minimum floor or room areas for each activity. Major activities are defined as those requiring rooms. Where floor area will be a function of development size or the specific context of a given development, only the activity is indicated. Generally, activity arrays and minimum floor areas are indicated both for housing for the independent elderly and the dependent elderly in congregate facilities. Required activities and their minimum floor areas are presented in this subsection for the dwelling unit, ancillary facilities, and common facililties.

Minimum floor areas are presented as an aid in programming, but they should also be used as a basic test of design effectiveness. The other major tests of design effectiveness, such as furnishability, functional suitability and relationship, minimum dimension, and efficiency are explored in the section on design.

DWELLING UNIT ACTIVITY FLOOR AREAS

Independent Elderly

The schedules on page 22 contain minimum area provisions for primary dwelling unit activities. It should be noted that the activities and their combinations listed are norms directed at conventional lifestyles; this structure should not, however, be assumed to preclude non-conventional housing activity requirements. Where the activities exist and are justified by valid requirements, these area minimums can be modified to suit the specific situation.

Because the diversity of lifestyles is as great among the elderly as it is for other age groups, significant variations in activity area sizes for given unit types should be used as one of the methods for providing alternative living arrangements to prospective occupants of any given development. Thus, varying both dwelling unit organization and activity area size provides choice and assists in the accommodation of a range of income levels. The provisions listed below are only minimum sizes and should, therefore, be exceeded where economically feasible.

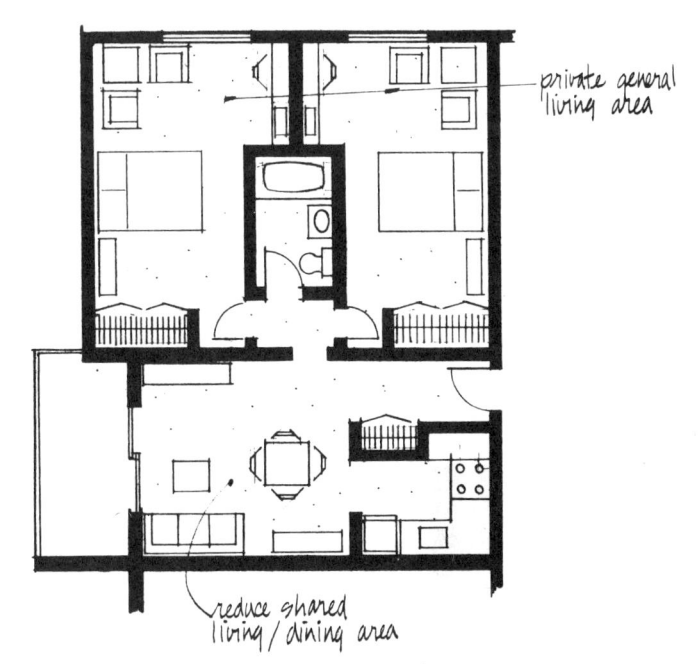

EXAMPLE - LIVING UNIT FOR UNRELATED ADULTS

private general living area
reduce shared living / dining area

Where justified by an identified requirement of use and an allowance in the financing program, reduction in activity areas may be acceptable where there is a compensating benefit. An example of this condition might be the circumstance of unrelated elderly who choose to reside together, where programming allows. To accommodate this situation, enlarged bedrooms (used as bed/sitting rooms) could be achieved by reducing the living/dining areas. Special circumstances such as this example should be reviewed carefully so that rational modifications to minimum requirements can be made.

Finally, the minimum requirements for provision of space in specific developments may be adjusted on the basis of unique location or housing type.

MEDIUM- AND HIGH-RISE APARTMENTS (3 STORIES OR MORE)

Bedrooms:

BEDROOMS	FIRST BEDROOM	SECOND BEDROOM
1	135 sq. ft.	
2	135 sq. ft.	100 sq. ft.

Some two-bedroom units could be planned for unrelated adults if programming allows, in which case the following provision applies:

2 Bdrms.	125 sq. ft.	125 sq. ft.

Living, Dining, and Food Preparation:

Several alternate arrangements are illustrated below. Other arrangements are possible and should be encouraged where they can be justified functionally. When an alternate arrangement is proposed, interpolation of the requirements should be carried out and/or additional evaluation standards established.

COMBINED LIVING-DINING, SEPARATE FOOD PREPARATION

TYPE	L – D	FP
1 Bedroom	210 sq. ft.	60 sq. ft.
2 Bedroom	230 sq. ft.	60 sq. ft.

COMBINED FOOD PREPARATION-DINING SEPARATE LIVING

TYPE	FP – D	L
1 Bedroom	130 sq. ft.	150 sq. ft.
2 Bedroom	145 sq. ft.	160 sq. ft.

COMBINED LIVING-DINING-FOOD PREPARATION

TYPE	L-D-FP
1 Bedroom	270 sq. ft.
2 Bedroom	290 sq. ft.

BALCONIES

TYPE	
1 Bedroom	minimum 50 sq. ft.
2 Bedroom	minimum 60 sq. ft.

TOWNHOUSES AND LOW-RISE APARTMENTS (2 STORIES OR LESS)

Dwelling units for the elderly should be increased in size as follows for townhouse and low-rise apartment configurations. The increases in floor area are required by the relative difference in accessibility of common facilities, or, where programming allows smaller developments, the potential absence of these facilities.

Bedrooms in townhouses and low-rise apartments shall be of the same size as those in high- and medium-rise apartments.

COMBINED LIVING-DINING, SEPARATE FOOD PREPARATION

TYPE	L – D
1 Bedroom	220 sq. ft.
2 Bedroom	240 sq. ft.

COMBINED FOOD PREPARATION-DINING SEPARATE LIVING

TYPE	L
1 Bedroom	160 sq. ft.
2 Bedroom	170 sq. ft.

COMBINED LIVING-DINING-FOOD PREPARATION

TYPE	L-D-FP
1 Bedroom	280 sq. ft.
2 Bedroom	300 sq. ft.

BALCONIES

TYPE	
1 Bedroom	50 sq. ft.
2 Bedroom	60 sq. ft.

Dependent Elderly Living in Congregate Facilities

Where programming allows and a development is planned to include formal congregate housing for the elderly, the following modification can be made to the guidelines for independent elderly people.

The table below applies only to medium- and high-rise apartment buildings as they are deemed the most appropriate type for congregate housing. The inclusion of congregate facilities and services, as defined at present, principally affect the food preparation and dining activities within the dwelling unit. Discussion of the design ramifications of other possible congregate facilities will be provided as these facilities become feasible. The table assumes that some light meal preparation and dining will be provided in the unit.

COMBINED LIVING-DINING, SEPARATE FOOD PREPARATION (KITCHENETTE)

TYPE	L – D	FP
1 Bedroom	190 sq. ft.	30 sq. ft.
2 Bedroom	210 sq. ft.	30 sq. ft.

COMBINED LIVING-DINING-FOOD PREPARATION (KITCHENETTE)

TYPE	L-D-FP
1 Bedroom	230 sq. ft.
2 Bedroom	250 sq. ft.

ANCILLARY ACTIVITIES and FACILITIES

Ancillary facilities can generally be viewed in two groups; those associated with housing developments for independent elderly people and those associated with housing developments for dependent elderly people. All of the facilities of independent elderly housing are contained in dependent housing as well as certain key additions. These two groups are discussed separately below.

Independent Elderly

As noted earlier, ancillary activities and facilities, although not residential in nature, are nonetheless essential to the residential function. Each development of 100 or more units must accommodate these activities and must include at least the facilities listed below. In developments where independent elderly are mixed with family housing, the development team should determine what ancillary facilities should be added to those normally found in a family development.

The floor area provision for each of these facilities will vary depending on development size, location, and design and should, therefore, be separately determined for each development. Minimum requirements, however, are given for each activity listed below.

Laundry: If a single central laundry room is provided, one washer and one dryer per twenty (20) dwelling units and appropriate laundry trays should be provided. If laundry space is provided on each floor of a multi-story building, one washer and one dryer per twelve (12) dwelling units should be provided. A washer and dryer and concomitant space occupy at least 30 square feet for each combination.

Management and Rental Office: At least 200 square feet should be provided.

Manager's Apartment: At least a standard one-bedroom unit should be provided.

Public Toilets: At least one men's (65 square feet) and one women's (70 square feet) toilet should be provided.

Mail Room, Package Delivery, and General Receiving Room: A complex of spaces occupying at least 250 square feet should be provided.

Trash Room: The type of facility provided depends on the type of equipment and methods used.

Tenant Storage: Each dwelling unit should have, either within the unit or at a central point or points in the building, a general storage closet or locker at least 12 square feet in floor area and no less than 100 cubic feet in volume.

Common Balcony: On all occupied floors of buildings designed for elderly residents where one or more dwelling units do not have private balconies, a common balcony accessible to all residents of the floor should be provided. The balcony should have an area of at least 60 square feet when only one unit on the floor is without a balcony and should be increased in size by at least 5 square feet for each additional unit without a balcony. This requirement should apply only to buildings of three or more stories.

In addition to the above designated ancillary facilities, all developments will, of course, have both horizontal and vertical circulation elements, mechanical and electrical rooms, and general storage and maintenance space. Ancillary facilities as a group should generally not amount to more than 135 square feet of floor area per dwelling unit.

Guides to the design of ancillary facilities will be found in the design section beginning on page 56.

Dependent Elderly Living In Congregate Facilities

The facilities for the delivery of congregate housing services are as varied as the types of potential services. It is not possible to define a precise and fixed set of services which can be classed as congregate. Each development that provides such services will have a different array depending on its particular situation and the needs of the elderly population to be serviced. Congregate services can be defined as those which are provided for occupants who cannot or do not wish to provide these services themselves. The broad objective in providing such services is to extend and enhance the length of time that an elderly person can, if he or she so chooses, live as independent a lifestyle as possible. The alternative to providing such services is to relegate all those elderly persons who are partially incapable of taking care of themselves to complete dependence.

All elderly housing developments will not, of course, include congregate facilities. The decision as to whether such facilities are necessary and should be provided should be made by the development team individually for each development.

The basic congregate services and facilities are as follows:

Central Food Service: For programming purposes, 20 square feet per meal served for food preparation, storage, and cleanup (including employee dining) are required. Fifteen square feet per seat is required in the dining room; these figures should not be simply multiplied by the number of meals to be served as great efficiency can be achieved by having two sittings.

Social Service and Referral Consultation: Size should be determined individually for each development. At least 150 square feet should be provided, however.

Medical Clinic (Outpatient): Size should be determined individually for each development. At least 350 square feet should be provided, however. At the present time it is not envisioned that nursing care facilities will be affordable within most developments for the elderly. Because such facilities may be required in the future, however, the design of each development should be so conceived as to facilitate the inclusion of nursing care facilities either by adding or converting space. For projection purposes it is reasonable to assume that nursing care beds and concomitant facilities for from 5 to 10 percent of the residents of a development might be required at any one time.

Housekeeping Assistance: The nature of these facilities should be determined individually for each development. However, facilities should certainly include a central janitorial room on each floor where this service is offered.

Central Laundry: If central laundry service is provided, only a pick-up point (100 square feet) for an off-site laundry service should be included in the development.

To administer congregate services it will be necessary to increase management office space. Some congregate services, however, such as those listed below, do not require special spaces because they can be carried out in common facilities:

Recreational
Crafts
Educational
Transportation
Work training/Job placement

COMMON ACTIVITIES and FACILITIES

These facilities are not essential to the residential function, but are provided for the convenience of tenants, and some will be required in all developments for elderly residents.

Housing for the elderly must include an indoor common facility within the development. The facility should be designed to support recreational and social activity. The size of the facility and the activities provided for in each development will vary according to the location of the development, its relationship to other accessible community and social services, and the nature of its site development.

The purpose of the common facility is not only to provide recreational activities for the elderly residents but to also serve as a means to a larger goal. The common facility serves as an important link which influences the ability of the elderly person to adapt to and redirect his or her lifestyle around the aging process. It provides an opportunity for social interaction with age peers within the development and with other persons and activity groups from the surrounding community.

The common facility must provide the elderly with a means to overcome the loneliness, isolation, and dependency which can be forced on the individual in the retirement process. A well-designed common facility can provide the resident with the opportunity for personal expression, service to others, a feeling of belonging, accomplishment, new experiences, continuation of past activities, and community action involvement.

The program for common facilities must respond to the diverse needs of different age groups within the elderly population. It must also respond to the varied backgrounds, cultural habits, and traditions of the residents. Community facilities, no matter how extensive, are extremely dependent on on-going, effective management.

The program of common facilities must be planned in terms of the services available in the surrounding community and those accessible to development residents. Lack of information about the community and its services and activities has several results. First, the developer does not have a clear picture of those persons who will be living in the development. He knows nothing about the particular needs, desires, or characteristics of the residents. Second, it lessens the opportunity for the participation of the local community in providing services for the elderly residents. Housing the elderly in any community means much more than mere physical structures; it requires a cooperative community effort. And, finally, lack of information can result

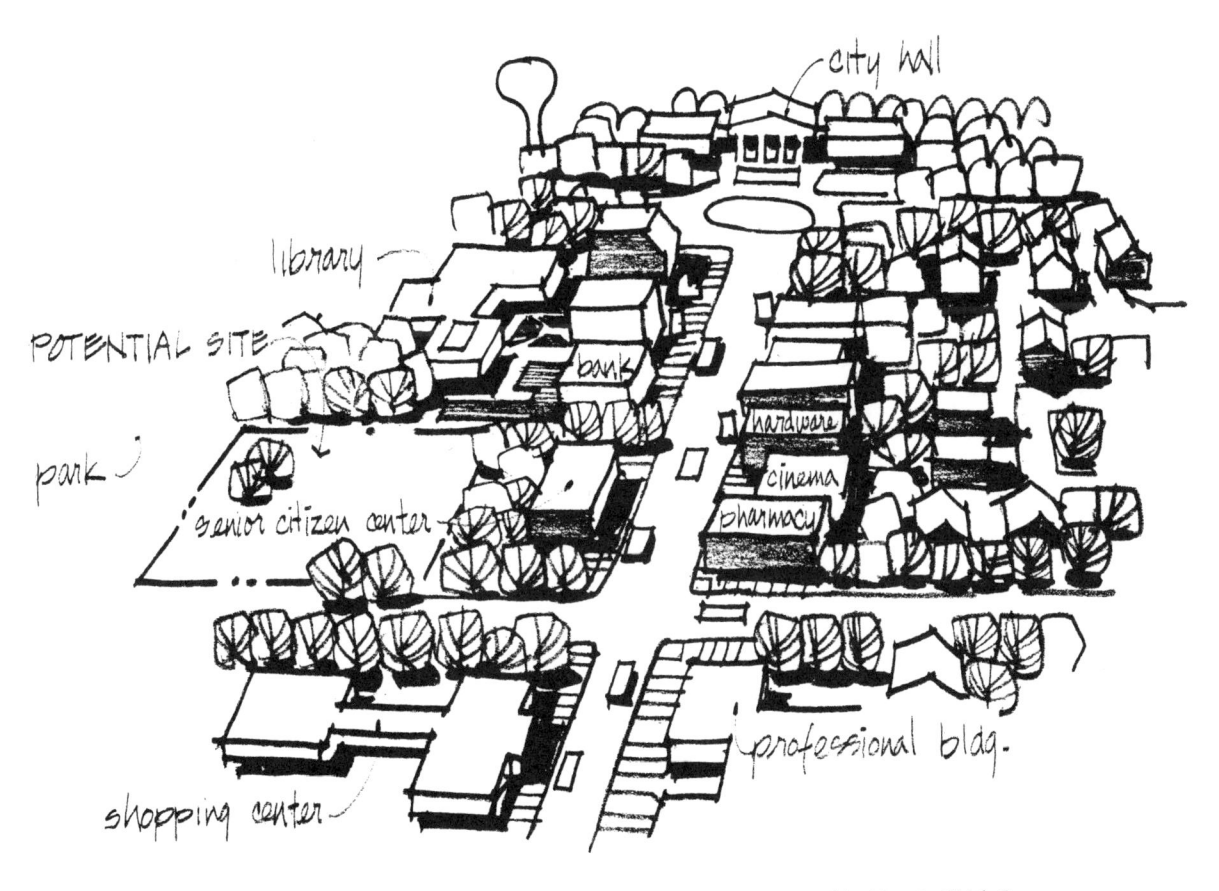

INVENTORY OF NEIGHBORHOOD FACILITIES

in an unnecessary duplication of program activities for the elderly.

It is difficult to predetermine what activities are going to be desired and enjoyed by the elderly population of any housing development without making an inventory of the community and an analysis of the given site.

Therefore, the determination of space provisions for common facilities must be made individually for each development. A minimum activity space requirement, however, has been established as a starting point.

Each development should contain at least the following spatial provisions in its common facilities:

Multi-Purpose Room: This space should be at least 1,000 square feet in area and it should be possible to divide the space into two smaller spaces.

Kitchenette: This serves the multi-purpose room and it should be at least 60 square feet in area.

Storage: Storage facilities supporting the multi-purpose room should include a cloak room (for at least 50 users), chair and table storage of at least 70 square feet, and closet and shelf storage for supplies of at least 100 cubic feet.

Because these are minimum requirements, most developments should be provided with additional facilities. Only where an existing, fully developed alternate facility is available immediately adjacent to the development would the minimum provision be considered sufficient.

The selection of additional facilities should be guided by an understanding of the activities desired by the elderly. A survey of recorded activity programs of sixty-five senior citizen centers in the State of Michigan indicates activities can be categorized into the following groups:

Mass Activities: Movies, dances, entertainment programs, mass informational meetings

Crafts: Painting, sewing, sculpture, ceramics, wood work, shop hobby activities

Study Groups: Discussion groups, educational classes, etc.

Table Games: Checkers, chess, card games, pool

Music and/or Drama: Bands, chorus, plays, poetry reading groups

Commercial: Barber/beauty shops, stores

The most frequently offered were mass activities and table games.

Common facilities as a group should generally not amount to more than 35 square feet of floor area per dwelling unit.

AMENITIES

It is recognized that each development will have its own market context and rent structure mixes. It is also recognized that differences between developments can exist in amenity level. Therefore, decisions as to certain residential amenities must be made based upon the specific context of each development.

Amenity items include a wide range of possibilities, some of the more common of which are:

Air Conditioning: This amenity is strongly encouraged and may be mandatory in some developments. In all developments air conditioning should be required in common facilities spaces (see section on technical standards, page 158). In addition, where air conditioning is not provided as part of the initial construction, rough-in provisions should be made to insure that air conditioning can be conveniently added at a future date (see section on technical standards, page 158, for specific guidelines).

Carpeting: This amenity is strongly encouraged and may be mandatory in some developments. The various locations where carpeting may occur include, but are not limited to, lobbies and hallways, dwelling units (generally only in living, dining, sleeping areas, and connective halls), common facilities, offices and clinics. Each development should have different requirements.

Full Draperies: As stated on page 143 in the section on technical standards, outer draperies are desirable in all developments. The provision of inner (or tenant) draperies may be a provided amenity in some developments. In such cases it is expected that the tenant would be given a limited range of choices (not less than three options).

Carports: In some developments carports may be provided as amenity options. The number and type will be determined separately for each case. It is not expected that any development having carports will have all tenant parking in carports. Carports will be paid for by the tenant by some additional monthly charge beyond the dwelling unit rent.

Frost Free Refrigerator: This amenity is strongly encouraged and may be mandatory in some developments.

Self-Cleaning Oven: This amenity is encouraged and may be mandatory in some developments.

CONCLUSION

The above program criteria were developed through careful evaluation of the special needs of the elderly. They represent a logical basis for defining the magnitude and scope of a proposed development. A comprehensive program basis for beginning the development process is necessary to create a firm foundation for the design of residential environments for the elderly which provide commodious living and personal dignity.

3
site selection

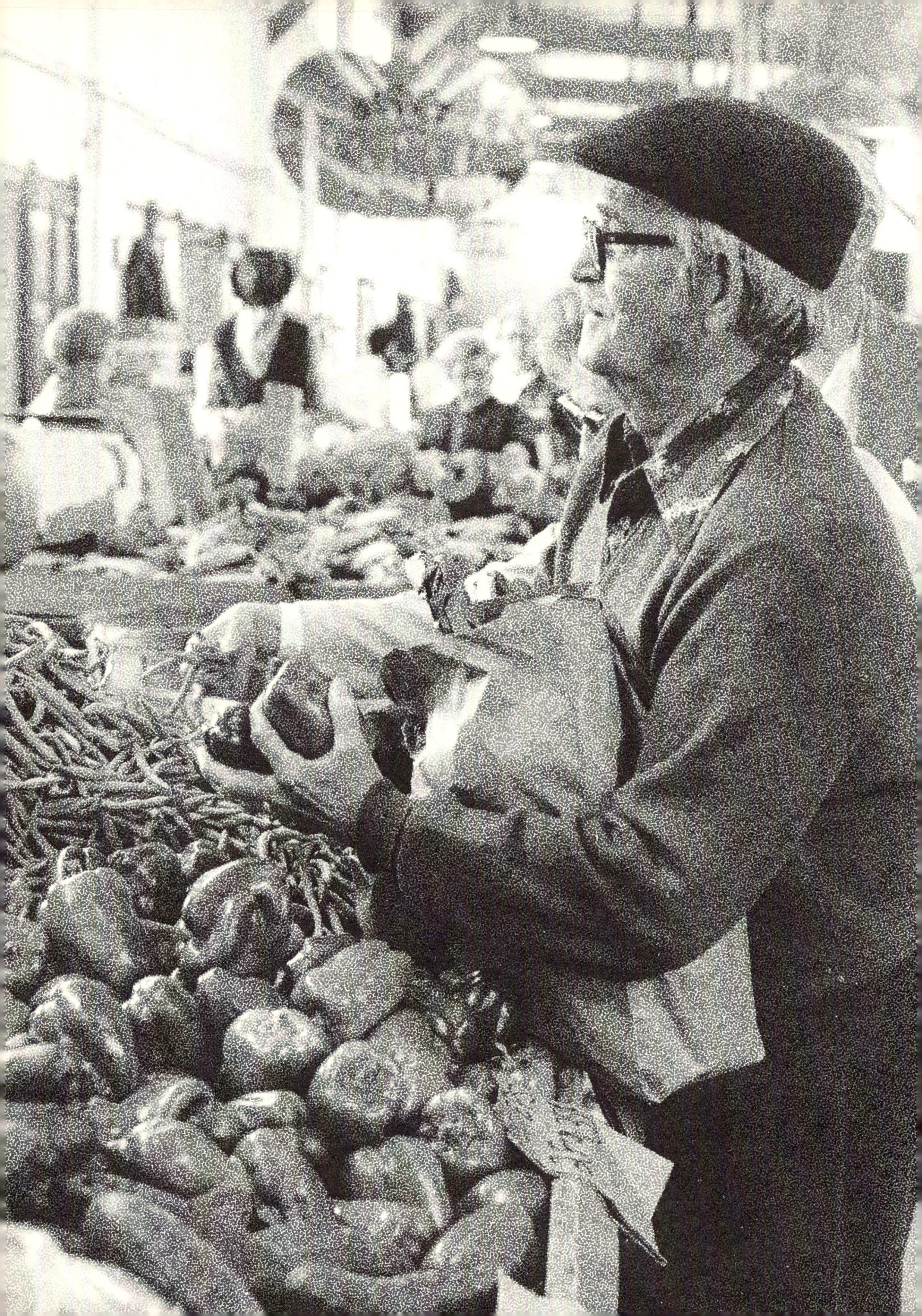

site selection

INTENT AND ORGANIZATION

The process of developing specific and measurable criteria for site selection involves understanding the human values and locational needs of the elderly and, at the same time, understanding the distinct contextual characterisitics of each site location. Specific site selection criteria have been derived through a comparison of this information, and this section will conclude with specific criteria. The section is divided into four parts:

1. ELDERLY NEEDS
2. THE COMMUNITY/REGION
3. THE NEIGHBORHOOD
4. THE SITE

ELDERLY NEEDS

What makes the elderly development site selection process uniquely different from other housing site selection processes? Special concerns in regard to the elderly have been listed on pages 10 through 12 in the section on programming. The following is a list of these concerns which have strong implications for the site selection process:

1. The elderly should be a part of the community. They should not be located on physically or socially isolated parcels of land.

2. The elderly desire autonomy and a sense of independence. In order to enable elderly people to achieve this, they need convenient services, especially full service shopping and health care facilities, social service and activity centers, public transportation, and others.

3. The elderly have time to participate in community affairs. They want to be able to control this participation, however.

4. The elderly are less mobile. They depend on public transportation more than younger people do.

5. Elderly people are limited in the amount of topography they can negotiate and the distance they can walk.

6. The elderly are concerned about physical and psychological security.

7. Elderly people are less mobile in terms of moving their households. Ninety percent do not move after they reach the age of 65.[1]

The above represents only some of the signficant differences between the elderly, people 60 and older, and the younger populace.

---

[1] U.S. Department of Health, Education and Welfare, *Patterns of Living and Housing of Middle-Aged and Older People,* Frances M. Carp, ed. (Washington, D.C.: Government Printing Office, 1965), pages 65-81.

Sites for housing developments for the elderly can be analyzed at three levels of urban development; the community/region, the neighborhood, and the site. These levels of urbanization are defined in more detail below:

The Community/Region: This area can be defined as the service area, which will provide community services for the residents of the development. This area could include, but not necessarily be limited to, the intended market area for the development.

The Neighborhood: This area can be defined as the immediate vicinity in which the site is located. It is defined by a characteristic land use and in some cases by a system of physical edges, that is, streets or highways.

The Site: This area can be defined as the land being considered for the proposed housing development and all its land use determinants, both natural and man-made.

These particular categories were devised to facilitate a logical methodology for the application of the criteria for site selection which have been developed.

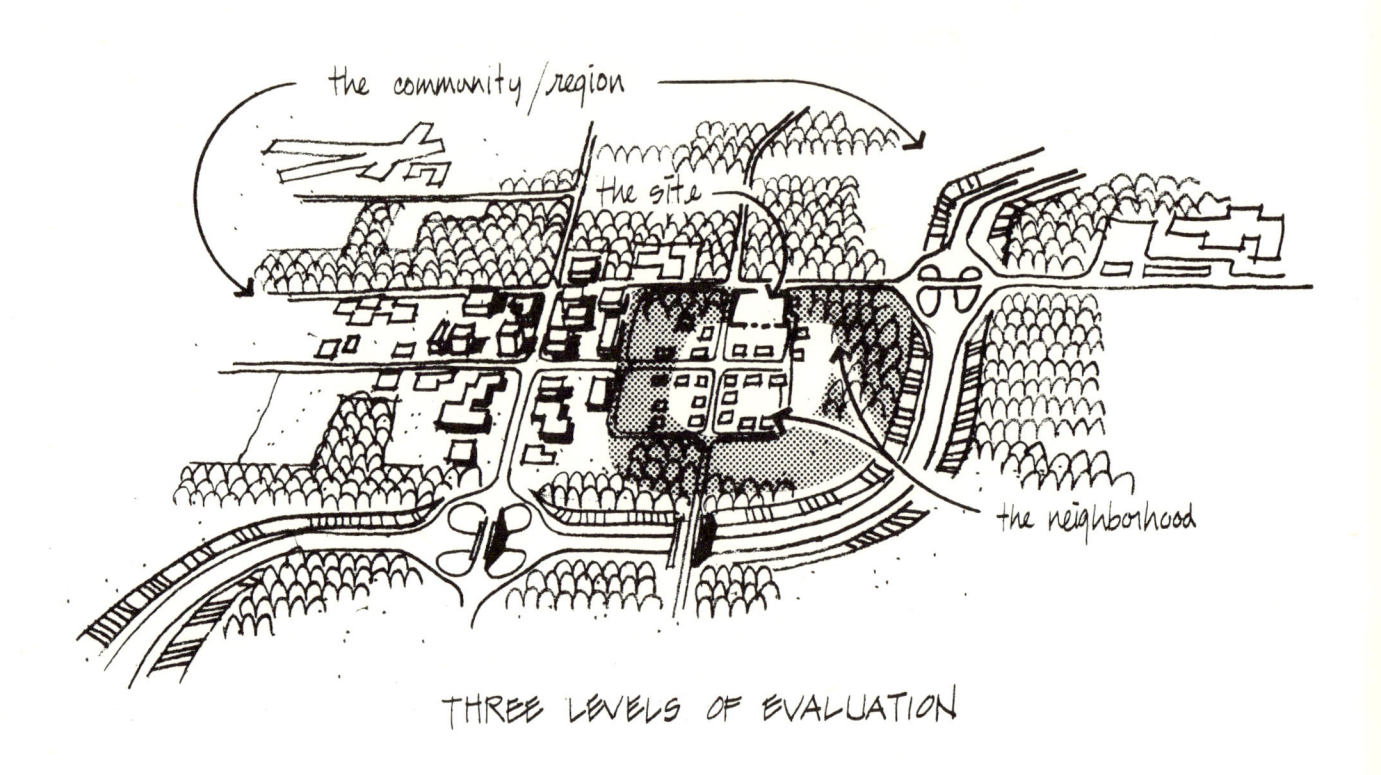

THREE LEVELS OF EVALUATION

THE COMMUNITY/REGION

The community or region within which the site is located shall contain certain services which are directly related to the elderly. It must be kept in mind that, although facilities might be available presently, they will come and go with the passage of time. The future evolution of all land use and services must be carefully considered. Commercial services tend to be clustered in communities in four ways:

Central Business Districts: These areas usually contain a full range of goods and services.

Community Service Centers: These areas tend to be located at the intersection of two major community thoroughfares. They are often located in close proximity to major expressway interchanges. Services usually include a department store, major food store or market, a drugstore, bank, hardware store, stationery, and other specialty shops.

Neighborhood Service Centers: These areas are usually located at intersections of major streets which define neighborhoods and tend to include a major food market, a drugstore, a hardware store, and other neighborhood services.

Strip Commercial Zones: These commercial facilities are usually oriented to the automobile driver with franchised food services, automotive services, and large appliance stores as well as the duplication of other services mentioned above.

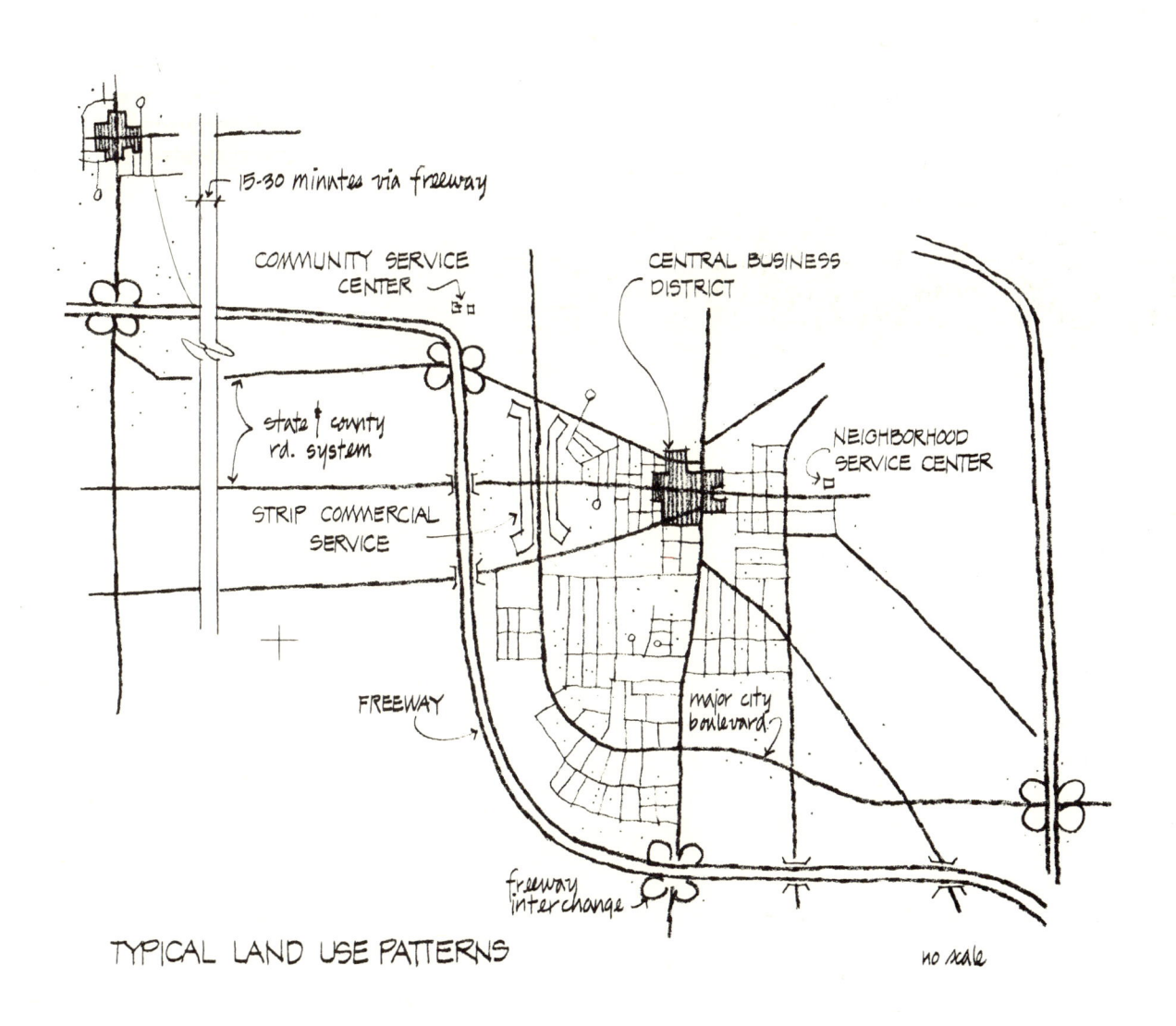

TYPICAL LAND USE PATTERNS

The following factors are of special concern at the community/region scale:

1. Major medical facilities should be available within a 20 minute driving radius of the site and these facilities should be connected to the site by a public transportation system where one exists. There must be ambulance service available.

2. Opportunities for community involvement should be available to the residents through existing facilities. Examples of some of these kinds of opportunities are listed below:
   a. Library
   b. Museum
   c. Churches
   d. Social services/community elderly center
   e. Historical societies
   f. YM-YWCA
   g. Adult educational program
   h. Community park system
   i. As many other related facilities as possible

These opportunities should be relatively accessible to the residents by a public transportation system where one exists.

3. Existing family and friend relationships are an important consideration. In many communities neighborhoods evolve in which the elderly tend to be the majority of the residents. These neighborhoods should be considered during the site selection process.

4. Future planning considerations should include the following land use and planning conditions:

   a. *Zoning*—There should be no expected zoning or building code restrictions which would hinder or prevent the sponsor from achieving his objectives.

   b. *Transportation*—There should be no highway, roadway, or mass transit proposal which would require that special easements be provided in the future either through or adjacent to the site.

   c. *Airports*—The site should not be located along an approach to an airport or be in a potential airport expansion zone.

   d. *Isolation*—The site should not be located in an area which is separated physically from the social/commercial community by such barriers as expressways, industry, thoroughfares, railroad rights of way, or large expanses of undeveloped land.

   e. *Pollution*—The site should not be near extensive or potentially extensive exposure to air, noise, or inordinate visual pollution.

   f. *Residential/Commercial/Community Services Mix*—The existing and future land use patterns in the vicinity of the site should be compatible with community development that provides immediate access to a variety of land uses appropriate and necessary for optimal residential living, as opposed to strictly commercial, industrial, or other uses.

For a small town community these considerations will be applied within the context of a region. A region can be defined as a network of small towns or villages connected by a major roadway system. It is emphasized again that the availability of these services and facilities must be assured for the future and related to the community's evolutionary trends.

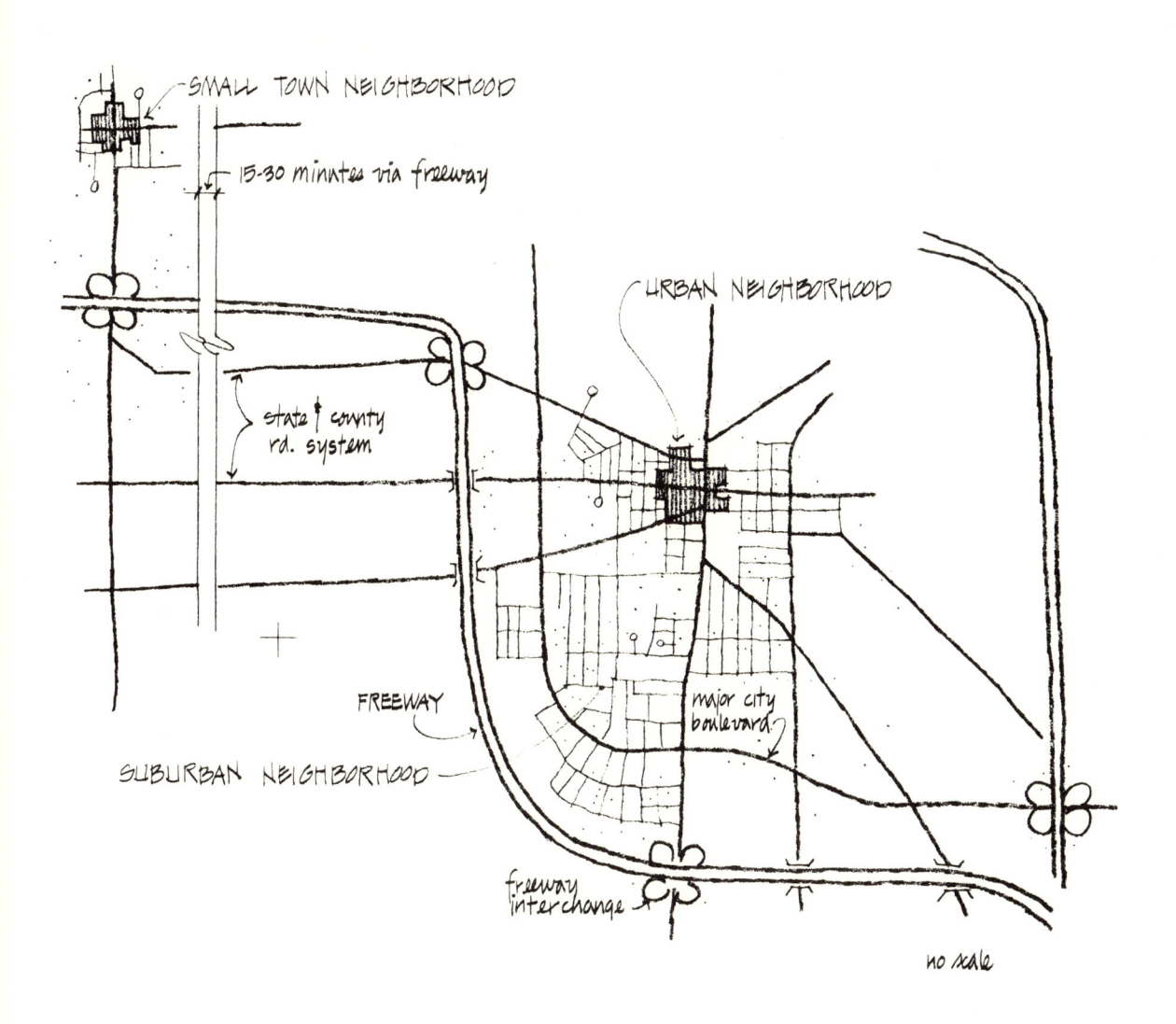

THE NEIGHBORHOOD

For purposes of clarification, the neighborhood has been organized into three subgroups each of which has different land coverage characteristics, visual character, and building heights. Each of the subgroups is defined below:

Urban Neighborhoods: Urban neighborhoods are represented at several different scales. Usually, sites in these neighborhoods are located within old central business districts, older residential areas adjacent to central business districts, or as a part of urban renewal areas.

Suburban Neighborhoods: These are the newer, outlying residential areas of our cities.

Small Town Neighborhoods: These neighborhoods may include all or part of communities with a population of 10,000 or less.

Each of the three neighborhood categories demands that special attention be given to certain considerations such as available services, scale (building mass and height relationships), pedestrian walkway systems, and optimum size of sites.

URBAN NEIGHBORHOOD SITES

Sites located in urban neighborhoods should offer options for passive recreation in nearby parks. These passive facilities will complement the highly active urban spaces found in this type of area. Of major importance is the existing and predicted crime rate in the neighborhood in question. Sites should be oriented toward the zone between commercial and residential development, thus providing the residents with the option to avoid the commercial area if they wish. Sites should not be located adjacent to industrial activities which cause environmental air, noise, or visual pollution.

Some of the key concerns regarding sites located in urban neighborhoods are listed below:

Security: What is the crime rate in the neighborhood? Is it safe for pedestrians to use the area at all hours of the day?

Pollution: What is the detrimental effect on the site of noise, air, and visual pollution?

Developability: Is the site large enough and of appropriate configuration so that an acceptable residential site plan can be developed?

Economic Stability: Are services that are within convenient walking distances diminishing, or will they remain stable and operative?

Precedent for Residential Living: Is the site in an area where families (other than elderly) live and want to live?

Availability of Public Transportation: Is a public transportation system accessible to the site and will it remain in operation?

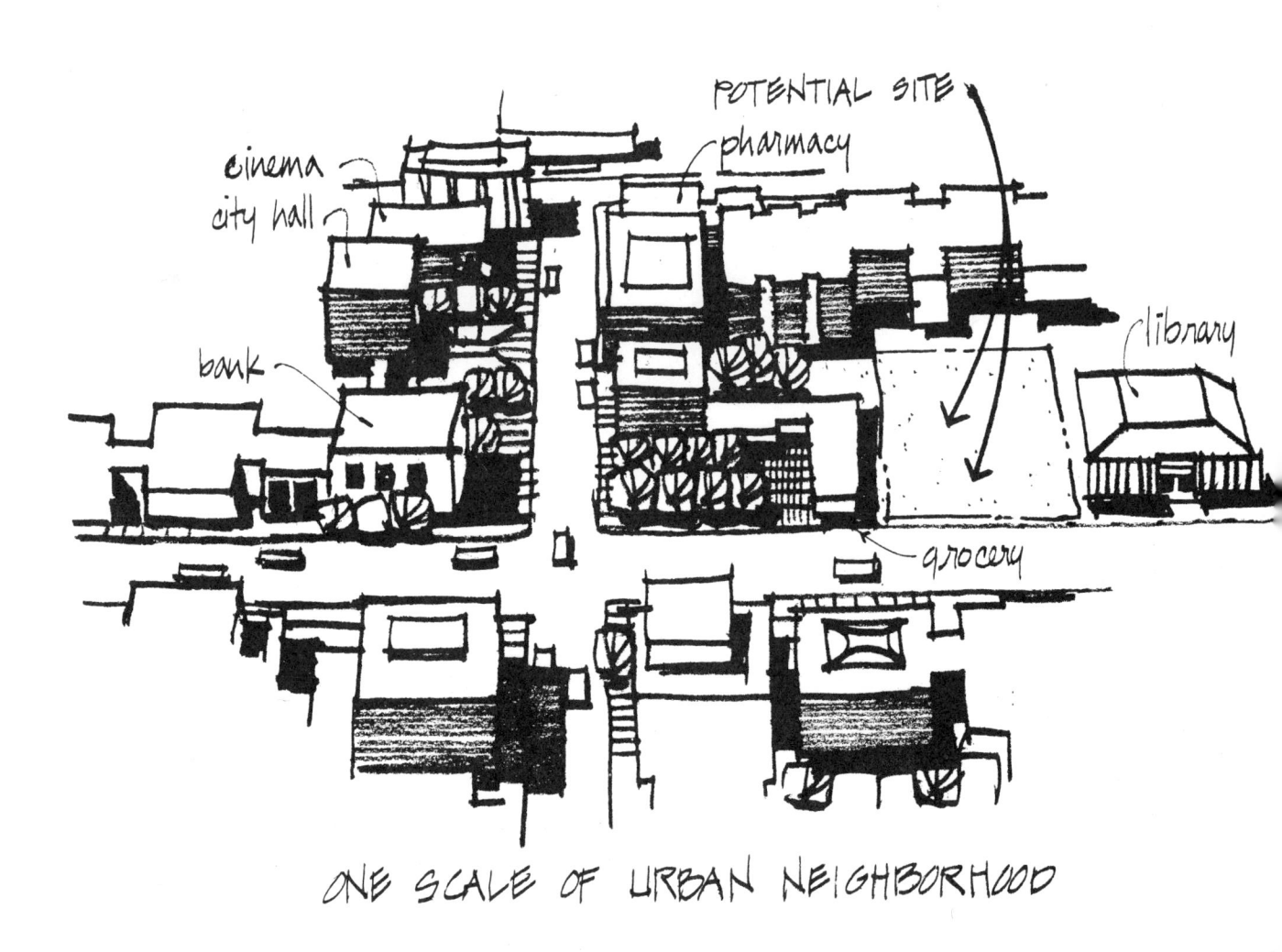

ONE SCALE OF URBAN NEIGHBORHOOD

A LARGER SCALE OF URBAN NEIGHBORHOOD

SUBURBAN NEIGHBORHOOD SITES

Suburban sites should be located in residential areas or along their edges. A desirable location would be in a residential area adjoining a commercial zone which offers shopping and professional services. Suburban shopping areas usually lack an adequate pedestrian access, and the fact the services are nearby is not sufficient to insure convenience for elderly residents. There must be a safe and convenient system of sidewalks and designated crosswalks that are well lighted and maintained to permit safe movement of residents to and from services.

Another important consideration is the relationship of the proposed building height to the heights of adjoining housing developments. To protect the privacy of adjoining housing developments, and respect the character of existing development, viewing angles from the proposed building must be considered.

Some of the key concerns regarding sites located in suburban neighborhoods are listed below:

Adequate Pedestrian Walkway System: Can residents get to where they need to go by walking?

Land Use Compatibility: Is residential land use appropriate in relationship to existing land uses? Will future land use of neighboring land be appropriate for proposed residential development on a particular site?

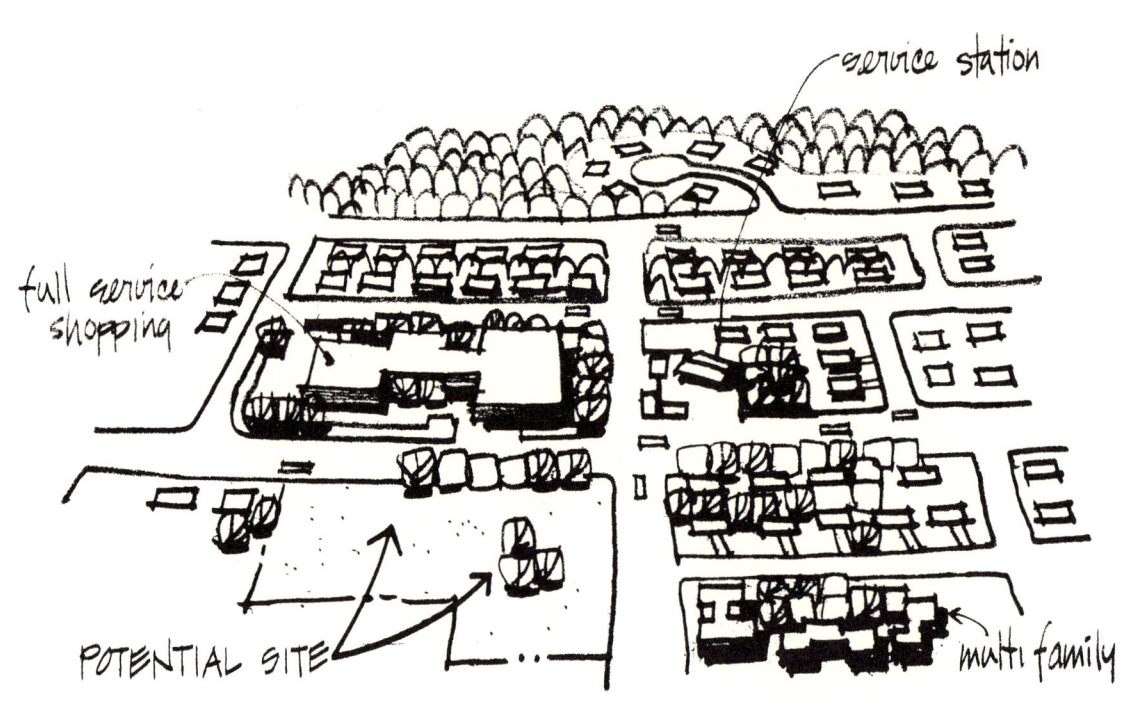

TYPICAL SUBURBAN NEIGHBORHOOD

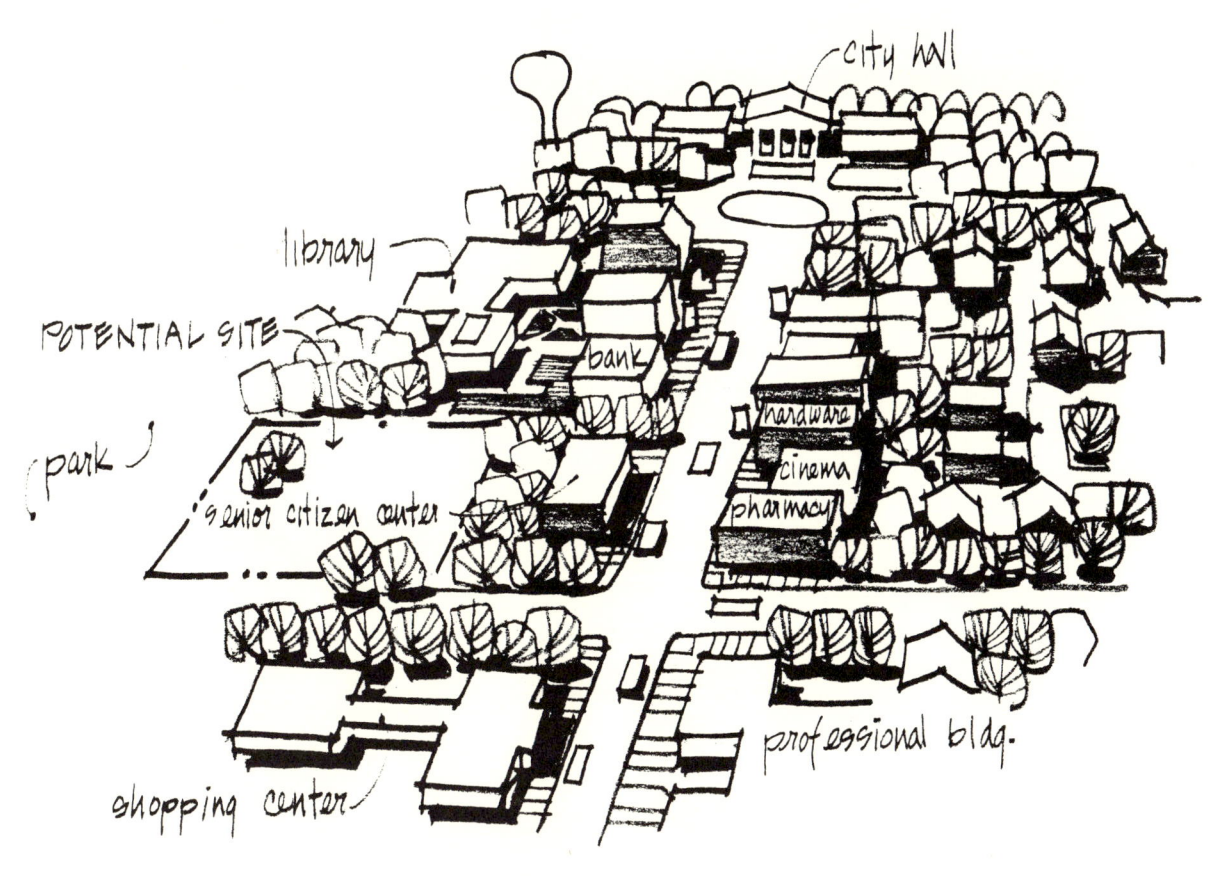

A TYPICAL SMALL TOWN SITE

SMALL TOWN NEIGHBORHOOD SITES

Smaller communities with a population of less than 10,000 offer potential sites for housing developments for the elderly. It is here that the distinction between community and neighborhood becomes less distinct because a neighborhood may encompass a major portion of a community. These smaller villages tend to be compact and efficient with a main street adjoining older residential areas. A general problem with small towns is that sites within the town limits are usually smaller than those found in larger, more urban areas. The visual character of these areas is very difficult, if not impossible, to match with a high-rise development for the elderly without destroying the charm and warmth of the neighborhood. Therefore, housing developed in small town neighborhoods should tend to be low rise in nature or, if a high-rise development is built, it should be executed with extreme sensitivity, utilizing proper site planning standards. Care should be taken to insure that there are potential opportunities for community involvement available in these communities where the pace of daily life tends to be slower than in larger communities.

Some of the key concerns regarding sites located in small towns are listed below:

Image: Will the small town image of the community be compromised by the development?

Availability of Community Involvement: Is access to social interaction obtainable from the site?

Sufficient Market Demand: Sufficient market demand for proposed elderly housing is always necessary, but this is a particular concern in small towns since the size of the total market might not be large enough to support an elderly development sufficient in size to be economically feasible.

In summary, these three neighborhoods pose different considerations for housing for the elderly, although some considerations generally hold true for all sites. A combination of both the needs of the elderly and site characteristics must be utilized as the criteria for selecting sites for housing for the elderly. This combination should stress proximity of the site to services and opportunities for further social involvement.

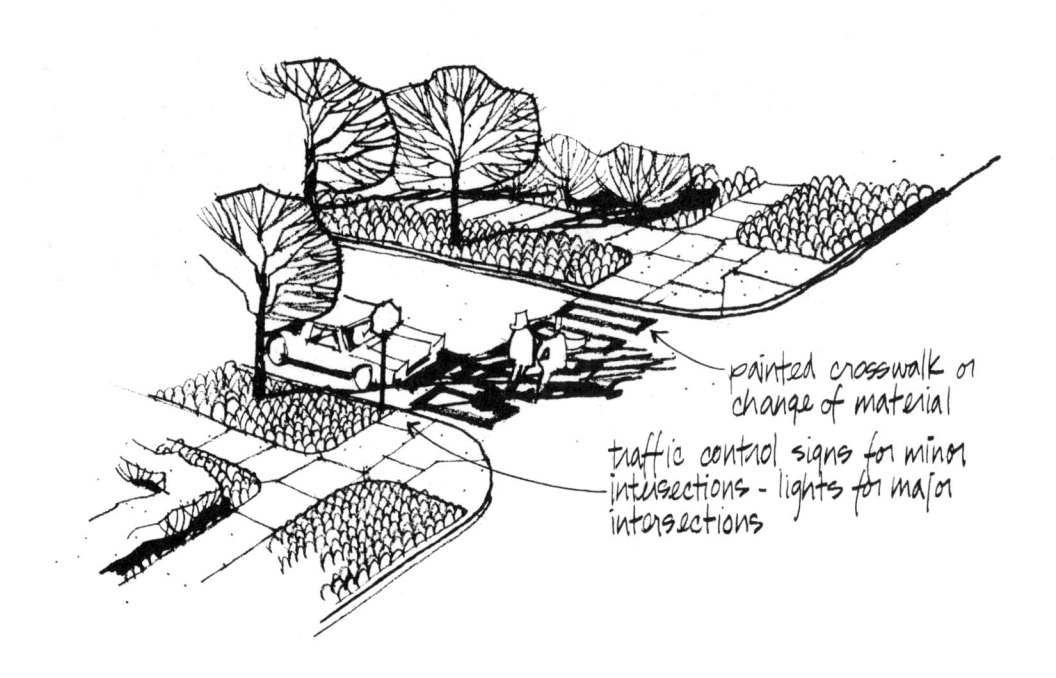

painted crosswalk or change of material

traffic control signs for minor intersections - lights for major intersections

PROXIMITY TO SERVICES and OPPORTUNITIES FOR COMMUNITY/SOCIAL INVOLVEMENT

Proximity To Services Relationship

Elderly housing sites should be located within a reasonable walking distance of services. Mere proximity in terms of short distances between the site and the service facility is, however, only one consideration in regard to the availability of services. There are three further criteria that must be applied to determine acceptable site proximity to services:

Adequate Walkway System: There should be safe and adequate paved walkways that are well lighted and maintained. Snow removal, which is of special concern, should be provided. Crosswalks must be delineated and, for crossings at streets or roads with heavy traffic, crosswalk control devices should be provided. If these walkway facilities are not available, close proximity to services is of little value to elderly pedestrians. In addition, it is recommended that shopping carts be made available to elderly residents.

Assured Pedestrian Security: The neighborhood within which the site and services are located should be a reasonably safe area where elderly pedestrians would be reasonably free from fear of bodily harm or robbery.

Neighborhood Topography Characteristics: Neighborhood topography can also influence the availability of services. Elderly people often have a fear of slipping on icy pavements and suffering injuries. Slopes between housing and services in question should not be greater than 10 percent, and these slopes should not run farther than 75 feet. Cumulative slopes between the proposed site and the services in question should not exceed an average slope of 6 percent.

Lighting min. 2 ft candles required

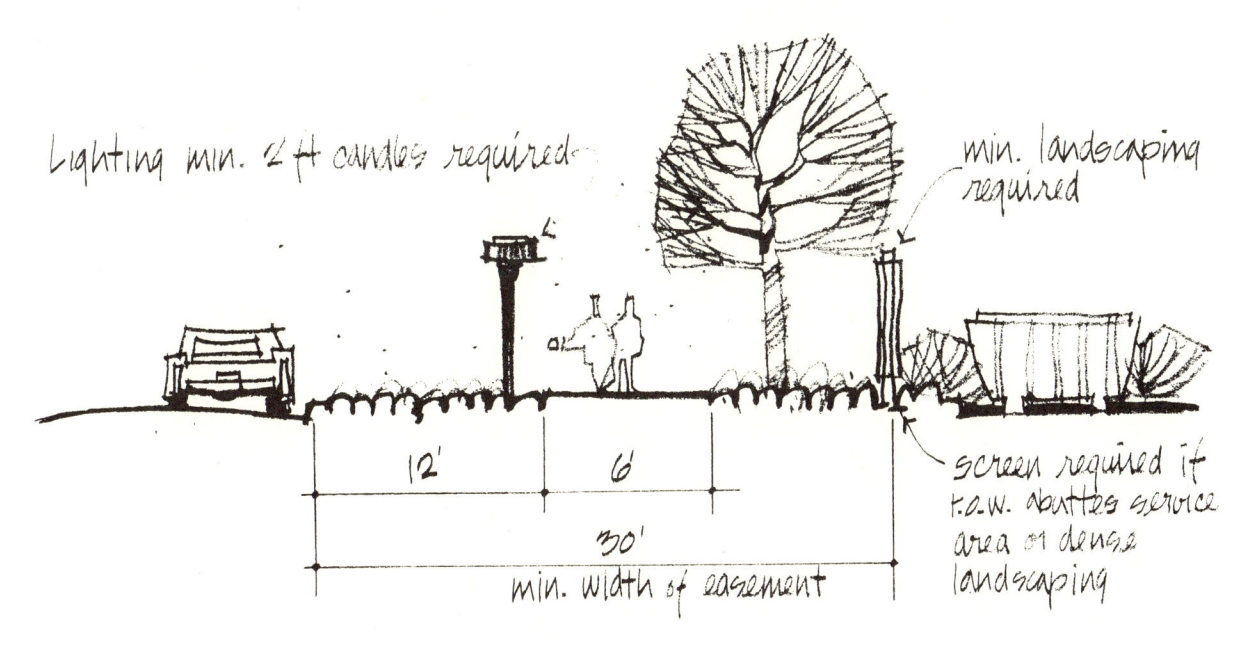

min. landscaping required

|← 12' →|← 6' →|

|←———— 30' ————→|
min. width of easement

screen required if r.o.w. abuttes service area or dense landscaping

DESIRABLE OFF-SITE WALKWAY CHARACTERISTICS

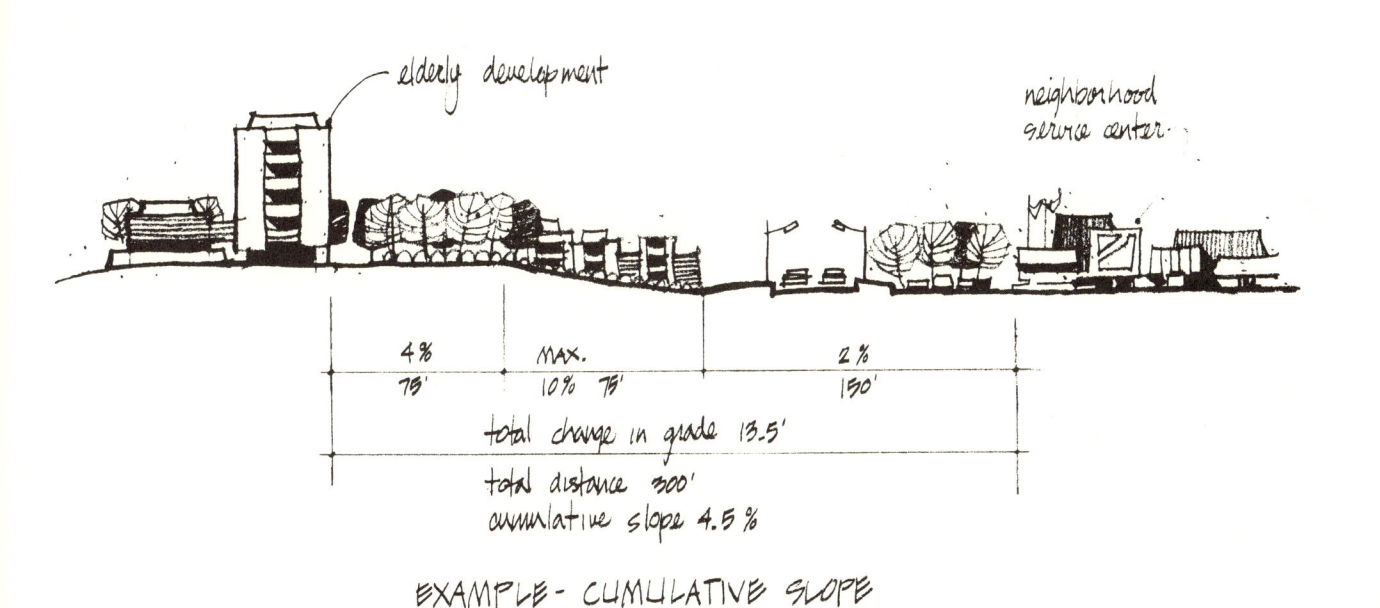

elderly development

neighborhood service center

| 4% | MAX. | 2% |
| 75' | 10% 75' | 150' |

total change in grade 13.5'
total distance 300'
cumulative slope 4.5%

EXAMPLE - CUMULATIVE SLOPE

Table D indicates specific definitions of what a reasonable walking distance is for specific housing types. It also specifies which services are vital and mandatory.

Proximity For Further Community/Social Involvement Relationships

The following is a list of cultural and recreational facilities which should be available to the elderly residents. It is desirable that these facilities be located within 2,000 feet of the proposed site with an adequate pedestrian walkway system available. Public transportation will, however, be acceptable as a valid link to these facilities if the transit stop is within 1,500 feet of the subject site and if the public transportation system is well established in the community.

    Social services/community elderly center
    Community park offering scheduled spectator events
    Neighborhood park offering active and passive activities
    Houses of worship
    Motion picture theater (except in small towns where none exists)
    Proximity opportunities for continuing family/friend relationships

TABLE D — CRITERIA FOR SITE PROXIMITY TO SERVICES BY DEVELOPMENT TYPE

SERVICES	TYPE I, Elderly Apts. (self-sufficient)	TYPE II, Elderly/Family Mixed	TYPE III, Congregate	TYPE IV, Self-sufficient/Congregate
Mandatory services:				
Supermarket or food store **	1,500 feet	2 miles	2,000 feet	1,500 feet
Drugstore	1,500 feet	2 miles	1,500 feet	1,500 feet
Transit stop †	1,500 feet	not applicable	1,500 feet	1,500 feet
Desirable services: ††				
Department or clothing store	2,000 feet	5 miles	2,000 feet	2,000 feet
Bank	2,000 feet	3 miles	2,000 feet	2,000 feet
Medical services	2,500 feet	3 miles	2,500 feet	2,500 feet
Beauty parlor	2,500 feet	3 miles	2,000 feet	2,500 feet
Barber shop	2,500 feet	3 miles	2,000 feet	2,500 feet
Restaurant	3,000 feet	5 miles	3,000 feet	3,000 feet
Post office	3,000 feet	5 miles	3,000 feet	3,000 feet

   *   Definitions for development types are given on page 12 in the programming section.
  **   Prices in this food store must be competitive with those found in other supermarkets within the community/region.
   †   Not applicable in small towns where public transportation does not exist.
  ††   Selection priority will be given to sites offering as many of these services within the prescribed distances, or shorter distances, as possible.

Distribution Of Developments

Natural community development patterns do not include large concentrations of elderly people at one location. A development for the elderly concentrated beyond certain limits encourages the isolation of elderly people. For this reason, it is generally recommended that not more than 300 units be located within any half-mile radius.

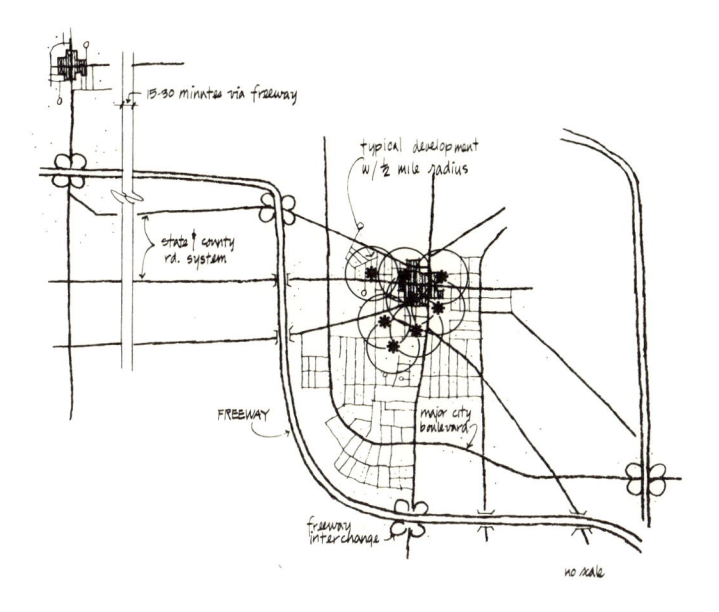

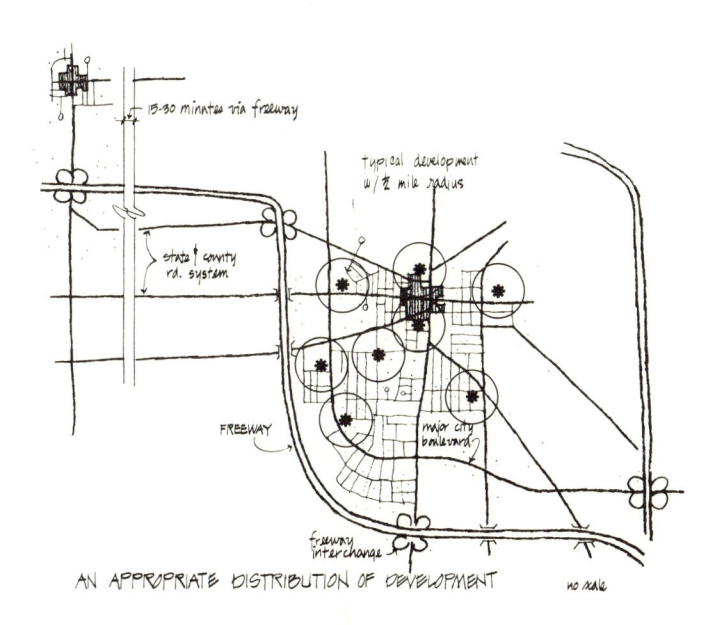

AN APPROPRIATE DISTRIBUTION OF DEVELOPMENT

THE SITE

The community/region and the neighborhood are crucial dimensions of concern that cannot be overlooked. The site itself is, however, the most basic unit of analysis considered here and, although community/region and neighborhood concerns must be addressed and met, the following criteria emphasize the primary importance of the proposed site.

Below is a list of categorical criteria that has been logically developed by analyzing the unique needs of the elderly and the characteristics of sites found within the context of an urbanizing landscape.

The categories of criteria include considerations of physical characteristics of the site in question, security in regard to personal safety, land use compatibility, and site density/distribution criteria.

SITE SIZE, FRONTAGE and CONFIGURATION, and TOPOGRAPHY

Site Size: The required size of a site is a function of building height, setback requirements, open space, parking, and services (see section on programming, page 16).

Public Right of Way Frontage: Development image is an important concern. The site should be self-advertising, and it should have market visibility to traffic passing by. The following is a list of specific frontage relationships which can be used as a guide in prescreening sites. Compensating locational and site characteristics may warrant special consideration in regard to frontage.

SITE FRONTAGE RELATIONSHIP

Size of Development	Required Continuous Feet of Frontage
Small development (24 units or less)	100 feet
Moderate development (25 to 90 units)	150 feet
Large development (100 units or more)	200 feet

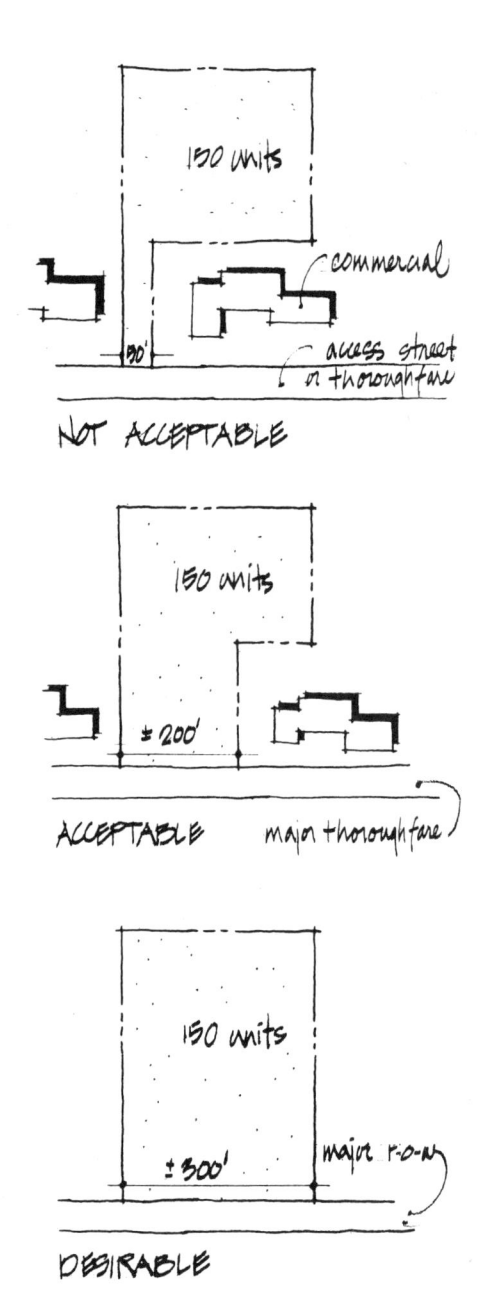

Configuration: The site configuration should permit proper site plan organization (see section on programming, page 17). Sites with simple, rectangular configurations are desirable.

Topography: Access to the site should not involve slopes greater than 5 percent. The portion of the site that is to be developed should not have a slope greater than 6 percent on any surface that is to be walked on by residents and the site development is to be free of steps. To accommodate these standards, the portion of raw site to be developed should be characterized by gentle slopes with an overall cross slope not greater than approximately 12 percent.

Site Ecology: Soils and vegetation should be considered in regard to the impact of site development on the overall forest and wildlife ecology of the neighborhood and community/region.

DENSITY

The designated density of a development is a function of currently available financing programs that prescribe the economic feasibility of a minimum number of units. Of equal importance, density is also a function of livability which is delineated through proper architectural and site development (see section on overall site/spatial requirements, page 15).

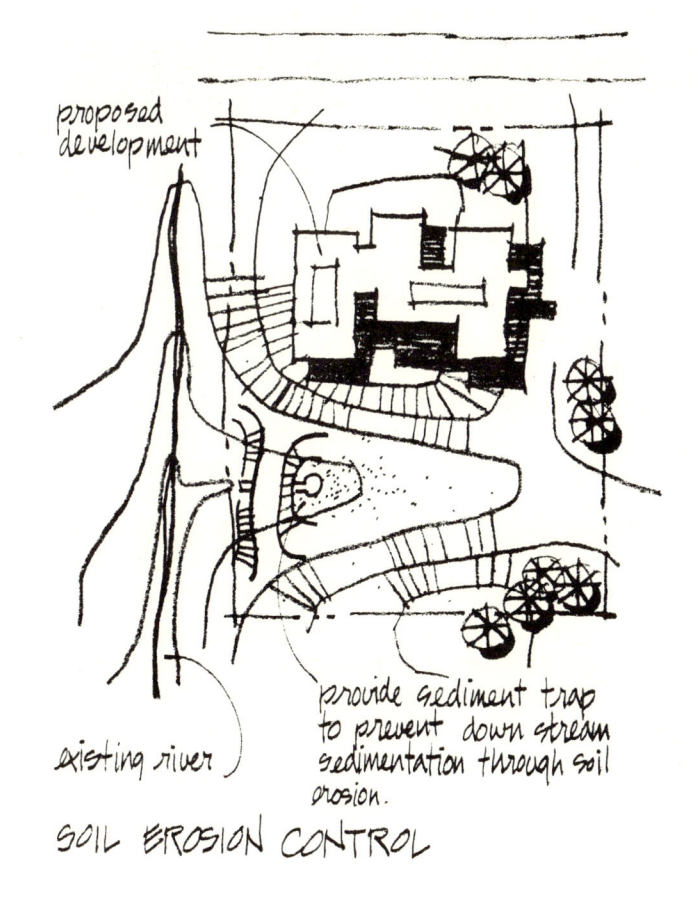

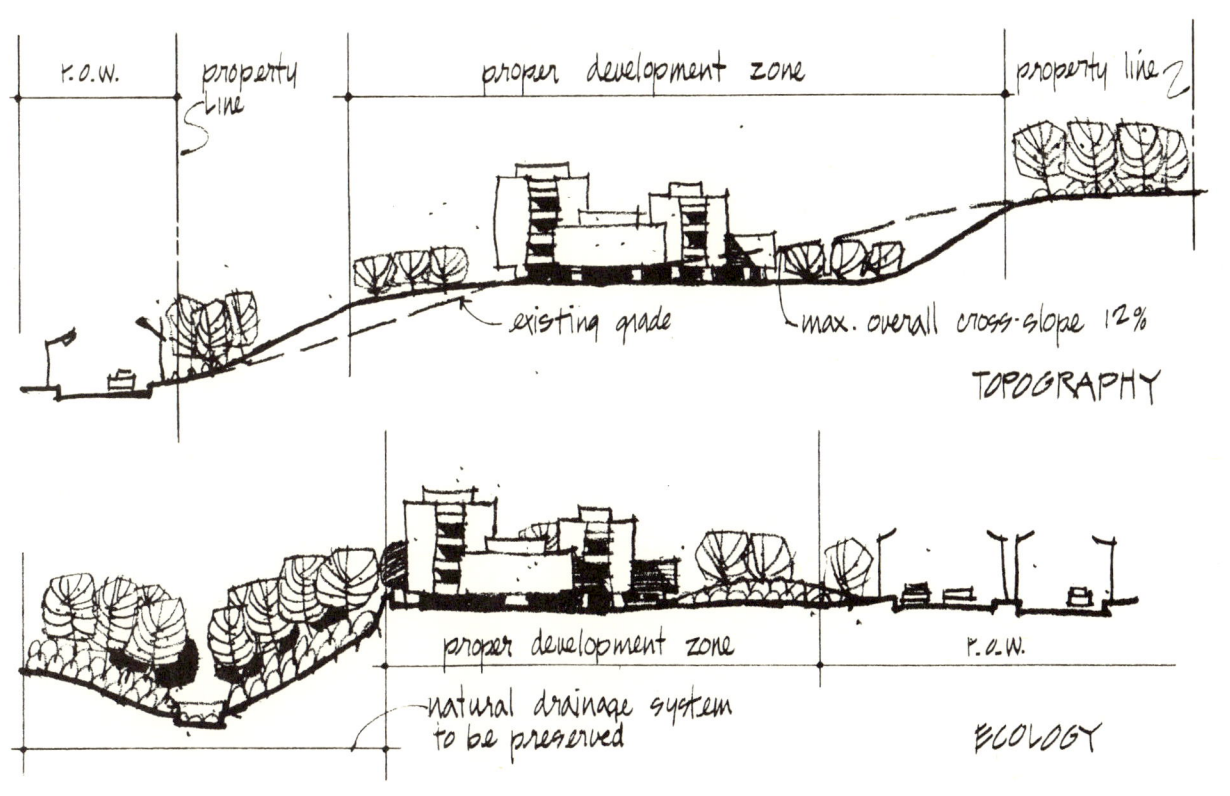

SOIL EROSION CONTROL

TOPOGRAPHY

ECOLOGY

ADJACENT LAND USE COMPATIBILITY

Sites should not be developed in areas which are not compatible with residential character even though zoning might permit such development. There are two categories of concern in considering the impact of site development on the adjacent properties in the neighborhood, and the effect of various adjacent land uses on the site.

Visual Impact of Site Development: If single family residential land uses occur on property adjacent to the proposed site, and, if the proposed structures for housing the elderly are more than two stories in height, the building(s) should be set back from the common property line a minimum distance equal to the height of the tallest component of the structure.

Implications of Adjacent Land Uses to the Site: Certain adjacent land uses often render a site unacceptable; these include the following:

Non-residential related, heavy strip commercial

Scrap storage or sanitary land fill area

Heavy industry

Fire/police/ambulance service or other similar noise generating land uses

Automotive service facilities larger than a service station

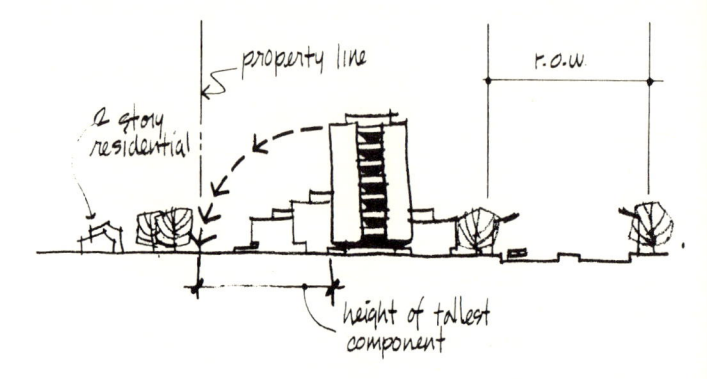

DEVELOPMENT SETBACK

CONCLUSION

These categories of criteria were developed through careful analysis of the unique needs of the elderly. They have implications at the community/region, neighborhood, and site levels. A logical and comprehensive approach to selecting appropriate sites involves a progression through these three levels. To look at the site alone is not enough and can result in an unsuitable environment for living. A more comprehensive approach to site selection is necessary to achieve an environment where elderly people can live in dignity.

4
design

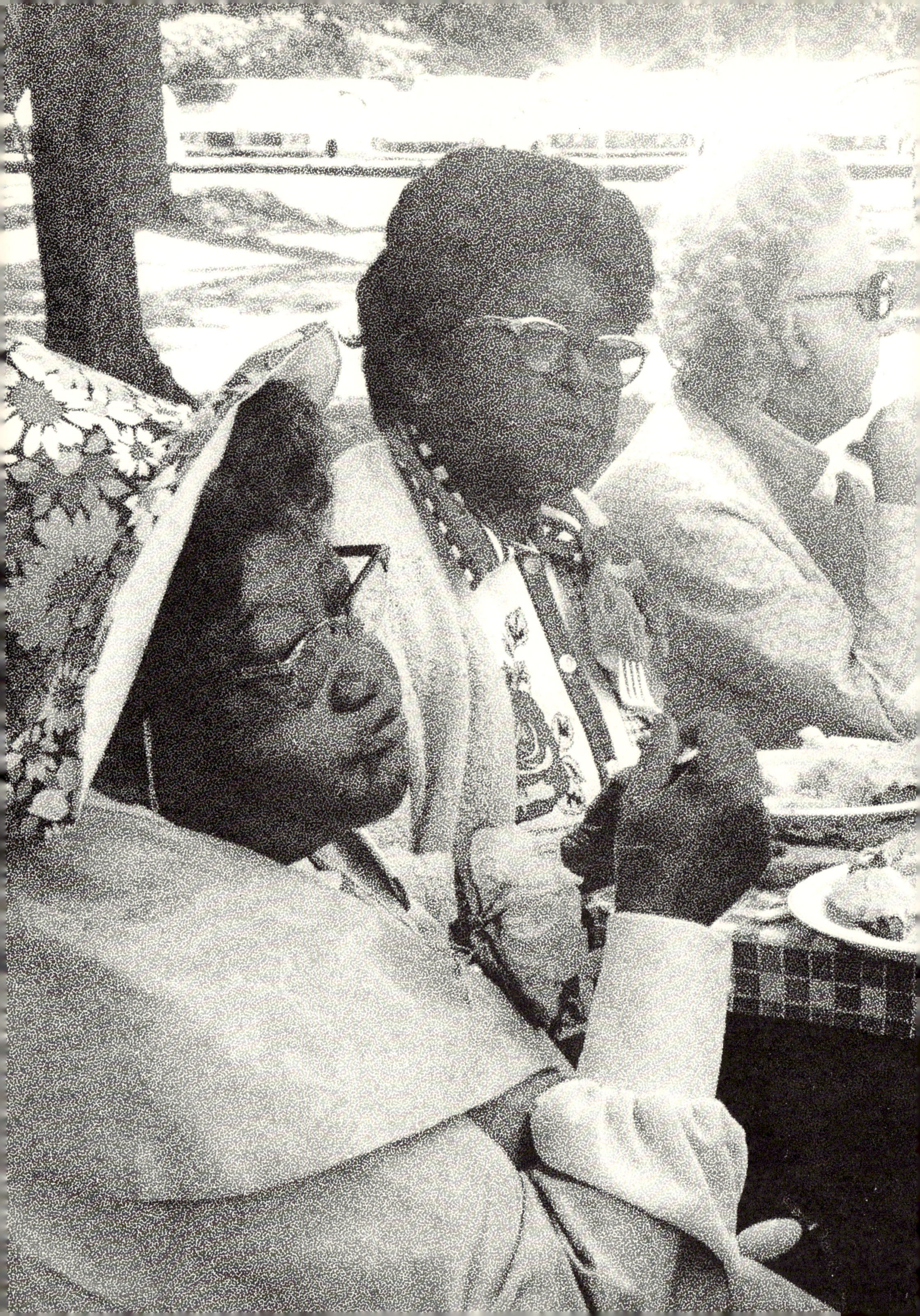

design

INTENT AND ORGANIZATION

This section is concerned with the physical design of residential buildings and their settings. It is assumed that, by the time the development team reaches this section, a development program will have been established and a site already selected. The purpose of the section is, then, to provide guidelines which help the development team in the process of translating the activity and numerical program into an effective residential design on the proposed site, in the same manner which Sections II and III guided the programming and site selection processes.

The preparation and presentation of design guidelines is necessitated by the fact that most development teams find that they have neither the time nor the money to conduct the basic research needed to understand the way in which dwellings function in relation to the elderly. The result can be designs which are based upon unsubstantiated, arbitrary, or intuitive judgments. To fill this void, the growing body of knowledge concerning housing for elderly persons has been abstracted here. The intention is to insure awareness of the basic functional and spatial requirements which allow the home and its setting to match the needs and aspirations of its user. This section thus becomes an operative standard to be used at the very earliest stages of conceptual design.

The design section is composed of three major subsections:

1. HUMAN NEEDS AND THE AGING PROCESS
2. DEVELOPMENT ACTIVITY COMPONENTS
3. DEVELOPMENT DESIGN

The first subsection is an attempt to give insight into what happens to a person as he or she grows old. Age-related perceptual and physical capability losses are explored in terms of their implications for the satisfaction of basic human needs. Emphasis is given to broad performance guidelines useful in relating the physical environment to needs of the elderly housing user. These guidelines form the basis of the detailed explorations of the other two subsections.

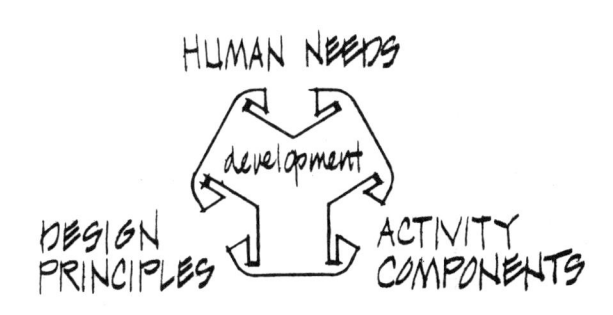

The second and third subsections are an exploration of the housing design process. The second subsection focuses on the activities which must be accommodated within a development, giving each functional and spatial definition. Activities are viewed within the broad context of the three major components of a development, namely, the site, buildings, and the dwelling unit. Pertinent performance characteristics for the facilities required by each activity are set forth emphasizing the limitations of the user. The subsection is concluded with an exploration of the overall functional organization of developments.

The subsection on development design deals with the aggregation of dwelling units into buildings and the formation of an effective site setting. Emphasis is given to the implications of various site and building types and to the creation of aesthetically appropriate building/site compositions.

In presenting design guidelines, the intent is not to restrict the creativity of the development team. Rather, the purpose is to spell out, before work begins, the nature of a desirable product.

HUMAN NEEDS AND THE AGING PROCESS

The development of appropriate and applicable design guidelines involves a direct response to the needs of the elderly resident. The basic human needs of the elderly are identical to those of any other age group. Human needs which relate to the environment can be divided into two categories:

Physical Needs: Those needs which involve using the environment in order to sustain acceptable physical health and comfort levels

Perceptual Needs: Those needs which involve a person's ability to process information about his environment and other people in that environment

In some cases it is difficult to clearly separate these two categories of need because there is a strong, symbiotic relationship between the two. It must be recognized that these needs are just as intense for the elderly as they are for anyone else.

Throughout the aging process, positive changes occur which provide a continuing growth in maturity and environment. As people age, however, they also experience losses with respect to their health, their senses (hearing, seeing, smelling, touch, and tasting), and their relationships to friends and loved ones. The table which follows illustrates this phenomenon.

The "Age-Loss Continuum" has the effect of making the elderly person less certain about the fulfillment of his needs. Many people face uncertainty in their day to day living and this can be exhausting. With a good night's sleep or by engaging in recreation most people are, however, usually able to bounce back. Elderly people are not as resilient and often do not bounce back as quickly. Therefore, the satisfaction of human needs, both physical and perceptual, must be approached with special care.

"THE AGE-LOSS CONTINUUM"

*LOSSES:	AGE	30	40	50	60	70	80	90
Separation of children					✱			
Death of peers						✱		
Loss of spouse						✱		
Motor output deterioration							✱	
Sensory acuity losses						✱		
Age related health problems							✱	
Reduced physical mobility							✱	

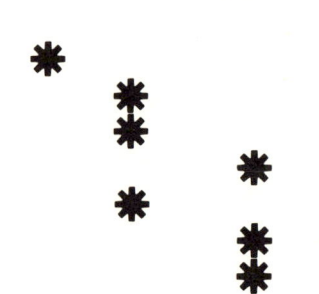

*The losses for each specific individual, of course, would not happen as precisely indicated for each age category. This is an abstraction used for analytical purposes only.

Source: L. Pastalan, "Privacy as an Expression of Human Territoriality." In L. Pastalan and D. Carson (eds.), *Spatial Behavior of Older People* (Ann Arbor: The University of Michigan Press, 1970), page 98. Used with permission of the author.

There are two factors involved in satisfying the physical needs of elderly residents; convenience and overcoming physical handicaps. The implications of these factors for the physical designer are more easily understood if presented in direct relationship to the component of the environment which they affect. Therefore, where applicable, the discussion of physical needs is contained within the guidelines for each housing development component.

To understand the process of gratification of perceptual needs, it is necessary to develop an understanding of how people perceive space and other people in space. To achieve a better understanding of how people perceive "places" and "other people" it is necessary to realize that people carry and maintain in their minds a map of the world with a "fix" relative to where they are.[1] In a similar manner people carry and maintain an "album" of social relationships. These friendships are built up over a lifetime. People develop and maintain their maps and albums

---

[1] D. Appleyard, "Styles and Methods of Structuring a City," *Environment and Behavior* 2 (1970): 100-116.
T. R. Lee, "Psychology and Living Space." In R. M. Downs and D. Stea (eds.), *Image and Environment* (Chicago: Aldine, 1973), pages 87-108.

using the same information processing method which involves obtaining answers to four sets of physical/social questions about their surroundings:[2]

1. Where am I? Who is it/he?
2. What will happen next? What will it/he do next?
3. Will it/he be good or bad?
4. What can I do about it/him?

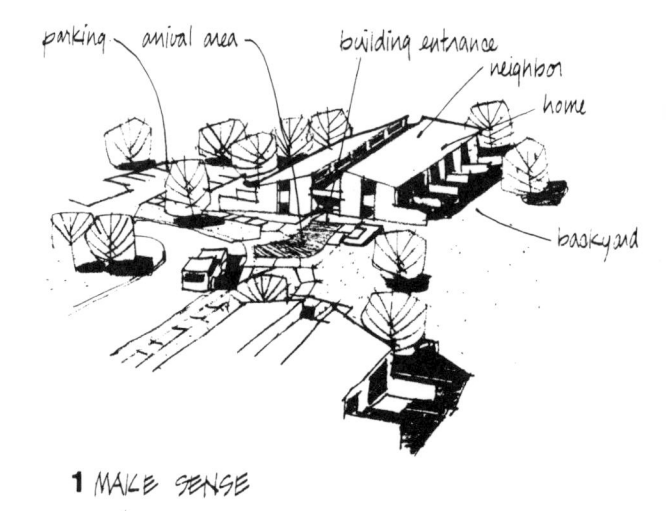

People use their five senses to absorb and process information about their physical/social surroundings. Perception and information processing is made easier for people, depending on how the physical environment is construed. Design facilitates this whole phenomena when it allows the physical environment to:

Make Sense: Making sense out of places involves being able to recognize what and where people are and how they relate to their mental maps of the world.[3] The same applies to people and their "people albums"....

1 MAKE SENSE

Offer Potential for Exploration: Places should provide a variety of physical forms, shapes, textures, and colors so that people can know where they are located within a place. Another important factor in exploration is mystery; that is, the attraction of the partially seen. Both variety and mystery can emphasize the desire for exploration.

variety

mystery

2 OFFERS POTENTIAL FOR EXPLORATION

---

[2] S. Kaplan, "The Challenge of Environmental Psychology: A Proposal for a New Functionalism," *American Psychologist* 27 (1972): 140-143.
S. Kaplan, "Cognitive Maps in Perception and Thought." In R. M. Downs and D. Stea (eds.), *Images and Environment* (Chicago: Aldine, 1973), pages 63-78.

[3] R. W. White, "Motivation Reconsidered: The Concept of Competence," *Psychological Review* 66 (1959): 297-333.
K. Lynch, *Image of the City* (Cambridge, Mass.: MIT Press, 1960).

Permit Role Choices: People do not want to feel manipulated by places. They want to be able to decide where and what they will do in a place, and they want to decide when and with whom they will do it. Relating to places and people involves certain amounts of risks. For example, places such as courtrooms can be threatening. In relationships with people, some people might be rejected and their feelings could be hurt. Not all people have the same capacity for risking. Therefore, the opportunities for risking must offer choices that accommodate a wide range of people.

I sat here — I could have sat up front

3 PERMIT ROLE CHOICES

These three factors cannot be separated in reality because they are closely dependent on one another. For example, a place that makes sense and has potential for exploration is "relaxing" and permits people to more easily decide on a role choice. It makes risking safer and easier. It is the combination of uncertainty about places and people and the capacity to risk relationships with places and people which becomes of primary concern to the designer.

Further, if the potential for exploration is allowed to dwindle, the motivation to relate to the physical environment and to other people begins to be less and less. This results in a common problem among the elderly, that of disengagement from the mainstream of life. By making sure that places make sense, offer potential for exploration (attractions), and permit role choices for users, designers can begin to create physical environments that are responsive to human needs.

Thus some of the ways in which physical design interacts with the perception of people's surroundings in satisfying human needs become clear. The behavioral theories stated above are general in nature. The following discussions are aimed at making the implications of these general principles of behavior more specific and applicable to the task of designing appropriate housing environments.

DEVELOPMENT ACTIVITY COMPONENTS

Site activities, development wide non-residential activities, and dwelling unit activities are each discussed separately. Each begins with a matrix diagram which lists the activities vertically. Each activity is analyzed in terms of the functional and spatial characteristics listed across the top of the diagram and guidelines for facilities which house the activity are developed. It is emphasized that not all of the characteristics are pertinent to all activities. Where this occurs, discussion of that characteristic is omitted.[4]

Each matrix diagram also contains a weighting system that measures the importance of characteristics for each activity and how they compare to each other. The purpose of the weighting system is to assist the development team in decision making. It is necessary that the various characteristics of each activity be accommodated. It is recognized, however, that unique circumstances of program, budget, or site may sometimes make this difficult to achieve. Therefore, the weighting system expresses three levels of importance.

Critical: Must always be achieved

Important: Should always be achieved unless some significant and outweighing benefit is gained by non-compliance

Dependent: Should be achieved but not at the expense of other requirements and may be varied to achieve benefit elsewhere

It must be emphasized, however, that the weighting system is used only where adherence to all given requirements would seriously jeopardize the economic or social viability of a proposed development. The weighting provides a method of choosing priorities.

It is recognized that occasionally consideration of a special program may require the accommodation of non-typical activities within a development which cannot be covered here. It is intended, however, that both the general information about design as well as the attitude toward the design of housing for elderly persons presented here will be used by the designer in dealing with special activities.

Before beginning the exploration of activities, it is necessary to emphasize that the material presented is not intended to create a series of "rote" design solutions. The understanding of activities and concomitant physical requirements should be the springboard of knowledge from which a wide variety of creative solutions will emanate.

SITE ACTIVITIES

The organization of activities on the site involves the consideration of relevant performance characteristics. The method of activity analysis has been explained in the introduction to this section. Briefly, site activities are listed vertically while the functional and spatial characteristics to be considered are listed across the top of the table on page 51.

---

[4] This system of presenting and analyzing activities was adapted from "Housing Design Criteria" by Theodore Liebman, Chief of Architecture, New York State Urban Development Corp., Joseph E. Brown, and A. Edwin Wolf, Harvard Graduate School of Design. New York: New York State Urban Development Corp., unpublished paper, page 6. Used with permission of the authors.

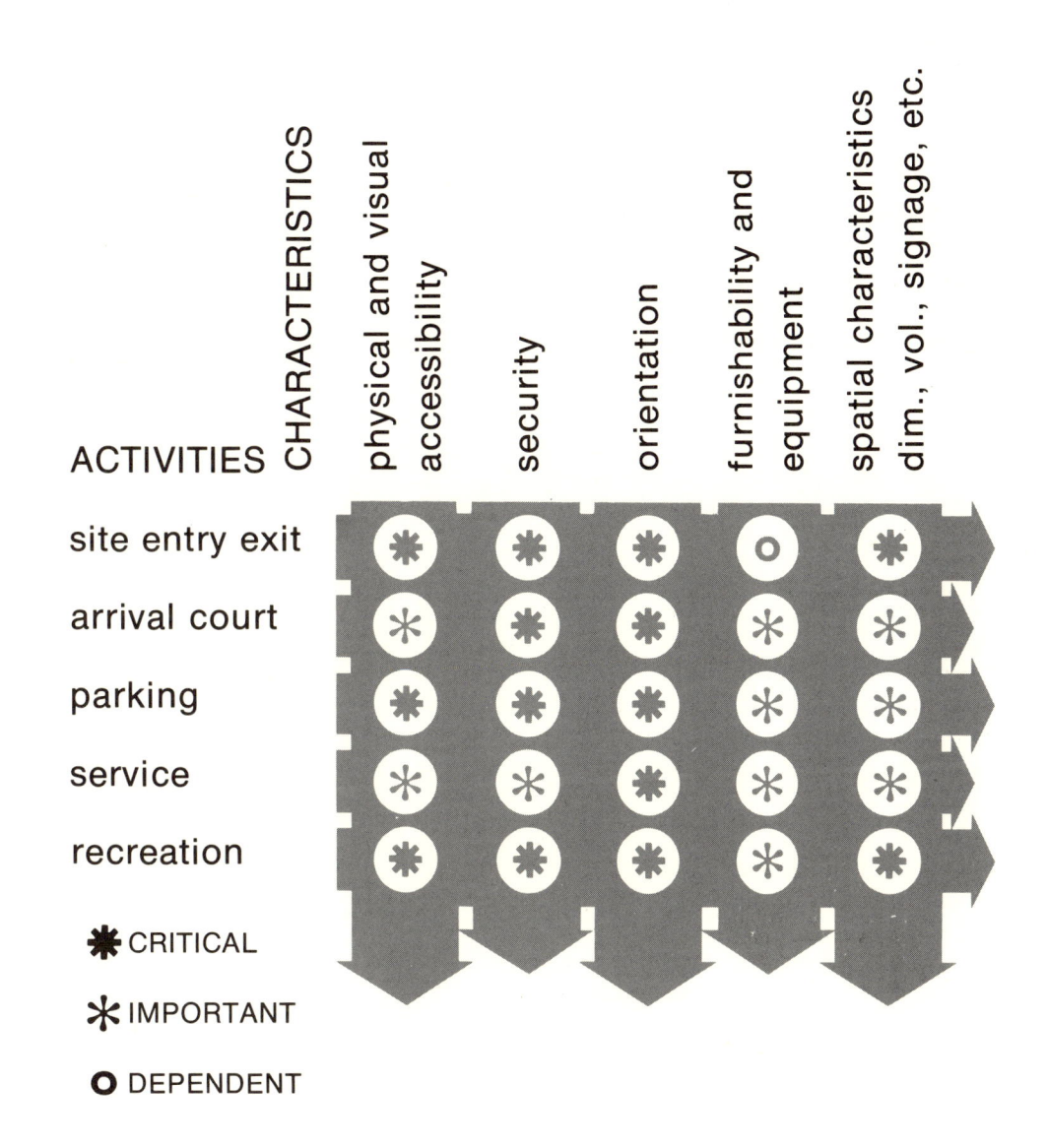

	physical and visual accessibility	security	orientation	furnishability and equipment	spatial characteristics dim., vol., signage, etc.
site entry exit	✸	✸	✸	O	✸
arrival court	✶	✸	✸	✶	✶
parking	✸	✸	✸	✶	✶
service	✶	✶	✸	✶	✶
recreation	✸	✸	✸	✶	✸

✸ CRITICAL
✶ IMPORTANT
O DEPENDENT

Matrix, activities, and characteristics adapted from "Housing Design Criteria" by Theodore Liebman, Joseph E. Brown, and A. Edwin Wolf. New York: New York State Urban Development Corp., unpublished paper, pages 11 and 81.

Site Entry/Exit

The entrance to the site is an important component of the development. There are two extremes of entrance access which are illustrated here, the entrance drive and the drive-by entrance. The key factors which usually determine the entrance are:

1. The type of roadway upon which the entrance is located and its traffic characteristics
2. The size and shape characteristics of the site

Accessibility: The entrance/exit point should be located so as to provide adequate sight distance in both directions. If the roadway upon which the entrance is located involves fast moving traffic an adequate apron or slow-down lane should be provided. Lighting should be designed to provide an even level of illumination to prevent glare at the entrance/exit.

Security: In some cases it may be desirable to locate a public transit waiting shelter at or near the entrance/exit point. Care should be taken to insure the security of this area. Planting should be high branching so as not to offer an opportunity for concealment.

Orientation: The question of orientation to a major or minor abutting street must be handled individually for each site. The issue to be considered involves a question of safety versus ease of recognition. An entrance might be located on a minor road to avoid the heavier traffic on a major road, however, this might cause problems in regard to people being able to find it.

Spatial Characteristics: The entrance/exit must be of adequate spatial proportion to the neighborhood setting to be recognizable and yet not overpowering. The entrance/exit should be designated by a sign stating the name of the development (refer to signing standards in the technical standards section, page 135).

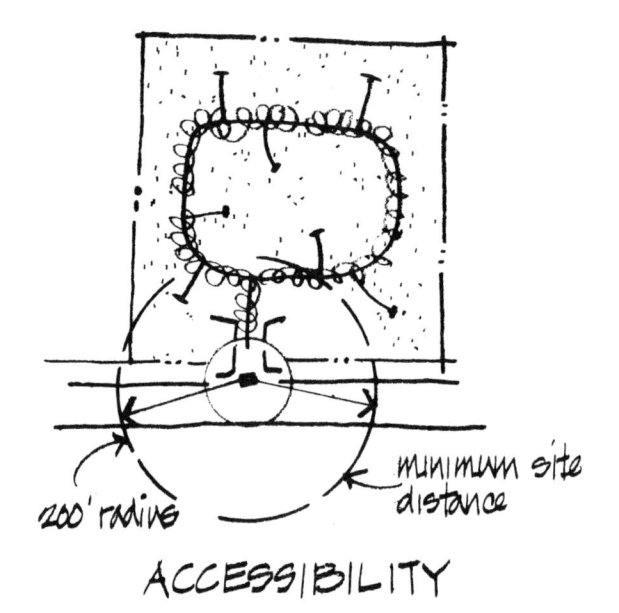

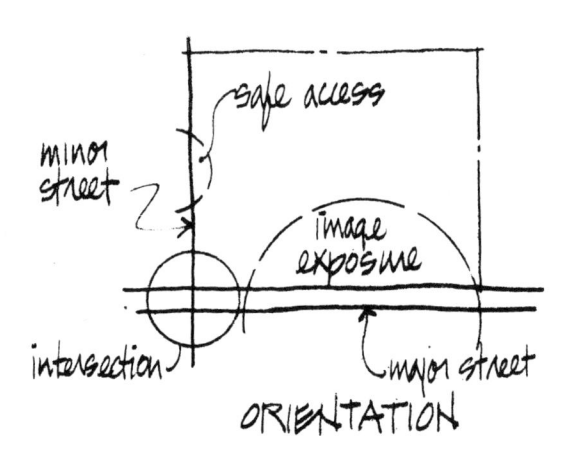

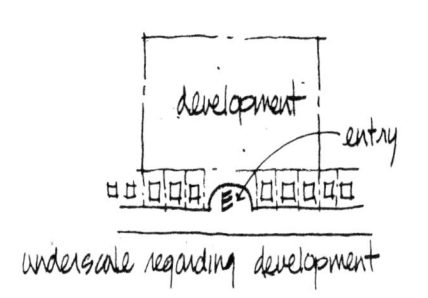

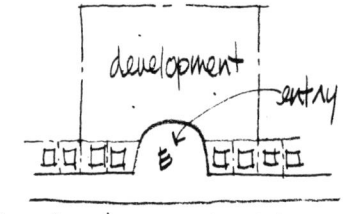

ACCESSIBILITY

ORIENTATION

underscale regarding development

balanced entrance scale neighborhood/development

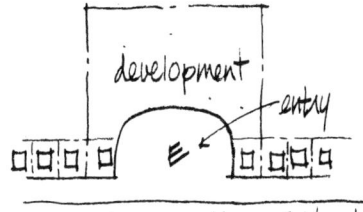

overpowering regarding neighborhood

Arrival Court

This activity includes the processes of dropping people off, loading and unloading residents' cars, short-term visitors' parking, and light servicing (mail and personal package delivery). It is an important image zone of the development.

Accessibility: The arrival court should be located so as to permit easy access to the main building entry/exit point. This connection should be covered utilizing either a canopy or a projection of the building.

Security: The area should be well lighted with an evenly illuminated distribution of light. Planting should be either high branching or low in habit to avoid creating the opportunity for concealment.

Furnishability: Vandalism and the possibility of theft must be considered in the neighborhood/community contact zone. For this reason, the furniture used in this area should be relatively immovable or fixed in place. For an urban site, the character of the street furniture should blend or match the character of the streetscape in the community. Specially designated short-term parking spaces should be provided for residents in the arrival area so that groceries or other purchases can be unloaded. These spaces would be provided at the following ratios:

NUMBER OF DWELLING UNITS	
Up to 100	6 short-term spaces
101 to 200	10 short-term spaces
201 to 300	12 short-term spaces

Spatial Characteristics: The turn-around circle should have radii which will permit easy maneuverability for both cars and buses. Where first floor dwelling units exist, there should be a buffering or screening device used between the entrance drive and the face of the building.

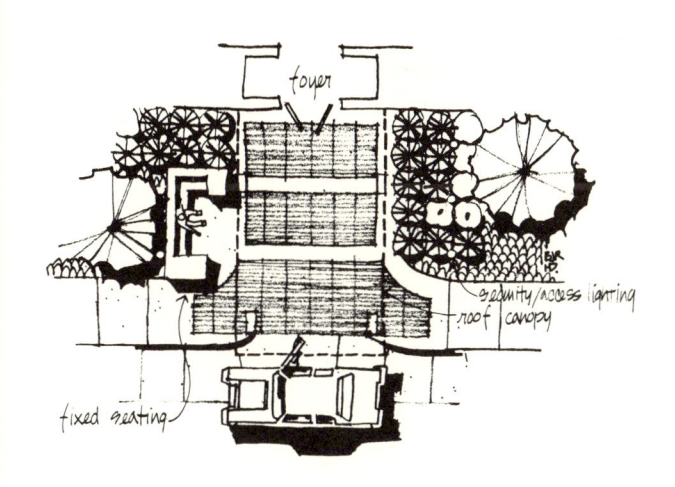

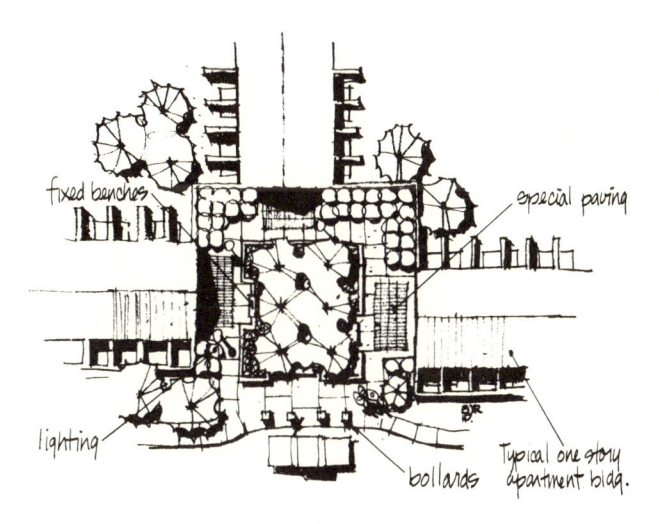

HIGH RISE ARRIVAL COURT

TOWNHOUSE/APARTMENT ARRIVAL COURT

TWO EXAMPLES OF ARRIVAL COURT IMAGE

Parking

The parking area is an important component in terms of an elderly person's being able to maintain his independence. It is his link to the services offered by the neighborhood and the community.

Accessibility: The parking area should be within convenient proximity to an entry/exit point at the building.

Security: The area should be well lighted and should have high branching plant material and low shrubs to avoid the potential for concealment. Surveillance of the area by residents from the dwelling unit is desirable; however, this must be balanced against the aesthetic concern of a dwelling unit being oriented to parking.

Spatial Characteristics: Where dwelling units exist at the same elevation as the parking area, the edge of the parking area should be located approximately half the height of the building away from the building to preserve a sense of visual foreground for the residents. This is not a hard and fast rule but rather a suggested goal.

Service

The service system should function so as not to cause any disruption to the residents' daily living activities.

Accessibility: The service entrance drive and building entrance should be accessible to the development entrance and parking road network. Where food service is available, large semi-trailer trucks must have easy access with limited backing movements.

Security: The service area should not offer the potential for concealment.

Orientation: The service area should be oriented away from major entry/exit points to the building. It should also be oriented away from the visibility of the outdoor recreation facilities. In addition, the image presented to the neighborhood should be considered.

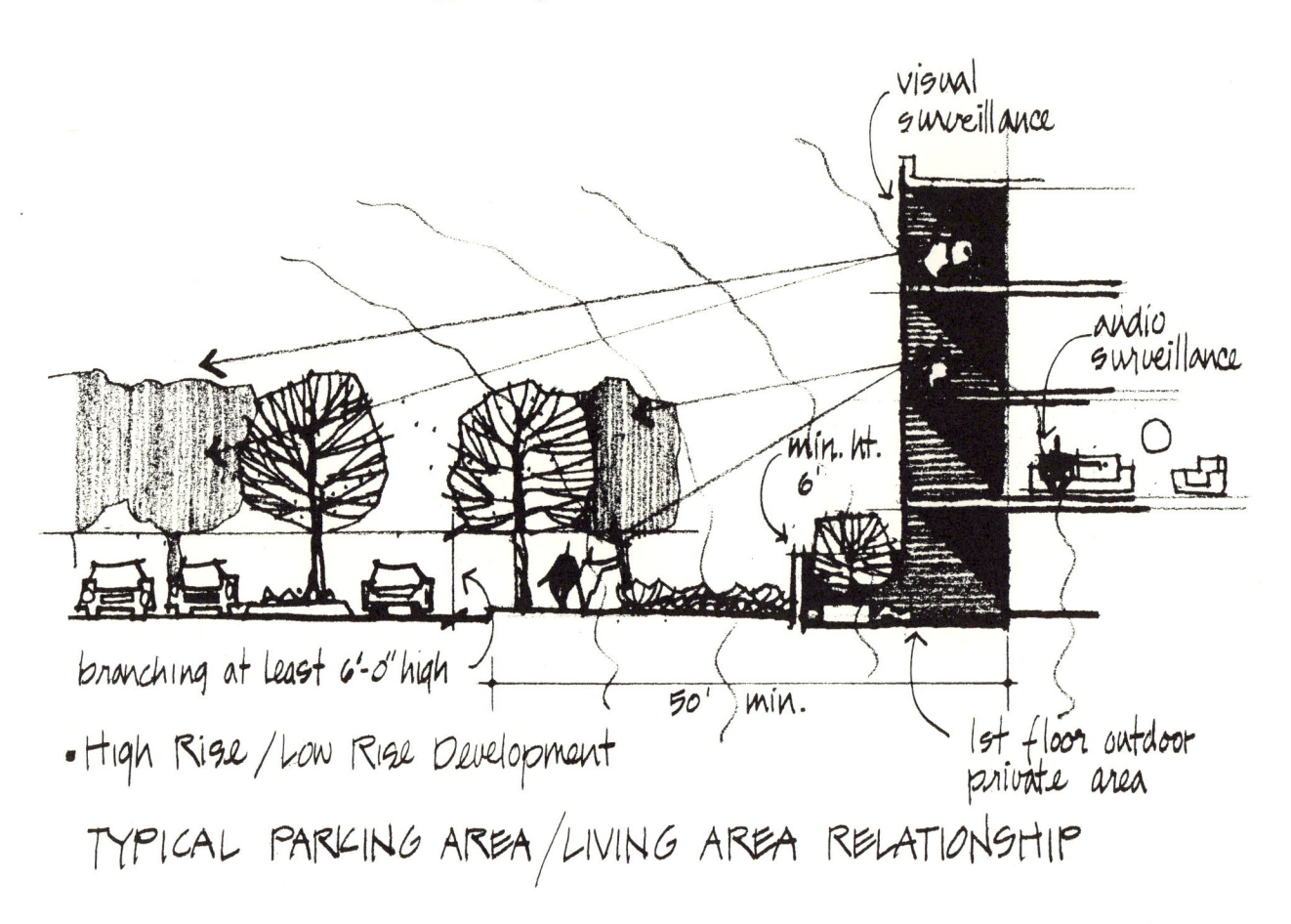

- High Rise/Low Rise Development

TYPICAL PARKING AREA/LIVING AREA RELATIONSHIP

Recreation

The outdoor recreation area should provide for a wide range of possible activities rather than a few rigid shuffleboard courts and a barbecue pit. Flexibility is a major consideration in this area.

Accessibility: This area should be protected and separate from adjacent properties and roads. It should be easily accessible to the building.

Orientation: The area should get some sun but it should be oriented and related to the building in such a way that the area does not become a heat trap, which can become uncomfortable on warm days.

Furnishability: The area should be designed to utilize portable furniture. Effort should be made to provide multi-use recreation potential.

Spatial Characteristics: The activities which can occur within a recreation area are divided into two categories, active and passive activities. It is important that a visual stimulus or attraction be a part of the passive activity area. One possibility is to organize passive and active areas so that the passive areas become a place to watch the active areas. There must be enough separation, however, so that active areas do not overpower the passive areas. A range of passive areas going from a quiet nook to a sideline seat at a volleyball court might be a solution to this problem. The outdoor recreation area should have human scale.

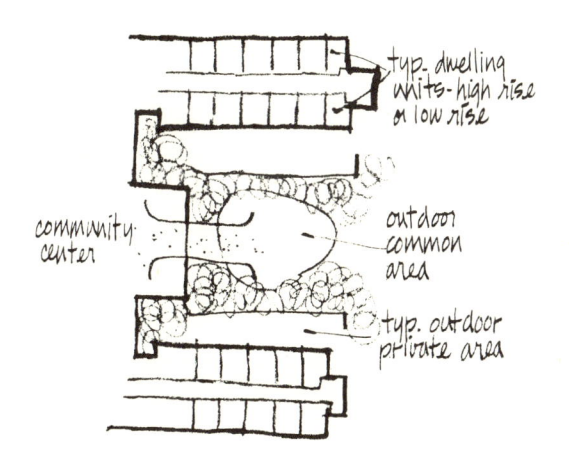

FUNCTIONAL RELATIONSHIPS

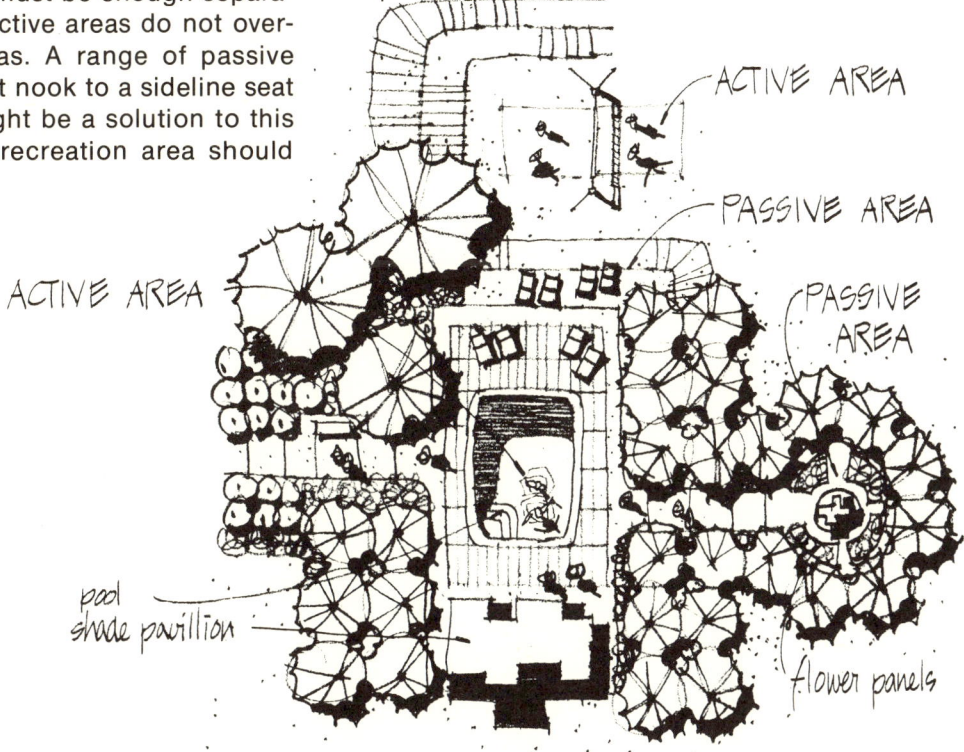

PASSIVE and ACTIVE AREAS RELATIONSHIPS for a TYPICAL HIGH RISE or LOW RISE

BUILDING ACTIVITIES

Each housing development for elderly residents will include an array of non-residential activities and concomitant facilities which are necessary to support the residential function and which enhance the lives of the occupants. It will be remembered that for programming clarity non-residential activities and facilities are of two types:

1. Ancillary, the category of activities all of which will always be required
2. Common, the category of activities of which the necessity will be determined individually for each development

Reference should be made to the programming section, page 23, for specific definitions.

The activities of these two categories are analyzed here with a view to establishing guidelines for the design of facilities to support them. The method of activity analysis is exactly the same as that used for the activities of the site and the dwelling unit. The accompanying diagram lists vertically the activities to be analyzed. The functional and spatial characteristics which form the basis of analysis are listed across the top.

A weighting of the relative importance of functional and spatial characteristics is provided here. Reference can be made to page 50 for a detailed explanation of the system.

Not all of the activities listed on the accompanying matrix diagram will occur in all developments. It should also be noted that some of these activities will be part of the dwelling unit in low density housing developments.

ACTIVITIES	physical, visual and audio accessibility	security	orientation	furnishability and equipment	spatial characteristics dim., vol., signage, etc.
building entry exit	✱	✱	O	✶	✶
management	✱	✱	✶	✶	✶
laundry	✱	✱	✱	✶	✶
mail package delivery	✱	✱	O	✶	O
trash disposal	✱	✶	O	✶	O
building maintenance service	✱	✱	O	✶	O
central food	✱	✱	✶	✶	✶
health care	✱	✱	O	✶	✶
social services	✱	✱	O	✶	✶
supportive public services	✶	✶	O	✶	✶
housekeeping assistance	✱	✶	O	✶	O
recreation and social	✱	✶	✶	✶	✶
common outdoor	✱	✶	✶	✶	O

✱ CRITICAL
✶ IMPORTANT
O DEPENDENT

Matrix, activities, and characteristics adapted from "Housing Design Criteria" by Theodore Liebman, Joseph E. Brown, and A. Edwin Wolf. New York: New York State Urban Development Corp., unpublished paper, pages 11 and 81.

Building Entry/Exit

This discussion is primarily directed toward multistory apartment structures. Accommodation of the entry/exit function in townhouses should be directed by the guidelines set forth for the dwelling unit, page 72. The design of single story apartment developments should respond to as many of the guidelines contained here as possible. It is recognized, however, that some of the locational and relationship requirements may have to be modified because of the sprawling, multiple entrance character of this building type.

It should be remembered that, because first impressions tend to be lasting, it is very important that the experience related to entering or leaving a residential building be pleasant for residents and visitors. The psychological response to building entry/exit points will either enhance or destroy the sense of residential appropriateness. All buildings should have at least one main entry/exit point as well as additional entry/exit points as dictated by the nature of the circulation system and/or the relative location of interior and exterior facilities. In these guidelines, the main building entry/exit function should consist of the following activities and/or spaces:

1. *Front porch:* outdoor sitting, viewing, and waiting area

2. *Foyer:* to serve as an air lock against the weather and the point where visitors are identified (in low density developments this may be only a sheltered outdoor area)

3. *Lobby:* primary circulation node to provide access to vertical circulation and public functions

4. *Lounge:* flexible space to sustain observation, waiting, visiting, chance meeting, and communal activities such as bake sales, activity sign-up, etc. (this may not be required in low-rise, low density developments)

Secondary building entry/exit points should have at least a foyer as a weather protection.

Accessibility: The main entry/exit point of each building in a development should occur at the focal point of both the internal and external pedestrian circulation systems, and should function as the transition zone between them. This point should be directly accessible to a vehicular drop-off/pick-up point. It should have continuous overhead weather protection from building to driveway, and should conform to applicable codes concerning the physically handicapped.

The normal arrival or departure sequence of events will best be accommodated by providing direct physical and visual accessibility (no intervening space or activity) between functional subcomponents in the following order:

1. Front porch
2. Foyer
3. Lobby
4. Horizontal and vertical circulation elements

The lobby is the focal point of this sequence and should provide direct physical and visual accessibility to the following other activities:

1. Management office
2. Mail and package rooms
3. Lounge

The physical and visual relationship between the lobby and common facilities may be indirect to the extent that access is through an intervening circulation element. This access should, however, be as simple as possible and should not include passage through other activity areas. Visual and physical access between entry/exit spaces and residential areas should always be through intervening circulation elements. Where

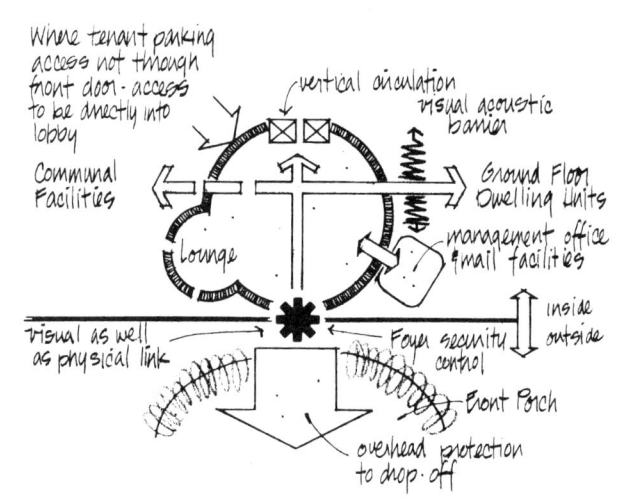

BUILDING ENTRY/EXIT

residential areas are located on the same floor as the entry/exit the circulation elements should provide positive visual and audio screening to insure privacy.

Where resident parking is not directly accessible from the main building entry/exit, a secondary entry/exit should directly connect the lobby and the parking area.

The visual and physical access between the lobby and the lounge must be such that access between the entry/exit and other activities does not require circulation through the lounge. At the same time it must be possible to observe the traffic in and out of the main entry/exit from the lounge. The main entry/exit point should be prominently visible from building approaches.

Security: Main and secondary entry doors should be locked. The door should be controlled and opened by a buzzer/call system located in each dwelling unit and in the management office.

All entry/exit points should provide a full view of the outside from behind the locked door in lobbies. The view should cover a sufficient field of vision to insure the resident or visitor that there is no danger before leaving the security of the building. Such a view should extend unobstructed all the way to potential destinations such as the parking lot, the public street in urban situations, and the vehicular pick-up point.

Orientation: The entry/exit spaces (especially the lounge) should be oriented to receive some sunlight each day. Northern orientations should be avoided where possible. The lounge and its windows should be organized to capture views of surrounding street life.

Furnishability: Lounges should be provided with comfortable seating for at least ten people in developments of 100 units or more; in very large developments several lounge areas may be a desirable solution. The lobby should provide adequate wall and floor area for displays, bulletin boards, information signs, bake sales, and the like without interference with circulation. The space should be such that alternate furniture arrangements and furniture arrangements which provide both private conversation areas and less private viewing areas are possible. The use of the space for a sale or sign-up activity should not totally negate its other purposes.

Spatial Characteristics: The foyer and the lobby should be bright, welcoming, and easy to maintain. They should project an image of spaciousness and residential activity and engender pride in residents. The spatial volume of the lobby, principally its height, should be greater than normal residential ceiling height. It should have sufficient floor area to accommodate both circulation and people standing still in chance meeting or decision making.

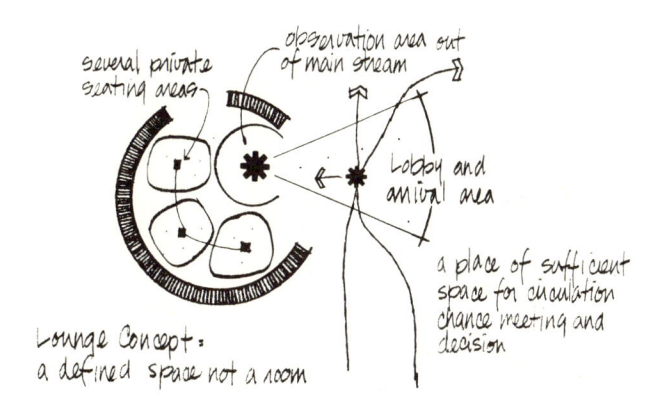

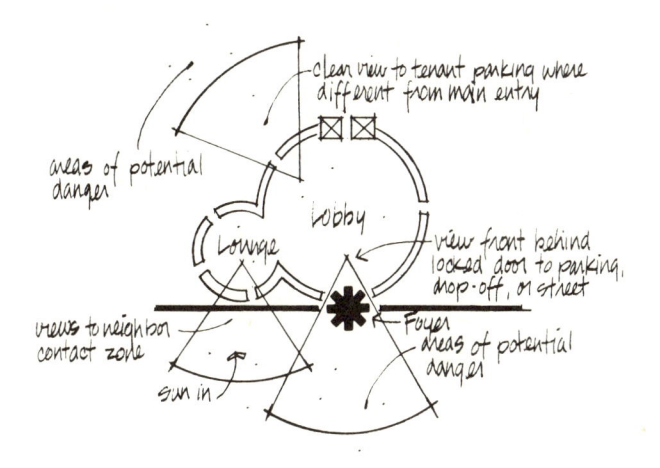

The lounge should be a more intimate space having a more nearly residential ceiling height. It should not be a room with doors, but rather should be a contained space with free opening to the lobby and surrounding circulation elements. Individual or small groups of people should feel comfortable in the lounge. Its spatial composition and furniture arrangement should provide both very private areas and less private transition areas to the very public lobby areas.

The overall spatial character and organization of all areas of the entry/exit activity should offer the resident the opportunity to choose between privacy or public contact in the conduct of the activity. The lobby and lounge should be capable of being adapted for a variety of short-term social activities. The latter requirement means more space will be required than that necessitated by circulation and furniture placement.

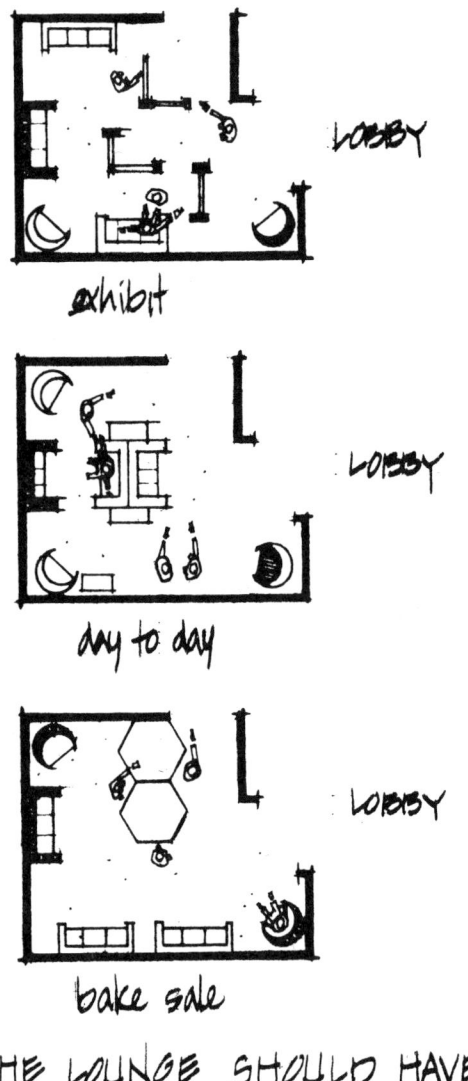

THE LOUNGE SHOULD HAVE MULTI-USE FLEXIBILITY

Management

There should be a space or spaces provided in each development for visitor reception, rental activities, and development administration.

Accessibility: The management office should be located with direct physical, visual, and auditory accessibility to the main building entrance and lobby, to common facilities when they are on the main floor, and to the mail/package room. Accessibility to residential areas should be through an intervening circulation element. Direct visual access is here taken to mean visual control.

Security: The management office in multistory structures should control the building entrance and lobby to discourage unwanted guests and add to the sense of security of the residents. This should be accomplished in an unobtrusive manner so as to avoid the feeling that all those who pass by are under surveillance.

Orientation: The management office should have natural light and also overlook critical areas of the site whenever possible, such as parking lots, entrance drives, etc.

Furnishability: This should be determined for each development, but it should at least include facilities for a manager and secretary, that is, two desks with chairs, filing cabinets, and several chairs for visitors.

Spatial Characteristics: The management office should accommodate its intended functions without becoming officious or overbearing in character. It should probably have normal residential ceiling height; and it should be enclosed with glass as much as possible, both to enhance surveillance and to achieve an open, welcoming quality.

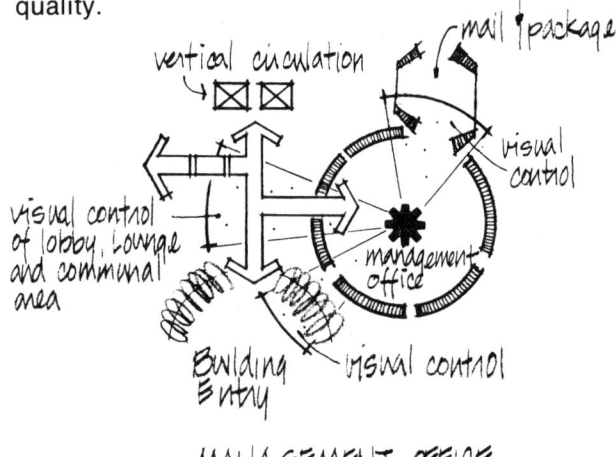

MANAGEMENT OFFICE

Laundry

Laundry facilities should be provided in all developments. Such facilities should provide for the mechanical washing and drying of clothes as well as soaking and sorting of clothes.

Housing for the elderly that is in townhouse form should have laundry hookups provided within the dwelling unit. For dwelling units in apartment buildings, laundry facilities may be contained in the dwelling unit or they may be centralized at one or more convenient locations to serve groups of dwelling units.

When laundry facilities are located within an apartment dwelling unit, no laundry tray is required, but the discharge from the washer must be separate from all sink and lavatory drains. Dryers must be separately vented to the outdoors.

Accessibility and Security: Where laundries are centralized in apartment developments, the location of such facilities should be convenient for use of the tenants. Whether they are located on each floor or at other areas of the building will depend on the size of the development and the number of dwelling units per floor. As a general rule, however, laundry facilities should be located on each floor of medium- and high-rise buildings to insure convenient access for all tenants.

Where dwelling units are in groups of buildings, an attempt should be made to provide a covered passageway to the laundry room.

There should be no audio accessibility between laundries and other areas of the building.

Entry doors to laundries should be designed with large glass panels through which the residents can see easily, and the room arrangement should not include areas which are totally screened from view from the hall or entry door.

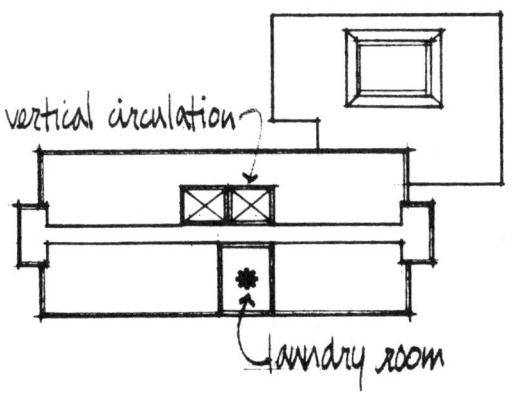

LAUNDRY ROOM ACCESSIBILITY

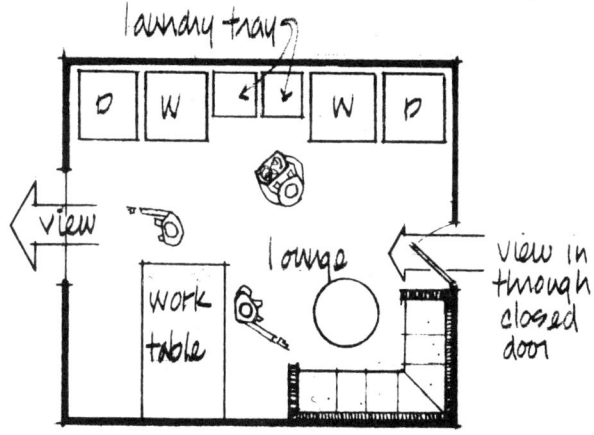

EXAMPLE OF LAUNDRY ROOM ORIENTATION

Orientation: Laundry rooms should be provided with natural light and views of the outdoors. It is also desirable to achieve a close visual link between the laundry and natural focal points in the building circulation system.

Furnishability: The suggested scale for washers and dryers is:

1. One central laundry room: one washer and one dryer for twenty (20) dwelling units
2. One laundry room on each floor: one washer and one dryer for twelve (12) dwelling units

Washers and dryers should be of the domestic size rather than the large capacity commercial size.

A large table (at least 3 feet by 5 feet) should be provided for folding clothes. An ironing board and extra convenience outlets are desirable. A water closet and lavatory basin in an appropriate room should be provided adjacent to laundries wherever possible. Seating should be provided both for waiting and to accommodate the natural social intercourse resulting from the gathering of people.

Spatial Characteristics: Laundry rooms should be designed with adequate clearance around the equipment for use and maintenance. Work space for using the laundry folding table should be provided such that circulation is not impaired.

The social functions of a laundry room can best be accommodated by room design which provides a natural lounge area.

Mail and Package Delivery

A facility for the delivery of mail and packages to tenants must be provided in all developments. In developments consisting of a large single building, a separate mail room should be provided.

Accessibility: These facilities should have direct physical accessibility from the entrance lobby and from horizontal and vertical circulation elements. They should also be directly accessible to the service entrance of the building for convenience of delivery. Visual and audio accessibility to the lounge should be indirect (screened). Visual and audio access to other areas will be determined by other considerations.

Security: These facilities should be overlooked and controlled by the management office. Control of the access door to the package room should be via a buzzer/call system.

Orientation: There is no particular need for natural light in this facility. Whether or not some natural lighting is included is entirely dependent upon the needs of other functions and it should only be included when convenient.

Furnishability: See section on technical standards, page 153.

Spatial Characteristics: In large developments, care should be taken to avoid the institutional appearance which results from a single large bank of mailboxes. Perhaps an island with mailboxes on several sides or a U-shaped configuration offers the opportunity to present small groups of mailboxes to which an individual resident can relate. It should be possible to reach this room without being forced into extensive public contact or unwanted interpersonal confrontations.

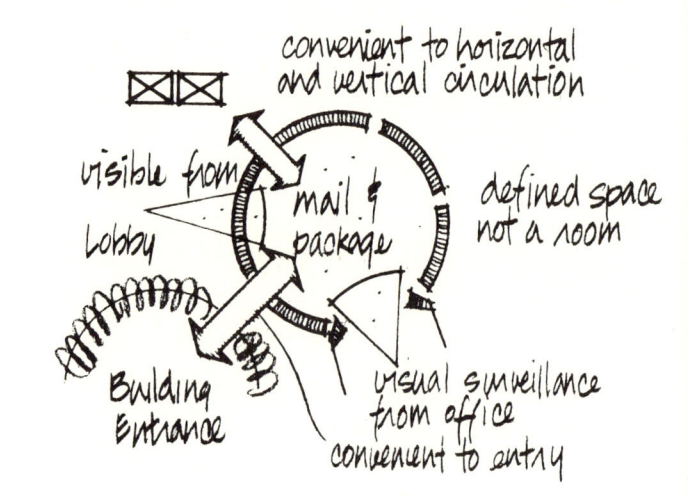

MAIL and PACKAGE

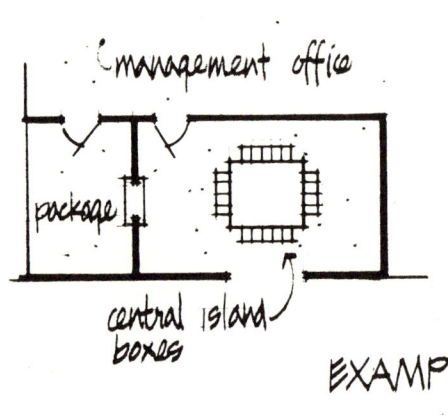

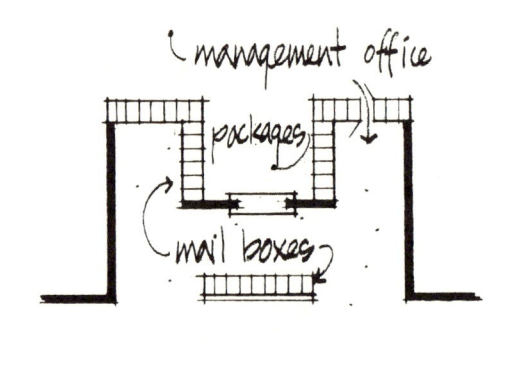

EXAMPLES OF MAILBOX ORGANIZATION

Trash Disposal, Building Maintenance, and Service

These facilities should be grouped whenever possible, forming a compact and efficient complex. This guideline can of course be waived where specific functional requirements so dictate. All floors of multi-story (except garden apartments) buildings will be provided with janitors' closets equipped with slop sinks; the closets should be sufficiently large to store the maintenance supplies and equipment normally required for the amount of floor area served.

Accessibility: Central facilities should have direct physical access to the service entrance of the building. There should be indirect physical access between these facilities (intervening circulation element) and other activity areas of the development. There should be no visual or audio accessibility between these activities and the residential and common activities of a development.

Security: Access to these facilities should be controlled by a locked door whenever they are not attended, both for the security and safety of the residents and for the security of the building.

Orientation: Whenever possible these facilities should contain windows but they are not essential.

Furnishability: Furnishability should be based on functional requirements of the individual development. Reference should be made to the section on trash disposal on page 134 of the technical standards.

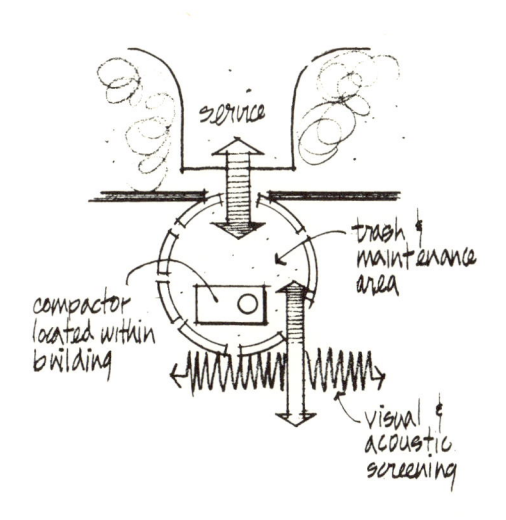

Central Food Service

Centralized provisions for the preparation and serving of meals may be provided in developments for the dependent elderly, or where the need can be substantiated on the basis of market and economic viability. The central food service facility should include: a dining room or rooms; a kitchen consisting of separate areas for food storage, food preparation and service, dish and utensil cleaning, and refuse storage and removal; and a chair and table storage room.

Care must be taken in the design and operation of a central food service facility to insure that the facility does not, by its existence, impart an institutional atmosphere to developments which should be strongly residential in character.

The kitchen should include an employee locker and lunch area.

Accessibility: The dining room should have direct physical and visual access to the food service area and the primary horizontal and vertical systems. In multi-story buildings, the distance between the dining room and elevators should be very short. Direct access should also be provided where outdoor patios or terraces which might be used for dining are included.

There should be no direct physical or visual access between the dining room and the food storage, preparation, or cleanup areas.

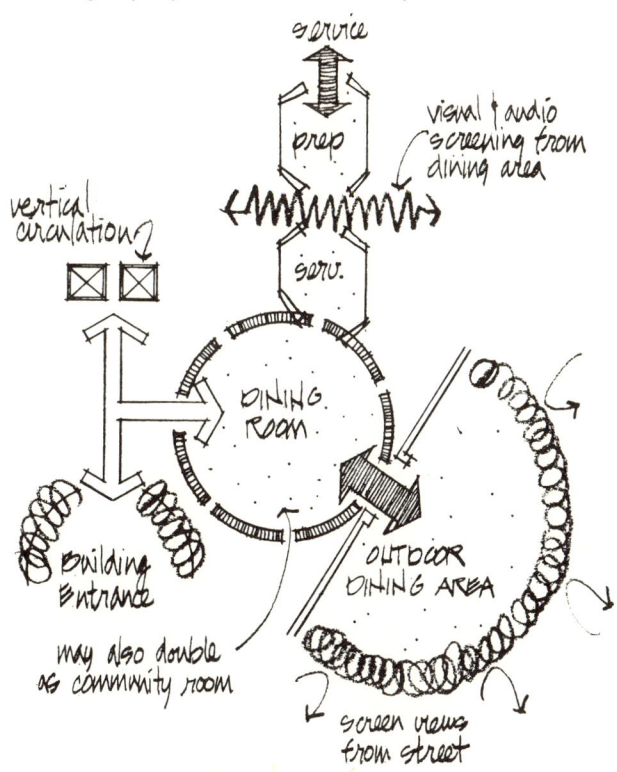

Audio access between the dining room and other building areas should be strictly limited. There should be no audio access between the kitchen and the dining room. The dining room should be visually screened from surrounding public streets.

Orientation: The dining room should be oriented to receive morning sun whenever possible. It should also be oriented to benefit from the best outdoor views available on the site. It is especially desirable if the dining room can overlook the outdoor common area. Such orientation should not result in a loss of immediate privacy for diners.

Furnishability and Equipment: The dining room should be so designed as to comfortably accommodate the programmed number of diners at tables which seat no more than four persons each. The kitchen should be arranged and equipped for adequate and efficient food storage, preparation, serving, and cleanup in the proper sequence. Kitchens should be planned by a qualified professional food service consultant.

All food service facilities should be designed to protect against contamination. Facilities should be easily cleaned and free from inaccessible areas.

Spatial Characteristics: The dining room should be bright and warm in image. Its physical size should never be allowed to destroy the normal levels of personal privacy required for pleasurable dining. Care should be taken to avoid the environmental feeling projected by institutional cafeterias. The desired image is closer to that of a restaurant. Depending on its size, the ceiling height should be somewhat greater than normal residential dimension. A large simple rectangle is not necessarily acceptable. A series of interlocking smaller dining areas is more desirable. At the very least, large simple spaces should be modulated with movable screens and planting boxes. Windows and lights should be placed to modulate the total space into smaller seating groups.

The dining room may be usable as a large group meeting and multi-purpose activities room where the room is so designed to allow convenient and rapid conversion to other uses. Where this capability is achieved, the dining room may function as an effective substitute for the community room.

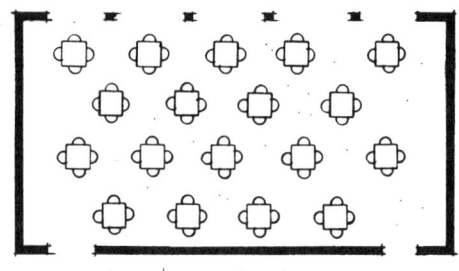

typical institutional dining

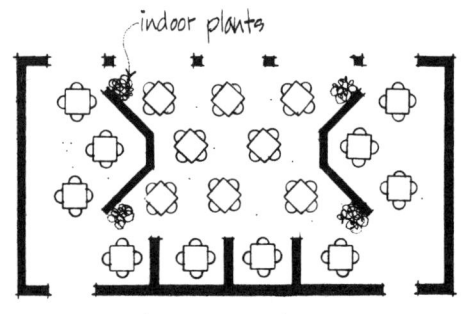

indoor plants

humanized dining

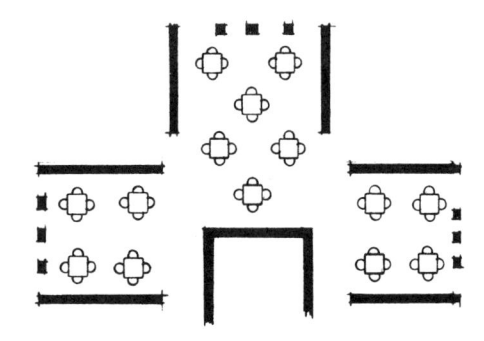

dining humanized by providing several separate spaces

DINING TABLE ARRANGEMENT

Health Care

An outpatient medical and/or dental clinic facility may be provided in some developments for the convenience and care of residents. When provided, the minimum installation should consist of a waiting area and two examination/treatment rooms.

Accessibility: This facility should have direct physical access to the primary building circulation system, especially in buildings with elevators. Visual access between this facility and other areas of the building should be carefully controlled to insure the privacy of users. Audio access should be strictly limited. It should not be possible to see into examination/treatment rooms from outside the building.

Security: This facility should be lockable when not in use.

Furnishability and Equipment: The waiting area should accommodate a nurse's station and seating for at least four users. The examination/treatment rooms should accommodate the equipment required by their specific function.

Spatial Characteristics: Examination rooms should be at least 8 by 10 feet in dimension.

This facility should be so located that it can be effectively converted to other uses if the clinic activity is no longer needed.

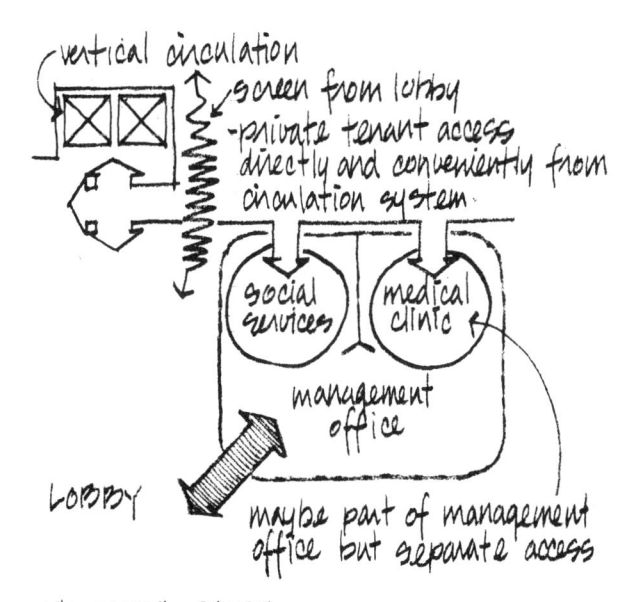

HEALTH CARE

Social Services

Spaces for the counseling of residents and the delivery of social services may be provided in some developments. In most cases these spaces can take the form of offices and should become part of the management office area. They should have the attributes of the management offices except that physical accessibility should be achieved while maintaining a high level of personal privacy for users. This means careful visual screening.

Supportive Public Services

Water fountains or coolers should be provided and should be located at such appropriate locations as lobbies, recreational rooms, etc.

Public telephones should be provided in lobbies. Phones should be adapted for use by both the physically handicapped and those people with hearing disabilities.

Housekeeping Assistance

In some developments where a high number of dependent elderly residents are anticipated housekeeping assistance services may be provided. The facilities required for this activity are simple. They include a small supply room on each floor, a central laundry pick-up and delivery point, a central supply and equipment room, and an employee locker room.

Accessibility: The supply rooms on each floor should be located adjacent to elevators and may be incorporated into the janitors' closets. The laundry pick-up point for off-site laundry service should be directly accessible from the lobby and service area but be visually screened. The central supply room and employee lockers should be incorporated into building maintenance facilities adjacent to the service area.

Audio screening should be provided.

Security: All rooms should be lockable and located so that residents do not enter them by accident.

Furnishability and Equipment: Service sinks should be provided in all supply rooms.

Recreation and Social

All developments should be provided with some common recreation, hobby, social, and meeting facilities. All developments should include a single, large, and subdividable community room. Most developments will have additional spaces serving the various functions discussed in the section on programming, page 24. The determination of the uses and scope of these facilities should be made individually for each development.

For the purpose of this discussion these facilities will be assumed to constitute a single complex containing spaces of various sizes related to their various purposes.

This complex should have as much use flexibility as possible to insure the accommodation of changing needs and to allow residents to choose activities for themselves. Secondary social spaces should be provided where use and desire can be assured. A good example of this latter case would be a small lounge area in a laundry room.

Public toilets for men and women should be provided convenient to this complex in quantities appropriate for the anticipated level of user population.

Accessibility: In large multi-story buildings, the recreational and social complex should have direct physical and visual accessibility to the building horizontal and vertical circulation system, the building lobby for guest and visitor convenience, and the outdoor common area. Visual control of the access to this complex should be possible from the management office.

Audio access between the complex and other building areas (especially residential) should be eliminated.

It should not be necessary to pass through this complex to gain physical access to any building activity area.

Each room or area within the complex should be physically accessible without dependence on circulation through other rooms or areas.

Where recreational and social facilities are in a separate building, access should be direct via the main pedestrian circulation system. The building should be visually prominent and easily identifiable.

Security: This complex should be so designed that residents will develop a sufficient sense of proprietary interest to insure self-policing. Access to the complex by non-residents should also be sufficiently controlled so that resident safety and enjoyment are insured.

Orientation: This complex should be oriented to receive sunlight for a portion of each day.

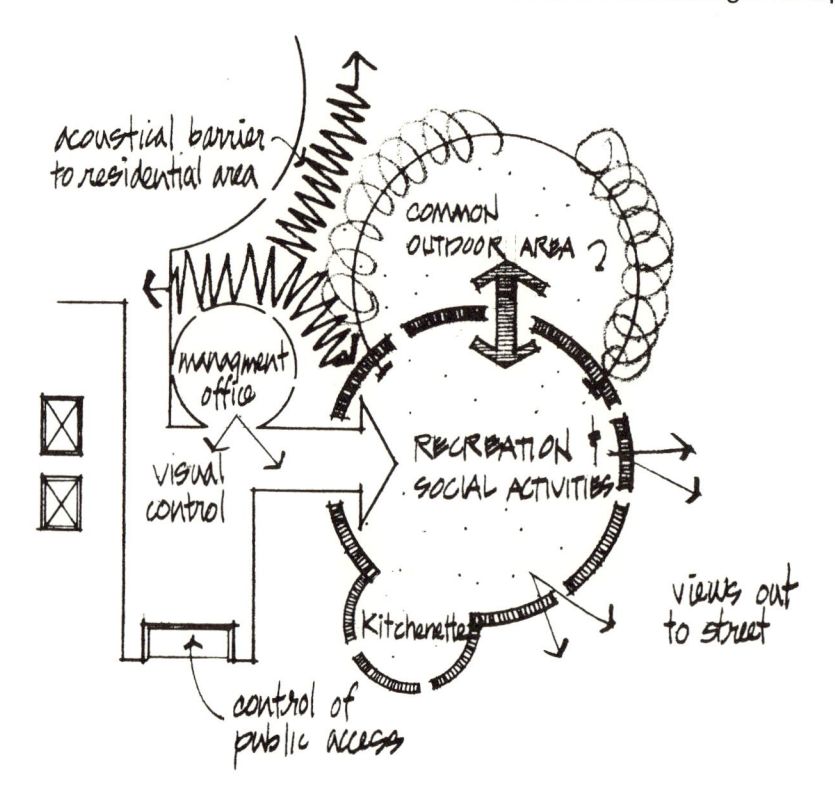

Views into the outdoor common area, the front yard, and in urban settings should be sought not only for pleasantness, but also to insure a strong sense of contact with the outside world.

Furnishability and Equipment: The furnishability of rooms and areas within this complex will generally be judged against proposed activities. Each space should accommodate the widest range of activities and concomitant furnishings and equipment as possible.

All rooms and areas should be provided with appropriate storage cabinets, closets, or shelving. The complex should contain a conveniently located chair and table storage room.

The main community room should accommodate a seating capacity for lectures, movies, etc., at least equal to the number of residents in the development. Seating arrangements should provide each person with an unobstructed view of the speaker or movie screen.

Spaces for craft or hobby activities should be equipped with service sinks and should be acoustically isolated from other areas.

All interior finishes in the complex should be easy to clean and maintain.

Spatial Characteristics: Spatial character will of course be determined by function; however, general character should be informal, bright, and warm. Spatial structure in terms of volume, sequence, and texture should enhance these qualities. The user should be able to immediately sense the organization of the recreation and social complex. Large group spaces should have proportionately higher ceilings.

Opportunities should be provided for residents to control the appearance of the complex through the use of wall decorations or other flexible design options.

It is essential that use flexibility be achieved in the design of the complex both in terms of short and long time frames. To this end consideration should be given in the design to the use of both movable and demountable partitions. Ceiling systems should accommodate the moving of walls.

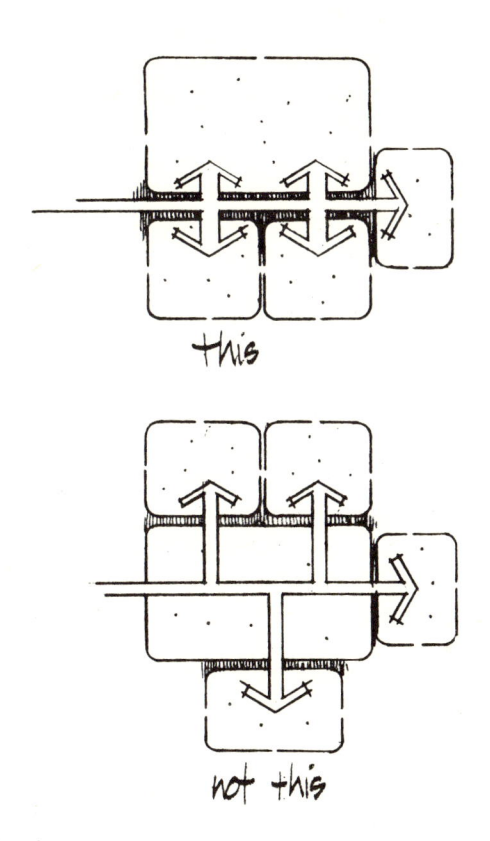

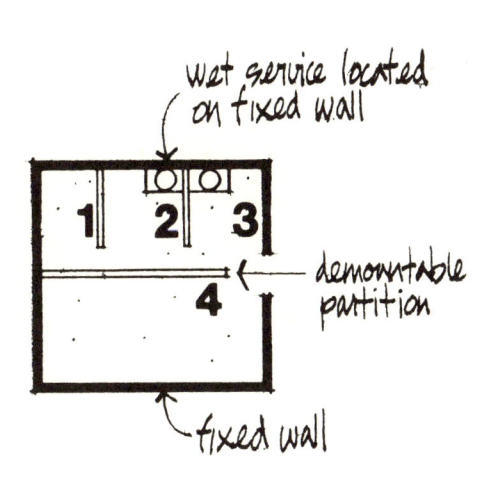

Common Outdoor

In buildings of three or more stories, where some dwelling units above the ground floor do not have private balconies, it is necessary to provide an alternate means of fulfilling both the life safety (see section on fire protection in the section on technical standards, page 154) and the amenity role of the private balcony. A common balcony located for convenient access from a public corridor can satisfy this need.

Accessibility: A common balcony should be located at a central point on the floor it serves. It should have direct physical and visual accessibility from the nodal point where the primary means of vertical circulation in the building intersects the primary means of horizontal circulation on the floor. There should be no physical or visual accessibility between the common balcony and dwelling units and private balconies. Visual accessibility between private and common balconies should be minimized.

Security: It should be possible to visually survey the common balcony from inside the building before entering. The common balcony should be physically safe for users. Handrails and enclosing walls should not only insure safety but create the feeling of safety. Handrails should be a minimum of 4'-2" high and be extremely sturdy (300 pound impact load).

Orientation: The balcony should receive sunlight at least 30 percent of each day during spring, summer, and fall. Its primary orientation should not be northerly.

Furnishability and Spatial Characteristics: Furnishability and spatial characteristics should be similar to that for private balconies (see page 87 of this section).

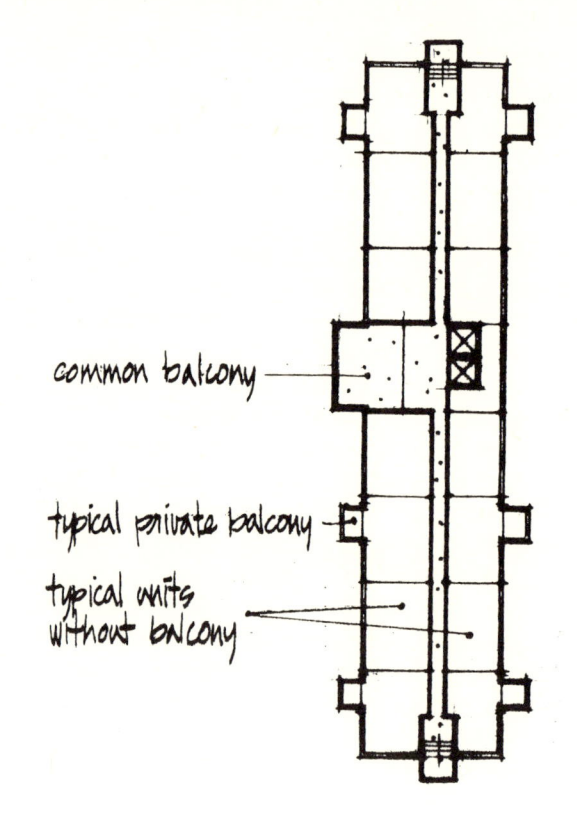

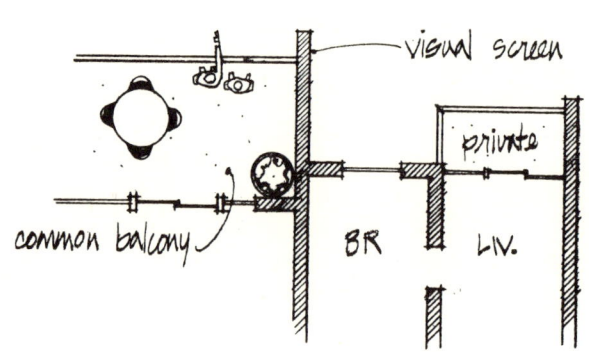

SEPARATION OF COMMON and PRIVATE BALCONIES

DWELLING UNIT ACTIVITIES

The dwelling unit is the common denominator of all residential developments for the elderly. For elderly persons, more than for any other age group, it is essential that the dwelling unit be efficient and livable. It is also essential that the dwelling unit provide both a physically and psychologically stable base from which the activities of life can be conducted.

The design of appropriate dwelling units must include the application of the three behavioral principles outlined at the outset of this section on design, namely, the environment must make sense, it must offer the potential for exploration, and it must permit a real choice of lifestyle for the elderly resident. These principles will be applied to the basic activities of the independent elderly which all dwelling units must accommodate. Where appropriate, modifications are indicated for housing for the dependent elderly person. The activity matrix and weighting system described on page 50 are used here.

ACTIVITIES	physical, visual and audio accessibility	orientation	furnishability and equipment	spatial characteristics dim., volume, etc.
entry exit	CRITICAL	DEPENDENT	IMPORTANT	IMPORTANT
food preparation	CRITICAL	IMPORTANT	CRITICAL	CRITICAL
dining	IMPORTANT	IMPORTANT	CRITICAL	IMPORTANT
living	CRITICAL	CRITICAL	CRITICAL	IMPORTANT
sleeping dressing	CRITICAL	IMPORTANT	CRITICAL	IMPORTANT
personal hygiene	CRITICAL	DEPENDENT	CRITICAL	IMPORTANT
private outdoor	IMPORTANT	CRITICAL	IMPORTANT	DEPENDENT
storage utility	IMPORTANT	DEPENDENT	IMPORTANT	DEPENDENT

✱ CRITICAL
✶ IMPORTANT
○ DEPENDENT

Matrix, activities, and characteristics adapted from "Housing Design Criteria" by Theodore Liebman, Joseph E. Brown, and A. Edwin Wolf. New York: New York State Urban Development Corp., unpublished paper, pages 11 and 81.

Entry/Exit

The entry/exit (or front door) is the critical transfer point from the least public area of the development to the least private area of the dwelling unit. If properly designed, it will insure the privacy of unit activities and contribute strongly to the sense of home. It must be a place, not just a door in a wall which opens directly into the living area or other such space.

Accessibility: The entry/exit area should be directly accessible to the following less private areas of the unit:

Food preparation
Living area, with spatial differentiation between the two functions
Storage/utility

The entry/exit area should be indirectly accessible (minor intermediate activity or a circulation path) to more private areas of the unit:

Dining
Private outdoor (optional)
Personal hygiene
Sleeping/dressing

The entry/exit area should have both visual and audio contact with visitors outside of the entry door; but visitors should not have visual contact and only controlled audio contact into the entry area of the dwelling unit. This maximizes the ability of the resident to keep out unwanted visitors and allows the resident to control the space just outside the unit.

All of the previously mentioned spaces with direct physical access to the entry/exit area should have visual/audio contact with this area for control and security within the unit. Other areas should have audio but not visual contact to minimize disruption of privacy.

Orientation: The orientation of this activity toward view and sunlight is governed by more essential concerns related to building type and the functional organization of other activities.

Furnishability: The furnishings and equipment necessary for this area are:

Storage for outer wear, that is, coats, galoshes, umbrellas, etc.; a closet at least 3'-0" by 2'-2" should be provided.
A place to sit while putting on outer wear.

Spatial Characteristics: The space should have sufficient wall area to accommodate a mirror; there should also be a clear dimension area of at least 3'-6" to 4'-0" square for putting on coats as well as greeting guests.

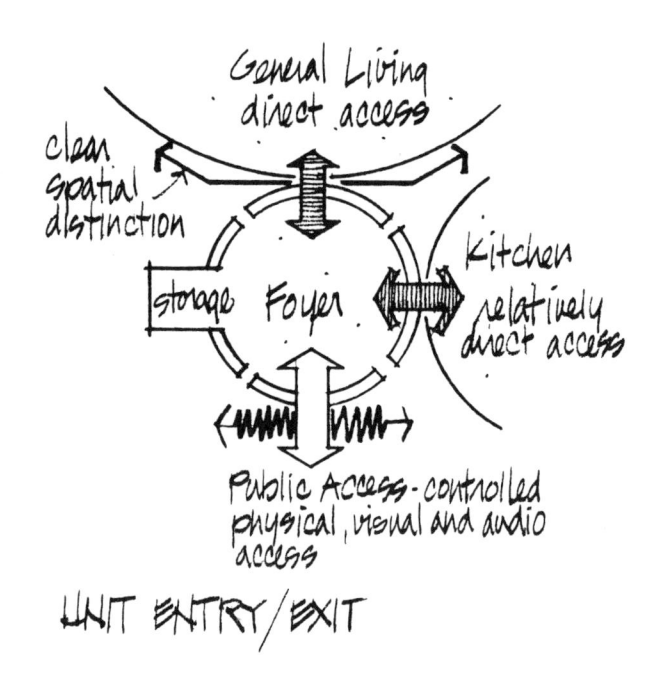

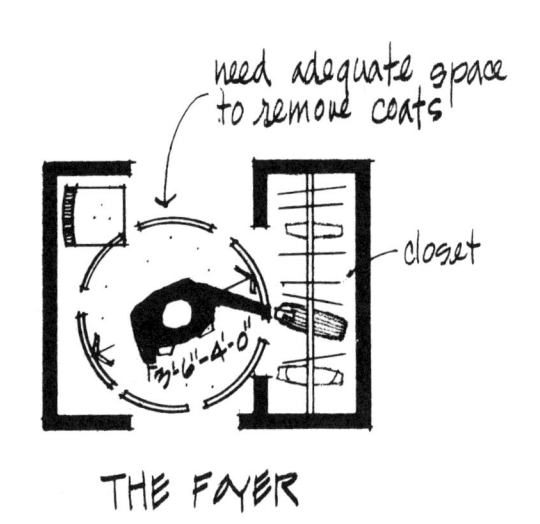

Food Preparation

The physical characteristics of the aged hamper the normal functions of food preparation, cooking, food and utensil storage, trash disposal, dish washing and drying, and eating. If appropriate physical design adaptation is not made to the food preparation space and facilities, cooking and related activities will become unpleasant, tedious, and possibly dangerous. The net effect will be the creation of a psychological barrier which deters the user from cooking and eating. This situation is particularly unacceptable because dietary problems can become acute for the aged.

Accessibility: The food preparation area should be directly accessible to the main entry/exit of the dwelling unit to facilitate carrying of packages. It should also be directly accessible to the dining area. If the dining area is outside of the kitchen, a small eating surface in the kitchen for breakfast or light meals should be provided. This can be a small table, counter, or pull-out shelf about 24 by 24 inches, set at table height and usable from a wheelchair. The food preparation area should be indirectly accessible to, but visually screened from, the living, sleeping, personal hygiene, and private outdoor areas of the dwelling unit. Of these areas, access should be most direct to the private outdoor space. In all cases, indirect access should be through easily traversed intermediate spaces or corridors.

Visual and audio contact to the entry/exit area should be maintained, while audio contact to the living, sleeping, and personal hygiene areas should be minimized.

Orientation: Often food preparation areas are located on an interior wall of apartment dwelling units, but, where possible, this should be avoided. The kitchen should be located on an outside wall with an interesting view from a window and it should have morning sunlight if possible.

Furnishability and Equipment: The necessary equipment for food preparation and related activities is:

- Ventilation, both mechanical and natural to eliminate heat and odors
- Sinks and associated work space
- Cooking unit and oven with associated work space
- Refrigerator and freezer with associated loading and unloading counter space
- Storage consisting of wall and base cabinets and pantry
- Dishwasher, optional but should be included where possible
- Dining counter (where formal dining space is outside of the kitchen)
- Clothes washer and dryer, location in the unit is optional, but the kitchen is a good location when this option is exercised

Detailed technical requirements for equipment can be found in the section on technical standards under kitchen equipment and mechanical systems, pages 148 and 155.

An example of a desirable organization of kitchen activities is shown in the accompanying diagram.

An L- or U-shaped kitchen is preferable to the pullman or corridor type kitchen. The corridor type is inconvenient for the elderly who, with advancing age and motor/sensory losses, find it difficult to repeatedly turn from one counter to another as they work. The table and diagrams contained below give necessary clearances and dimensions.

FRONTAGES FOR WORK CENTERS

WORK CENTERS	ONE BEDROOM	TWO BEDROOMS
Sink	24"	24"
Counter and base cabinet at each side	18"	21"
Range	24"	24"
Counter and base cabinet at one side	18"	21"
Refrigerator (space)	30"	36"
Counter at latch side	15"	15"
Mixing		
Base and wall cabinet	30"	36"

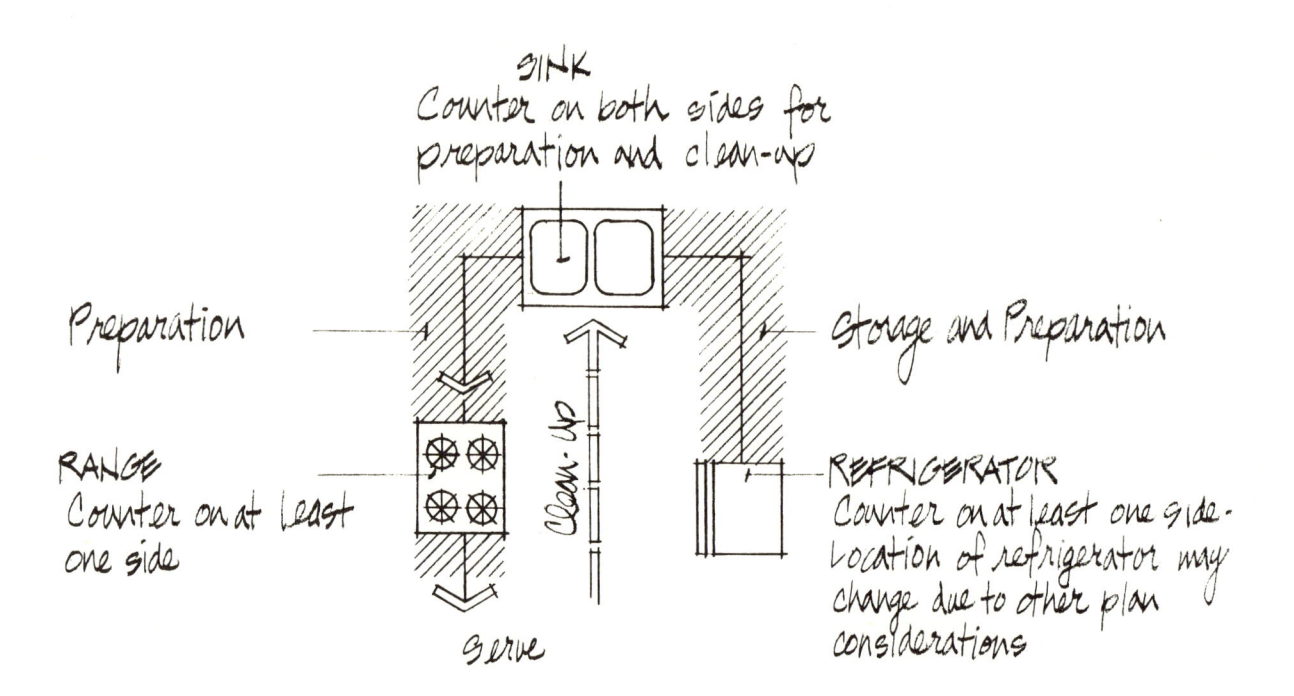

KITCHEN ACTIVITY PATTERN — MEAL PREPARATION and CLEAN-UP

Equipment should be placed so that there is sufficient operating room between it and any adjacent corner cabinet. At least 12 inches from the edge of the sink and range and 15 inches at the side of the refrigerator are recommended.

A minimum of 42 inches should be provided between base cabinets or appliances opposite each other. This same minimum clearance applies when a wall, storage wall, or work table is opposite a base cabinet.

Desirable kitchen layouts and work area frontages are illustrated in the accompanying diagrams. There should be no through circulation in the kitchen work area.

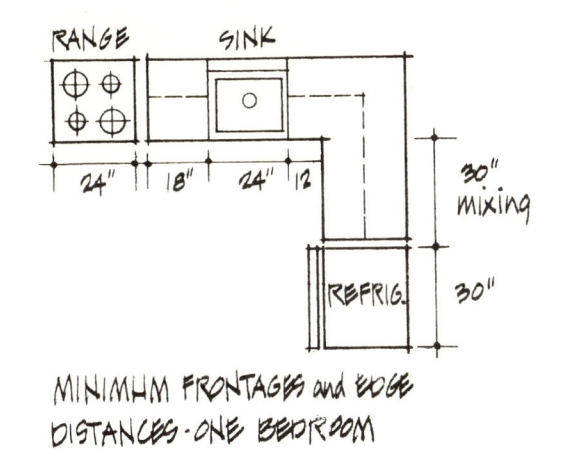

MINIMUM FRONTAGES and EDGE DISTANCES - ONE BEDROOM

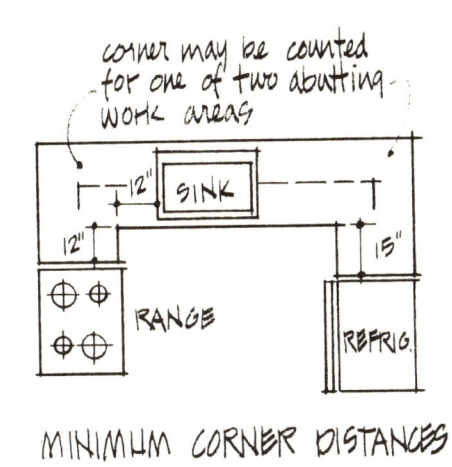

MINIMUM CORNER DISTANCES

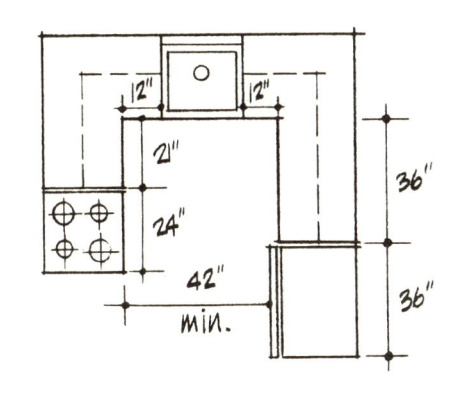

Spatial Characteristics: To insure that this space is enjoyable to work in, it is necessary to provide adequate artificial light at all work areas (see section on technical standards, page 160) and to create a spatial volume of appropriate scale. These criteria can be translated to mean that the ceiling height should be no lower than 7'-6''. Color should be used carefully and be tied to visual identification. It should not create the impression of a closed-in, constricting place. Where ductless range hoods are used, another means of ventilation should be used to carry away cooking heat. Where the main dining function is combined with food preparation, there should be clear spatial distinction between them, perhaps even a difference in ceiling height.

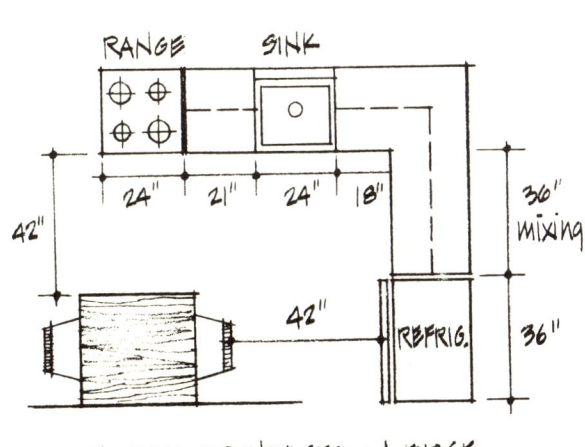

MINIMUM FRONTAGES and EDGE DISTANCES - TWO BEDROOM

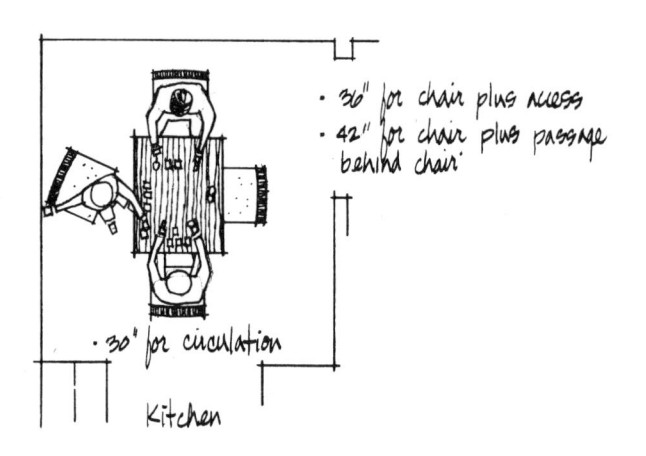

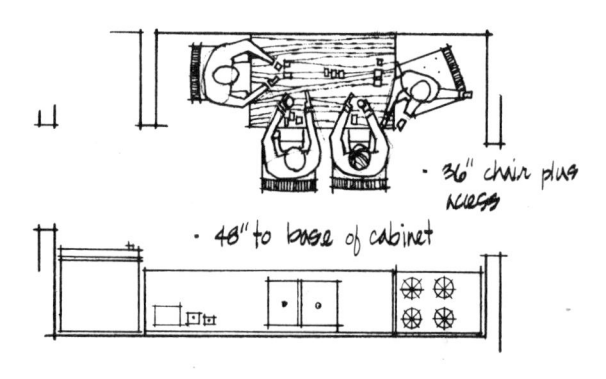

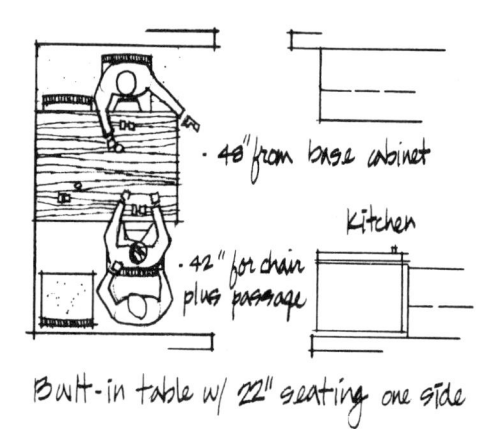

[Diagrams with annotations:]
- 36" for chair plus access
- 42" for chair plus passage behind chair
- 30" for circulation
- kitchen

- 36" chair plus access
- 48" to base of cabinet

- 48" from base cabinet
- kitchen
- 42" for chair plus passage

Built-in table w/ 22" seating one side

MINIMUM CLEARANCES for DINING AREAS in KITCHENS

Dining

There must be a permanent dining place within each dwelling unit for the independent elderly. Depending on the program, the space may be eliminated from units which are part of formal congregate care programs. This place may be within or outside of the food preparation area. Secondary activities will naturally occur within this area such as table games, letter writing and paper work, and hobbies.

Accessibility: Because of the array of activities that will be carried out, the dining area should have direct accessibility to:

Food preparation, to facilitate serving of food and cleaning of dishes
Living area

The dining area may have only indirect (minor intervening activity or circulation path) accessibility to:

Entry/exit
Private outdoor

These relationships should be subordinated to the requirements of relationship to the food preparation and living areas. There should be no direct accessibility between the dining activity and:

Sleeping/dressing
Personal hygiene

There should be direct visual/audio accessibility between the dining and the food preparation areas. Dependent upon unit organization, there may be direct visual/audio relationship between the dining and living areas; however, in such a case there should be no visual connection between the food preparation and living areas through the dining area. Visual/audio contact between the dining area and the very private areas such as sleeping/dressing and personal hygiene should be minimal or entirely eliminated.

Orientation: Wherever possible, the dining area should have views out of the dwelling unit and should also have morning sunlight. Where the orientation is western, it is important to control the harsh effects of the setting sun. Because other functional relationships must be achieved (such as entry/exit to the living and food preparation areas, and the food preparation area to the dining area) these orientation criteria must be subordinate and may not be achievable. At the very least, views out should be possible through other activity areas.

Furnishability: Each dining space must contain sufficient space to accommodate four people. It is desirable if sufficient space is available to expand this accommodation to six persons for special circumstances. Appropriate space should be provided for the storage of china and large dining articles. There should be space to accommodate the following items of furniture:

Dining table with a minimum width of 3'-0", and 2'-0" of edge length for each diner (tables should be no less than 3'-0" by 3'-0" square, or 3'-6" in diameter)

Dining chairs of 1'-6" by 1'-6" sufficient for the number of diners that can be accommodated

Buffet or storage unit of 1'-6" by 3'-6"

Size of the individual eating space on the table should be based on a frontage of 24 inches and an area of approximately 2 square feet. In addition, table space should be large enough to accommodate serving dishes.

The following minimum clearances from the edge of the table should be provided:

36" for chairs plus access thereto
42" for chairs plus access and passage
42" for serving from behind chair
30" for passage only
48" from table to base cabinet (in kitchen)

In sizing a separate dining room, provision should be made for circulation through the room in addition to space for dining.

Spatial Characteristics: As noted above, the dining activity space may be located separately or combined with living or food preparation spaces. Because of economic considerations, a separate dining space seems unlikely but, nevertheless, it is desirable that developments offer both arrangements to provide a variety and choice in responding to the differences between formal or informal lifestyles of various tenants.

The ceiling height of the dining space in a dwelling unit may be raised or lowered for spatial effect; it should, however, be no lower than 7'-6".

The dining table location should be permanent, requiring no rearrangement of furniture at mealtimes, and use of this space should not infringe upon other activities. Wall area should be available for hanging pictures and the like. It should be possible to see the outdoors from the dining table.

Where cabinets are used to separate the food preparation area from the dining area, some of the cabinets should open from both sides to facilitate table setting.

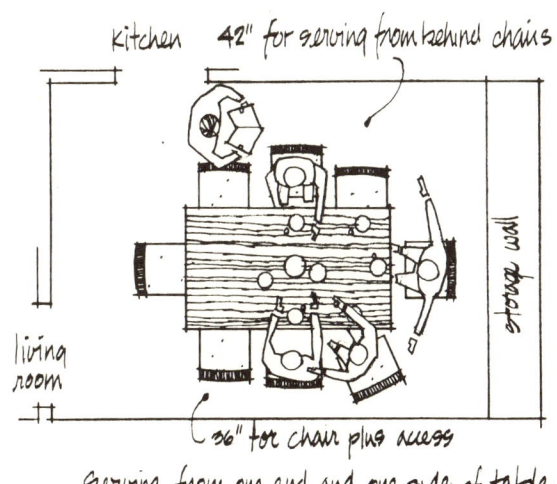

MINIMUM CLEARANCES for DINING AREAS

General Living

Each dwelling unit should have an area or areas which are organized and furnishable for a wide range of activities such as:

Conversation
Entertaining
Reading
Television viewing
Radio/record listening
Contemplation
Lounging

In most units, more than one of these activities will be provided for in a single space. In larger than standard units or in two-bedroom units, however, it may be desirable to provide more specialized spaces.

Acessibility: Direct physical accessibility (no intervening spaces) should be provided to:

Entry/exit (planning can be too open, therefore, there should be a definite spatial distinction between the living and entry/exit)
Private outdoor, for the extension of general living activities
Dining, where these spaces are combined, accessibility should not impair either activity

Indirect physical accessibility (minor intervening activity or circulation path) should exist between:

Food preparation
Personal hygiene, for visitor use (this accessibility should not impair the privacy of the sleeping/dressing areas)
Storage/utility
Sleeping/dressing

Visual and audio contact with equally active areas (entry/exit and private outdoor) should be encouraged. Visual and audio contact to the food preparation area should either be minimized or controllable so that it can be minimized or maximized as desired by the resident. The visual/audio relationship between the dining and living areas will vary with the location of the dining area. Visual/audio contact to sleeping/dressing and personal hygiene spaces should be minimized.

Orientation: Living spaces will be occupied many hours of the day and should, therefore, be provided with interesting views out of the unit. Windows should be located so that a seated person can see out. In first and second floor units, windows should also be carefully located to avoid loss of internal privacy from outside of the unit. On upper floors, close views from one unit to another should be avoided.

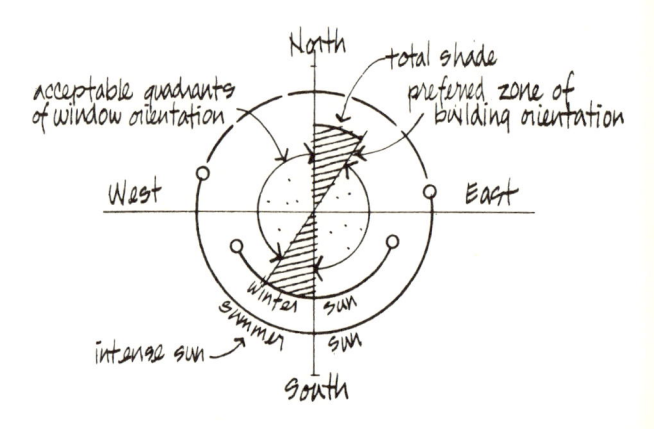

TYPICAL APPROACH TO SPACE ORIENTATION
varies throughout the world

Sunlight is important to both physical and mental conditions and, therefore, planning should insure that living spaces will receive some sunlight during each sunny day (probably no less than 30 percent of the day). Northern orientations should be avoided. Reference should be made to the accompanying diagram for acceptable sun orientations.

Furnishability: Furniture that should be accommodated in the living area should include the following items (sizes are minimums) for one-bedroom units:

One couch, 3'-0" x 6'-10"
Two easy chairs, 2'-6" x 3'-0"
One television set, 1'-4" x 2'-8"
One table, 1'-6" x 2'-6"

For two-bedroom units one easy chair should be added as well as:

One desk, 1'-8" x 3'-6"
One desk chair, 1'-6" x 1'-6"

Because of the diversity of activities which may occur in this space or spaces, and because provision must be made for a wide variety of lifestyles, special provision should be made in the design process to allow for many alternate furniture types and arrangements. The location of doors, windows, and other openings should be carefully considered so as not to unnecessarily limit furniture arrangement. A substantial amount of uninterrupted wall length is required. It should be remembered that many elderly residents will come from single family or larger rental housing and many of them can be expected to have much more furniture than described above.

The following specific design criteria should be used:

60" minimum clearance should be provided between facing seating.

30" minimum clearance is required for use of a desk.

60" minimum distance is necessary between the television set and seating. The designer should make sure that it is possible to locate the set opposite the main seating area.

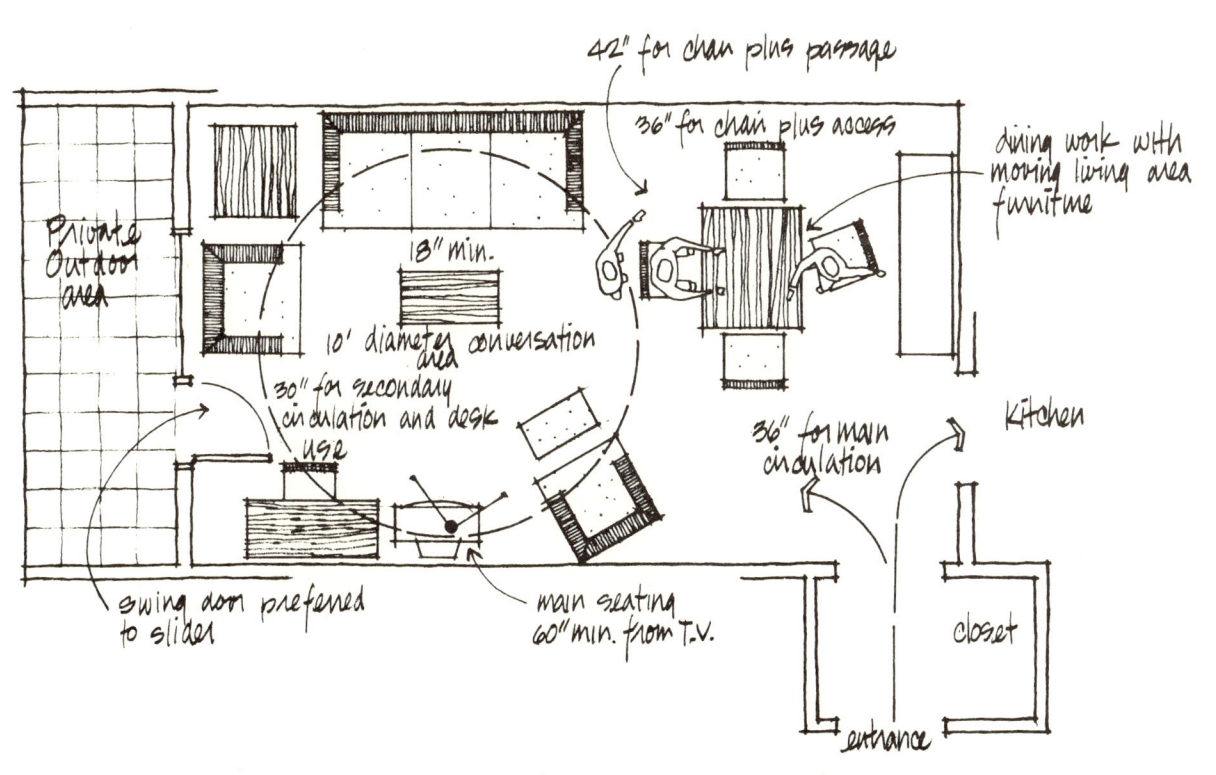

MINIMUM CLEARANCES, CIRCULATION and CONVERSATION AREAS for LIVING ROOMS

People gather during social activities in relatively small groups and a desirable conversation distance is rather short; an area approximately 10 feet in diameter is workable.

The accompanying diagrams illustrate the desired circulation and furnishability requirements.

The living area or areas will most probably have to sustain both intra- and interspace circulation. Adequate circulation space which is direct and non-disruptive is important because of the tendency toward infirmity of movement and loss of visual acuity in the elderly. The following criteria pertain:

36" minimum clearance should be possible for main traffic paths. This dimension will also accommodate a wheelchair.

30" minimum clearance should be allowed where secondary circulation occurs between furniture.

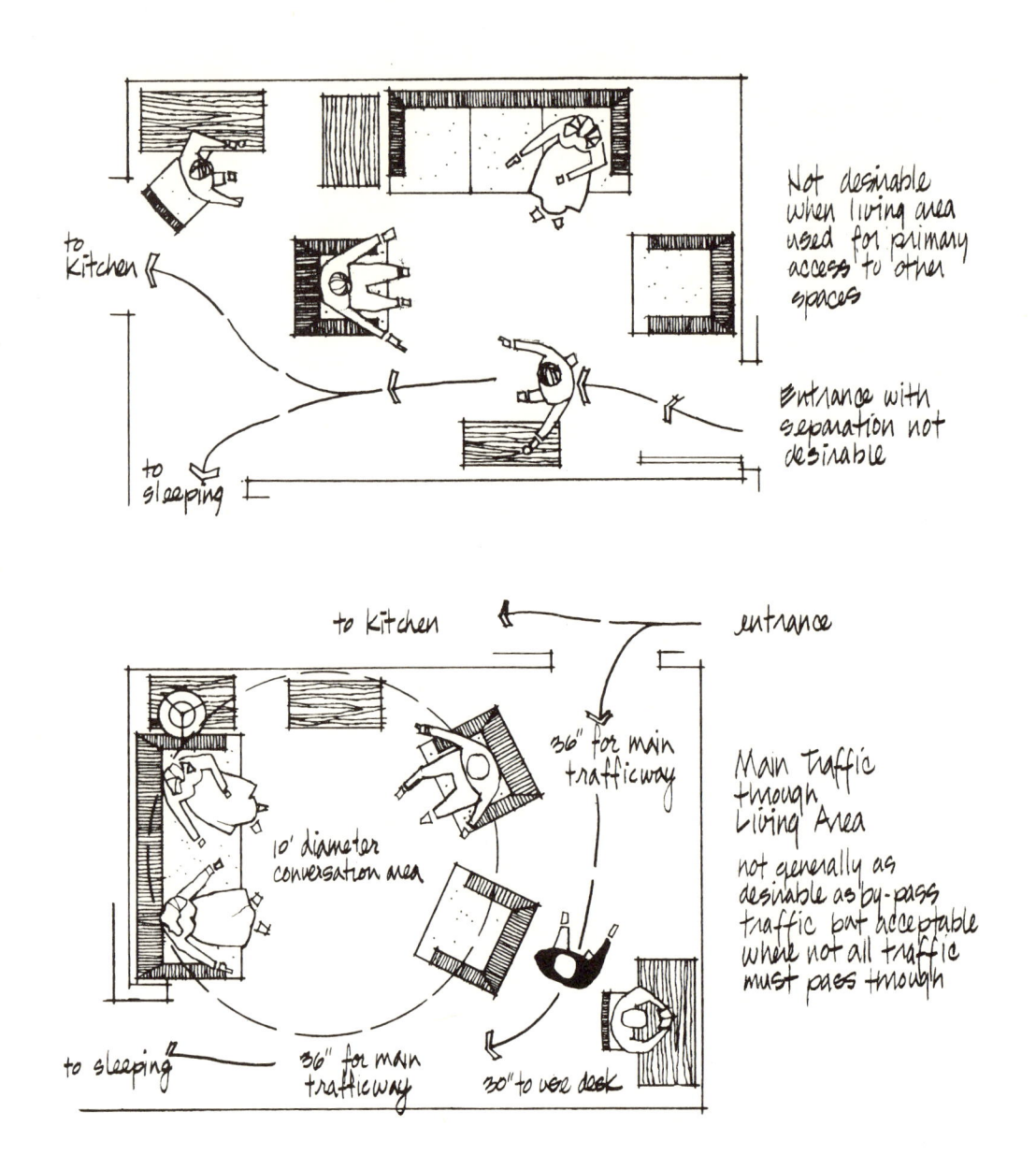

LIVING ROOM CIRCULATION APPROACHES

LIVING ROOM CIRCULATION APPROACH

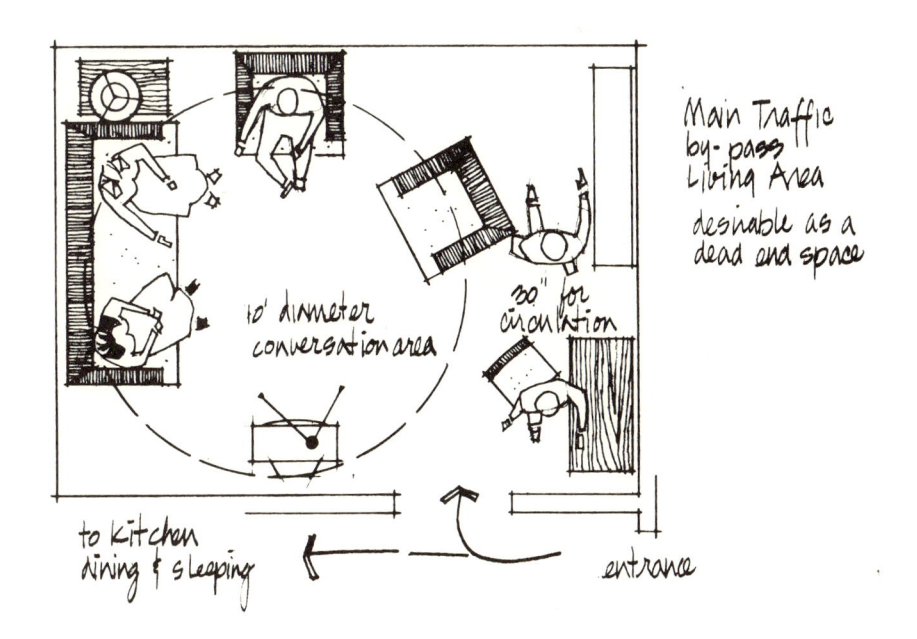

(Diagram: floor plan showing a living room with a 10' diameter conversation area, 30" for circulation, entrance, and arrow indicating path to kitchen, dining & sleeping. Annotation: "Main Traffic by-pass Living Area desirable as a dead end space")

Spatial Characteristics: The living area is likely to become the focus of the dwelling unit for many residents. The size of the space, however, is often not as important as good planning which effectively accommodates the living activity while also accounting for circulation, doors, windows, and furniture. This does not mean, however, that a small space is desirable; in fact the living area should be of sufficient size as to allow some excess in floor area for such temporary activities as exercises, ironing in front of the television set, etc. Provision of floor area beyond the minimum space required by the furnishability test will also insure the accommodation of a wider range of lifestyles and activity patterns.

The living activities area may be greatly enhanced in spatial character by a higher than normal ceiling if the building type permits.

As a general rule, it has been found that a width of less than 12 feet is difficult to utilize effectively. It has also been found that rectangular rather than square space is easier to furnish and to zone for different activities.

Consideration should be given in dwelling units of larger than standard size to subdividing the living activities area into two separate areas such as a living room and den/sewing room combination. This can also be accommodated by room configurations (such as L-shape) which are easily subdivided by furniture arrangement. This approach is particularly effective where there are two residents in a unit who wish to carry on different activities simultaneously.

Sleeping/Dressing

The elderly make greater use of the bedroom than any other age group except babies. An efficient and commodious bedroom is important for any household but for older people it is absolutely necessary. This is partly because of the need for rest periods but also, as people grow older, many become more susceptible to illness and are bedridden more frequently than younger people.

Accessibility: This activity is one of the most private in the dwelling unit. In dwelling units containing two residents it is essential that one resident be able to carry on normal living activities (including entertaining visitors) without serious loss of privacy to the other person in the bedroom. Because of this basic need, direct physical accessibility (only minor intervening space) should only exist between the sleeping/dressing area and:

    Personal hygiene
    Personal clothing storage

The bathroom may also be accessible through a hall.

In some cases provision for personal living activities may be located within the bedroom. Direct accessibility to private outdoor space may also be acceptable under some circumstances.

Indirect accessibility (through intervening circulation) should exist to:

    Food preparation
    Storage/utility

No direct accessibility should exist between the sleeping/dressing area and:

    Entry/exit, for protection of privacy
    Living
    Dining

Because of the privacy factor and the desire to be able to entertain guests without having to make the whole dwelling unit tidy, the sleeping/dressing area should be isolated from most visual and audio contact with other areas in the dwelling unit. The level of visual/audio contact between the bathroom and the sleeping/dressing area should be controllable to insure bedroom privacy when a guest uses the bathroom. It is desirable that a circulation space serve as a buffer between the sleeping/dressing area and the rest of the dwelling unit.

Like the living area, this area should have excellent views from its windows. Windows should be placed so that a person can easily see out while lying in bed. This space requires direct exposure to the sun for at least 30 percent of the day. Reference should be made to the accompanying diagram for desired sun orientation.

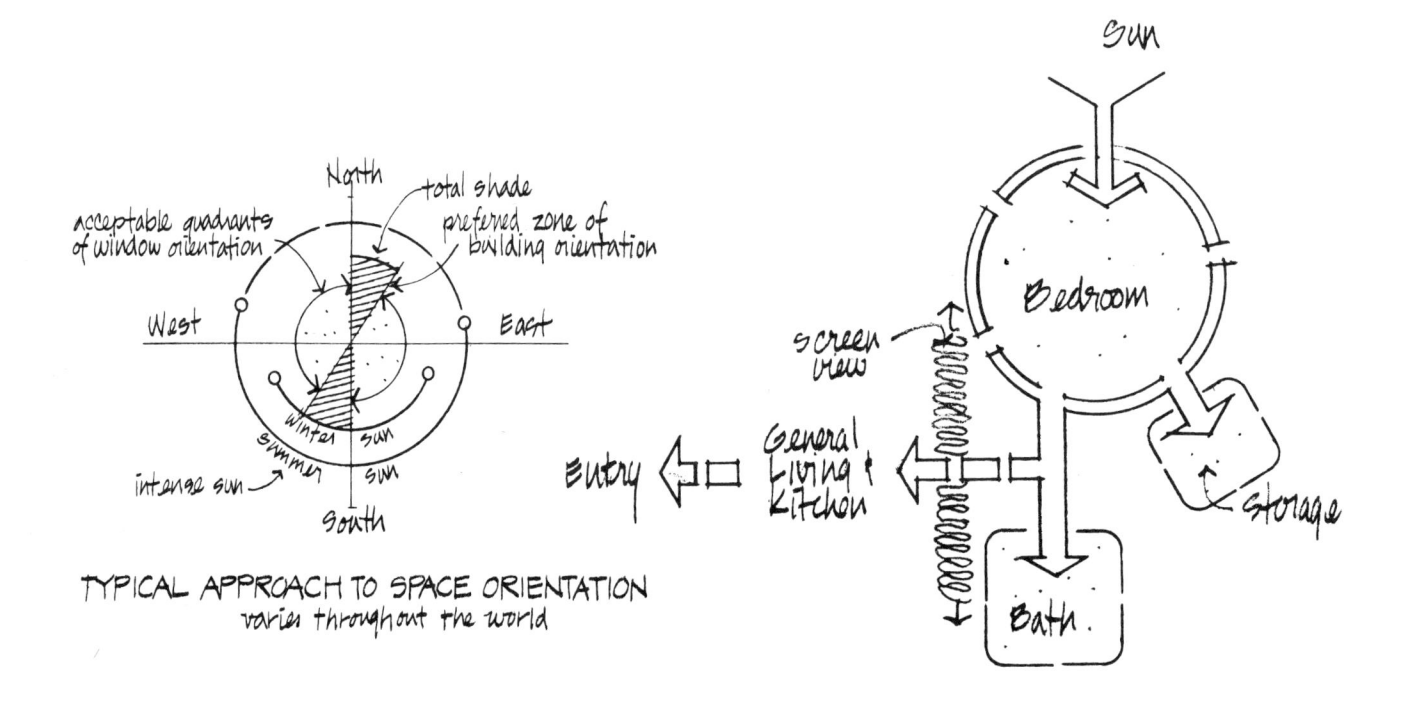

TYPICAL APPROACH TO SPACE ORIENTATION
varies throughout the world

Furnishability: In addition to the sleeping and dressing functions, the bedroom should have provisions for such passive living activities as:

Television viewing
Reading
Sewing

The minimum furniture to be provided for is as follows:

Two twin beds (3'-3" x 6'-6") or one double bed (4'-9" x 6'-6")
One dresser (1'-6" x 4'-4")
One chair (1'-6" x 1'-6")
One table (1'-6" x 2'-6") for sewing or other work (optional)
Two night stands (1'-6" x 1'-6")
One portable television set

Where both bedrooms of a dwelling unit are primary (as in unrelated occupancy), the above requirements apply to both.

Twin beds should be possible even in the bedroom of a unit programmed for single person occupancy.

A secondary bedroom for single occupancy should have circulation space and accommodate furniture of the following sizes:

One twin bed (3'-3" x 6'-6")
One dresser (1'-6" x 3'-6")
One chair (1'-6" x 1'-6")
One night stand (1'-6" x 1'-6")

The location of doors, windows, and closets should be planned to allow for the best placement of the bed and other furniture.

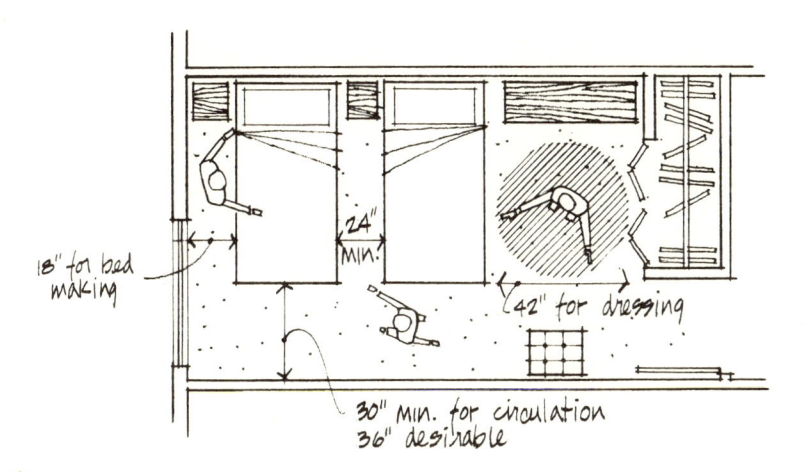

TYPICAL STANDARD BEDROOM - with twin beds

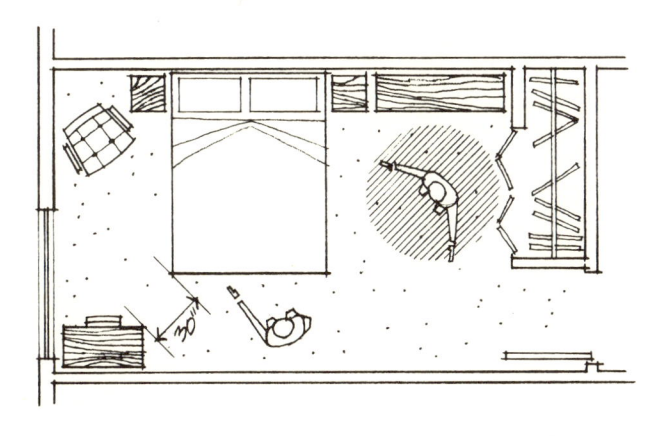

TYPICAL STANDARD BEDROOM - double bed

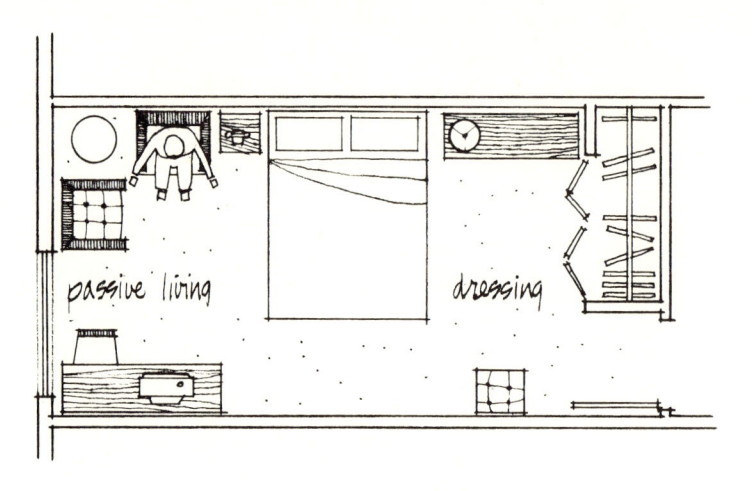

LARGER THAN STANDARD BEDROOM
may be applicable in larger than standard unit or in two bedroom unrelated occupancy

The closet should be placed next to the door into the bedroom because the use of available wall space is minimized in this way.

For reasonable access to and use of bedroom furniture and equipment, the following minimum clearances should be observed:

42" at one side or foot of bed, for dressing
24" clearance for least used side of double bed
6" clearance from side of bed to side of dresser or chest of drawers
36" clearance in front of dresser, closet, or chest of drawers
30" clearance for major circulation path (door to closet, etc.)
24" clearance between twin beds
18" clearance between twin bed and wall for ease of bed making

It should not be necessary to move beds in order to make them up. Bedrooms should be sufficiently large and so designed as to permit alternate arrangements of furniture if at all possible. There should also be space provided for working privately or resting.

Each bedroom should have a storage closet at least 2'-2" × 6'-6" with a shelf and hanging bar approximately 55" above the floor. In two-bedroom units occupied by related adults, the second bedroom closet may be somewhat reduced in length.

Spatial Characteristics: As a guide to space formation, it is noted that bedrooms with the smallest dimension of less than 9'-6" tend to be difficult to furnish, and circulation in the bedroom may also become difficult.

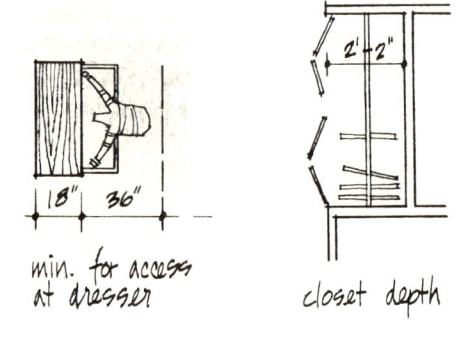

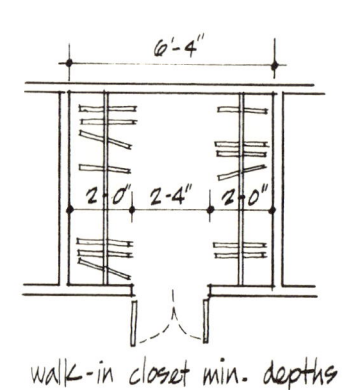

min. for access at dresser

closet depth

walk-in closet min. depths

Personal Hygiene

The bathroom is the subject of much public and private research. What is set forth here is not ideal but rather an attempt to synthesize the most current thinking on the subject as it relates to the elderly user. In addition, requirements for bathroom facilities for use by permanently disabled persons are included. It is recommended that at least 10 percent of the units in developments of 100 units or more should be adapted for use by the handicapped.

In general, bathrooms in developments for the elderly should be given great care in design as this space can, if poorly conceived, cause both serious health hazards and, through its inconvenience, great frustration. The general lack of mobility and slow reaction time of the elderly make it mandatory that hygiene spaces be inherently safe, free from sharp edges and slippery floor surfaces, and that they do not require excessive bending, leaning, or twisting to carry out necessary activities.

Accessibility: In addition to more frequent than normal use during the day, frequent use of the bathroom at night is common. Therefore, consideration should be given to direct accessibility between the bedroom and the bathroom. Hopefully, this accessibility would not require passage through an intervening circulation space. If it does, the route should be direct, unobstructed, and of sufficient width for a wheelchair to pass easily. Indirect accessibility should also exist between the bathroom and the more general living areas of the unit for use of the bathroom by guests.

Visual/audio contact between the bathroom and other areas should be minimized. It should not be possible to see into the bathroom from the living, dining, or food preparation areas.

Orientation: Views to the outside and natural light are not necessary to bathroom functions. Where windows are used, the following criteria pertain:

The designer should make sure that no loss of privacy occurs.

Windows should not be located over bathtubs.

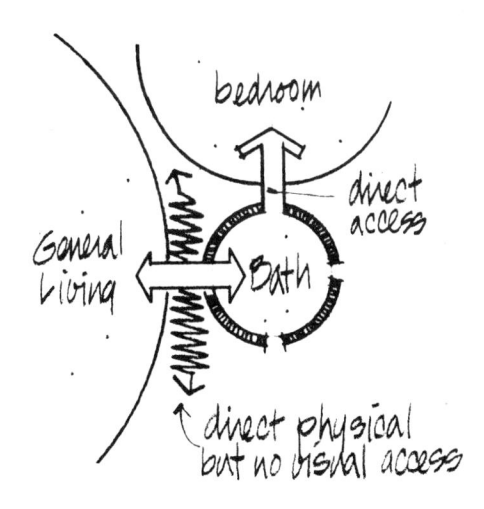

Furnishability and Equipment: All personal hygiene spaces should have the following equipment:

Lavatory basin (preferably in a vanity counter top)
Water closet
Bath or shower (see section on technical standards, page 151)
Appropriate grab bars
Storage space and mirror
Toilet-paper holder
Towel bars

The requirements in detail for this equipment are contained on page 151 of the section on technical standards.

It is essential for the successful functioning of the bathroom or lavatory that certain minimum clear working areas be provided around fixtures. These requirements are:

Lavatory Basins: 3'-6" × 3'-6"; the sink should be centered on one dimension and at the extreme of the other.

Water Closet: 2'-6" × 4'-4"; the water closet should be centered on the 2'-6" dimension and located at the extreme of the 4'-4" dimension.

Tub and/or Shower: 2'-4" clear dimension extending out from access point of fixture and at least 2'-8" along its length; the length dimension should begin from the central end of the fixture.

An emergency call system should be included in all developments. An alarm button should be placed in the bathroom in a convenient place, but not where it can be set off accidentally.

All bathrooms and lavatories, whether naturally ventilated or not, should have air exhaust fans venting to the outside and sized according to the code for an interior bathroom.

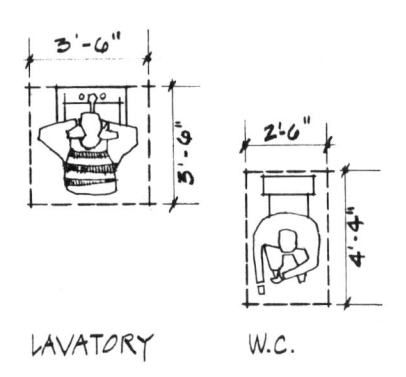

LAVATORY   W.C.

MINIMUM CLEARANCES - PERSONAL HYGIENE

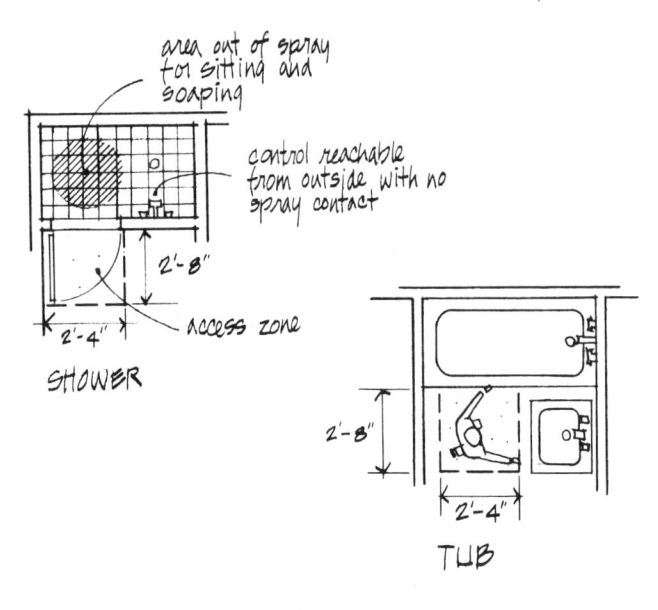

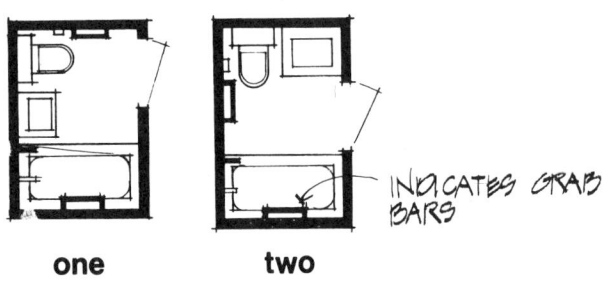

SHOWER

TUB

one   two

ILLUSTRATIVE HYGIENE SPACE LAYOUTS

ALL DOORS 2'-8"

Spatial Characteristics: All personal hygiene spaces, both bathrooms and lavatories, should have privacy locks which can be easily unlocked from the outside in case of emergency. The key type of emergency release is not desirable because there may not be sufficient time to locate the key in an emergency. Outward opening doors should be used so that people can get in easily to help someone who is lying on the bathroom floor, perhaps unconscious or helpless.

Non-slip, easily maintained floor surfaces which are free from changes in level should be provided.

The vertical surfaces of bathrooms should be free from sharp corners and edges, unnecessary projections, and breakable materials. This requirement has particular bearing on room layout and the location of bathroom accessories, such as towel bars, paper holders, etc.

Many bathroom layouts are possible but two are the most common, offering solutions to a wide range of concerns. Each has its own advantages. These layouts are described for illustrative purposes below.

Layout 1: In the first layout, the toilet is placed by the wall with the lavatory next to the bathtub. This arrangement allows easy placement of the toilet-paper holder and grab bar on the wall while, at the same time, the edge of the lavatory can be used as a support for getting into and out from the bathtub.

A vertical grab bar mounted on the wall near the bathtub in addition to grab bars on the bathtub wall is recommended. An angled grab bar should also be provided on the wall by the toilet.

Layout 2: In the second layout the bathtub is placed against the wall opposite the lavatory and toilet. As in layout one, separate grab bars should be provided for the toilet and tub. In this layout the lavatory can be installed in a vanity counter top with sides. The vanity arrangement can support a toilet-paper holder next to the toilet, a towel rack, and perhaps a small grab bar.

Other layouts, such as the standard sequence of bathtub, water closet, and lavatory, tend to require the use of floor-mounted grab bars at the water closet. This is not desirable because it adds a projecting element in the space which may be a real hazard if someone should fall. Such bars also preclude the use of the toilet as a seat while using the lavatory.

Private Outdoor

Many older people, either by choice or by limitations of their physical conditions, are largely confined to their dwelling units and access to a private outdoor space over which they have control is very desirable. It offers a welcome change of atmosphere, a chance to grow flowers, cook out, and enjoy the sun. In the event of fire, a balcony can provide refuge and access to fresh air. Provision for private outdoor activities may take the form of balconies or patios. Requirements for patios are discussed in the *Townhouse Development Process*.[5]

Accessibility: The private outdoor space should be directly accessible to the main general living area of the dwelling unit. If possible this area should also be directly accessible to the food preparation area; however, if this is not possible the indirect accessibility between the outdoor space and the food preparation area should be via a non-circuitous circulation path. Accessibility to all other areas should be indirect and placed as dictated by the functional organization of the dwelling unit, except that there may also be direct accessibility to the sleeping/dressing area.

To protect the privacy of private outdoor areas on the ground floor, direct access from them to the public outdoor area should be avoided by creating an identity for the outdoor private areas. There should be no direct accessibility between the private outdoor areas of separate dwelling units. In areas where security is an issue, private outdoor access should be totally and securely enclosed.

Visual accessibility between the private outdoor area and interesting views on and off the site should be maximized, while at the same time loss of privacy from views outside the outdoor area should be minimized. The visual accessibility between the general living area of the unit and the general outdoor area should not be impaired by the design of the private outdoor area.

Orientation: The configuration and orientation of the outdoor space should be such that sun falls on the space for at least 30 percent of each day during the prime spring, summer, and fall months.

Furnishability and Spatial Characteristics: On-grade patios and/or private areas should be well defined. Location and design should provide spatial privacy from other living units and from adjacent walks or drives in public space.

Overhead protection of balconies is very desirable but not required. A shelf for plant pots should be included for all balconies at a height of 24 to 30 inches above the floor.

Access doors to balconies or patios should be fully draftproof and should not be the only source of natural ventilation to the room. The door sill should be kept as low as possible. Passage doors of the swing type are preferable to sliding glass doors and should be used when economically feasible to eliminate large sills.

Balconies or terraces above the twelfth floor are generally undesirable and should not be provided except in special or unique circumstances.

Where private balconies are not provided for all the dwelling units on a floor, a common balcony should be provided at a central location (see page 68 of the section on design).

All balconies, terraces, and patios should be provided with artificial lighting which can be switched on from within the dwelling unit. At least one duplex electric receptical which is weatherproof should be provided in each private outdoor space (see section on technical standards, page 160).

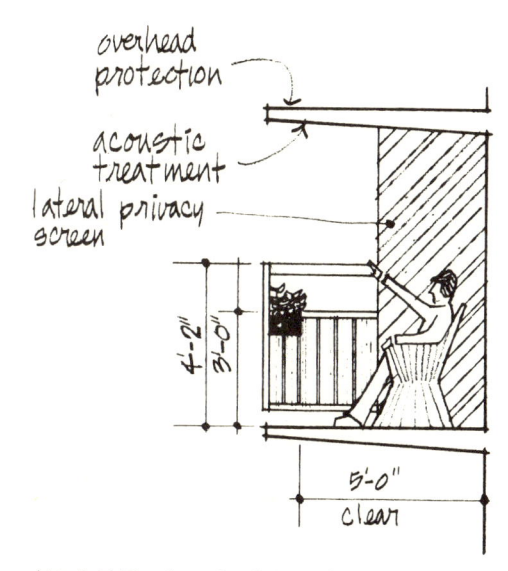

EXAMPLE OF BALCONY

---

[5] Michigan State Housing Development Authority, *Townhouse Development Process*, 1970.

The criteria for minimum privacy require that screening walls at the sides of outdoor spaces be provided to protect the space from being overlooked by adjoining dwelling units and their private outdoor spaces. The side of the space opposite the building wall may be partially closed and/or defined by planting.

On-grade private space should have a least dimension of 12 feet, extend the full width of the unit, and include a paved patio of at least 100 square feet. The remaining area should be lawn or planting beds.

Private on-grade outdoor spaces may become a security problem if their design provides the potential intruder with a space completely free from observance and control. Therefore, completely enclosed patios should themselves be secure as illustrated below. Partially enclosed patios should be designed so that they can be controlled visually from public areas.

The paved surface in outdoor spaces should be smooth and free from unexpected changes in level. All steps required to provide a transition from unit floor level to ground level should have handrails (see section on technical standards, page 140).

Private outdoor spaces above grade (raised terraces and balconies) should be included in the integral design at the beginning of the design process and not added later as an afterthought. Only in this way can the problems traditionally associated with balconies be overcome. Balconies should have a least clear dimension of no less than 5 feet and a total clear area of no less than 50 square feet for one-bedroom units and 60 square feet for two-bedroom units. Because the elderly are particularly concerned about security and heights, balconies must not only be safe, but they must also feel safe. The use of solid balustrades is desirable. Where this is not possible, a sturdy railing with a large solid top rail should be used. In either case care should be taken to avoid obscuring views out from the interior of the dwelling unit. For this purpose a solid balustrade to a height of 24 inches with an open handrail above is a good solution. Railings or balustrades should have a minimum height above the balcony surface of 42 inches (50 inches is desirable) and should extend completely along all open sides of the balcony.

Whenever possible balconies should be recessed behind the main face of the building because this technique provides a strong sense of enclosure, privacy, and security. Where this is not possible, and where there are adjoining balconies or the balcony is exposed to broad public view, balconies should be provided with screening walls or devices at their sides which achieve privacy and security.

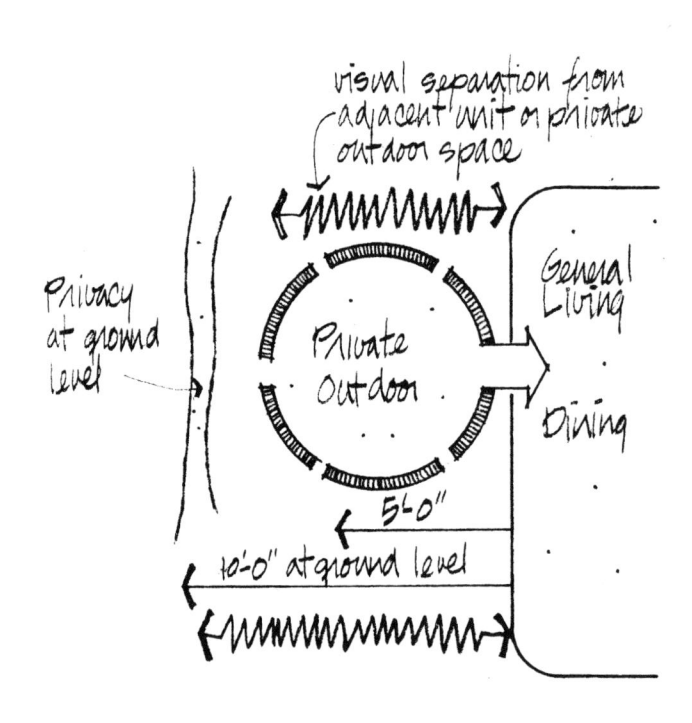

Storage Utility

Each dwelling unit should be provided with a facility for the storage of items that are not used in daily living, such as suitcases, off-season clothing, etc. This general storage area may be contained in the unit or it may be located at some central point in the development. In townhouse and low-rise apartment type units, this storage is best contained in the unit. However, as residential buildings increase in height, it may become more economical to provide one or more central storage rooms and eliminate such storage from the unit itself.

Physical and Visual Accessibility: If the general storage area is located within the unit, physical accessibility should be safe and convenient. The area may be best located either adjacent to the entry or within the bedroom, but in either case visual screening from other living areas should be complete. Access to this space should not require the removal of other stored objects such as clothes in a required closet.

If the general storage area is centrally located, physical access should be direct and dependent only upon major building circulation elements. When a central storage area serves more than one floor, it should be located adjacent to an elevator with only a short horizontal traverse required. Visual screening from other areas should be complete except for security requirements.

If the area is centrally located, the room should be locked at all times with entrance gained by use of the dwelling unit key. It should be possible to survey the room visually through a window in the door before entry.

Furnishability and Spatial Characteristics: Tenant general storage, whether it is within the dwelling unit or centrally located, should be at least 12 square feet in floor area and 100 cubic feet in volume for each dwelling unit. If located within the dwelling unit, it may take the form of a closet.

If located in a central room, each tenant storage area should be individually secure and enclosed as a closet or cubicle by walls or heavy duty, small-mesh screening. The access door should be at least 30 inches wide and be capable of being locked securely.

Storage cubicles should not be stacked one upon the other because this arrangement would require stooping and/or reaching for use and this may be beyond the physical capabilities of the elderly.

Each storage cubicle should be well lighted. Interior surfaces should be painted or otherwise treated to allow for easy cleaning. Floors should be covered with a durable and washable material—exposed, untreated concrete is undesirable because of dust.

Conclusion

The foregoing subsection views the dwelling unit through its component activities. Assembling these components in an effective and commodious manner is the creative role of the designer. In this endeavor, care should be taken to project possible dwelling unit designs forward into the design of the building to evaluate their implications for building organization and massing. A critical concern in this regard will be the sun orientation of the unit and the relationship to public outdoor areas and unpleasant views.

Although many dwelling unit organizations are possible, a generalized synthesis of necessary activity patterns most commonly produces organizations such as those illustrated here. It should be noted that these naturally produce and require clear distinction between the public and private face of the unit and, internally, between the private and less private living zones. In the case of the apartment dwelling unit, the distinction can also be made between an inner and outer zone. These factors have a critical effect on building design and should be carefully considered by the designer.

It should also be noted that placement of the entry and related circulation paths genuinely affect the success of the dwelling unit. In this regard the second example is less desirable because of entrance placement relative to the kitchen and the private zone, especially in double occupancy one-bedroom units and in two-bedroom units.

These examples are not intended to preclude other organizations consistent with the activity requirements either of this section or those specially established for a given development. Rather, they are examples directed at giving some summarized understanding of the foregoing.

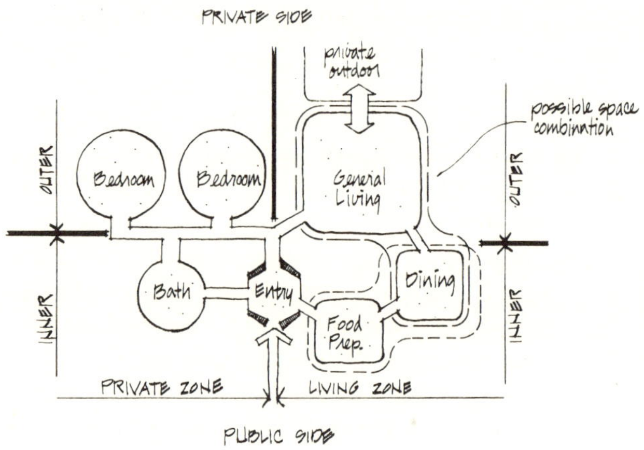

EXAMPLE OF ACCEPTABLE DWELLING ORGANIZATION

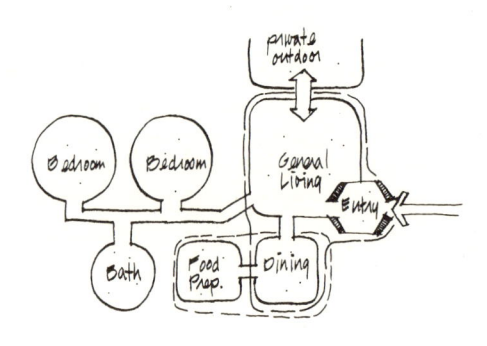

POSSIBLE DWELLING UNIT ORGANIZATION NOT AS DESIRABLE BUT ACCEPTABLE

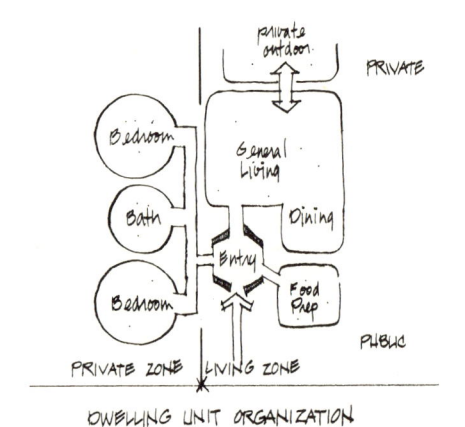

DWELLING UNIT ORGANIZATION

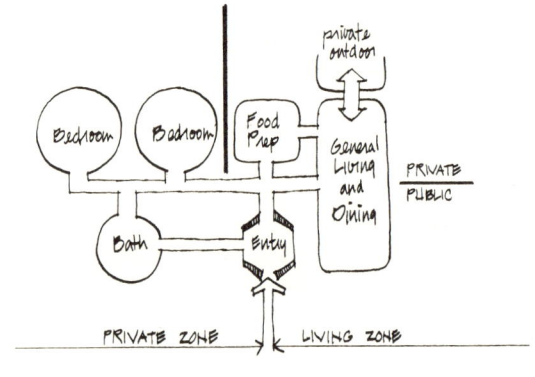

DWELLING UNIT ORGANIZATION

FUNCTIONAL ORGANIZATION OF ACTIVITIES

Each activity which can reasonably be expected in a housing for the elderly development is individually analyzed in the section on development activity components, pages 56 and 70. But these analyses do not give a comprehensive insight into how a housing for the elderly development can or should function as a whole entity. The various activities of most housing developments for the elderly will naturally organize themselves into five site and building zones.

Neighborhood/Development Contact Zone: This zone provides the interface between the development and the neighborhood within which it is located. The zone can be referred to as a front yard or, for an urban site, as the front porch. This zone has two-way visual implications. It must be a visually recognizable place which can be easily picked out by elderly residents. It should be a place to observe the comings and goings in the neighborhood and of fellow residents.

Outdoor Common Area: This area can be thought of as the development's back yard. It includes outdoor activities which are available to the elderly residents. It should be defined and separated from the neighborhood/development contact zone and abutting properties. It should be defendable and feel separate from the general public although, as with the building, it is sometimes a shared zone.

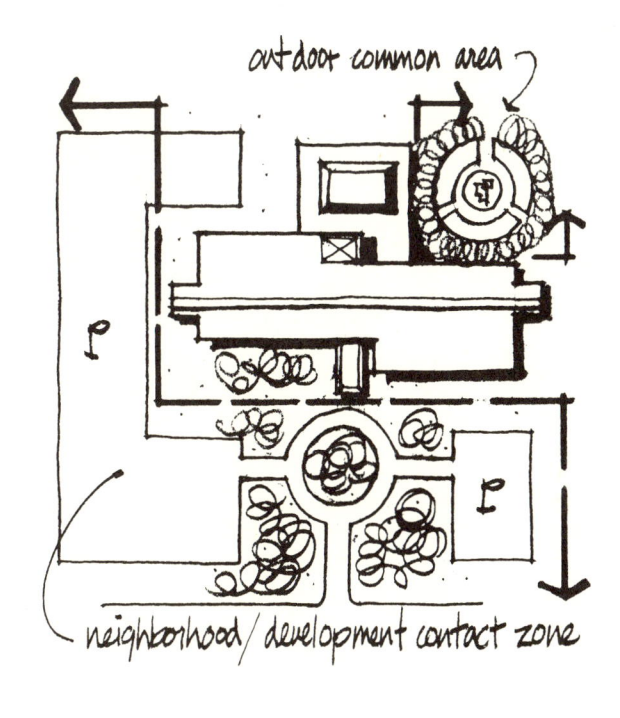

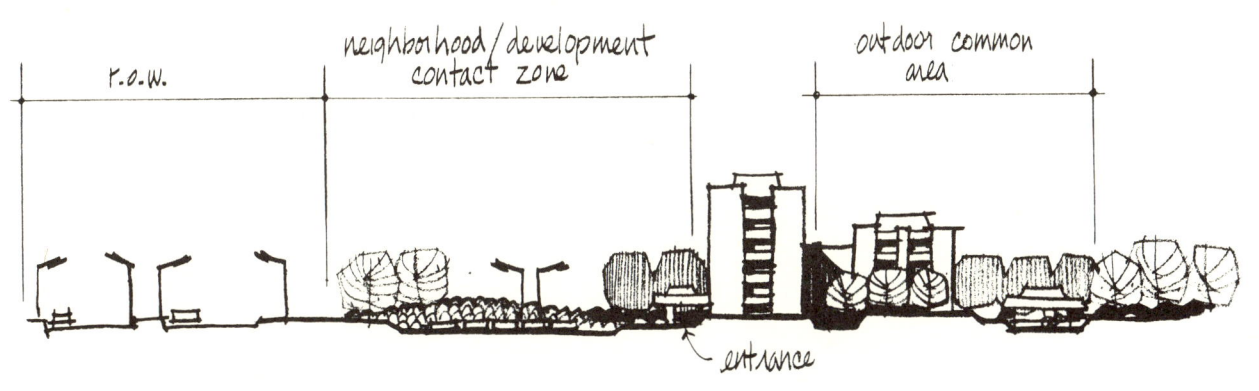

OUTDOOR ACTIVITY ZONES

Indoor/Outdoor Contact Zone: This zone is the interface between the exterior environment and the interior of the buildings of a development.

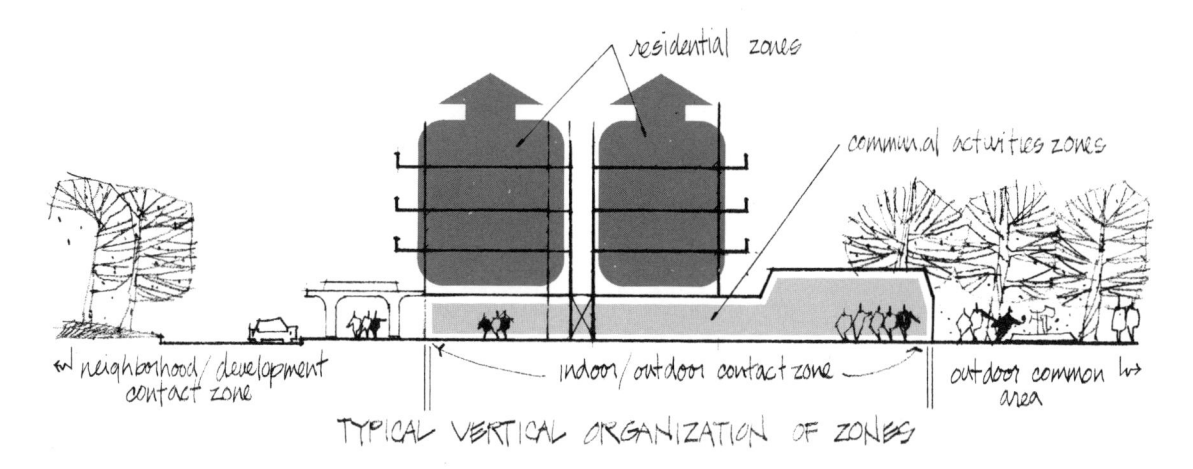

TYPICAL VERTICAL ORGANIZATION OF ZONES

Indoor Communal Activities Zone: This is the most public zone of the interior in a development. It may, like the residential zone to be discussed next, be a series of zones with a range from places where certain activities or facilities shared by all residents are located and the general public is excluded to places where certain communal activities occur in conjunction with the general public. If the public is included in the activities, the zone performs a transitional or linking role, joining residential zones to the outdoor surroundings. This zone will and should be identifiable and separate from the residential zone. It should also feel safe and be defendable from the outside world. This zone should become the focus of communal life in a development without becoming overwhelmingly closed or demanding of communal participation where none is desired.

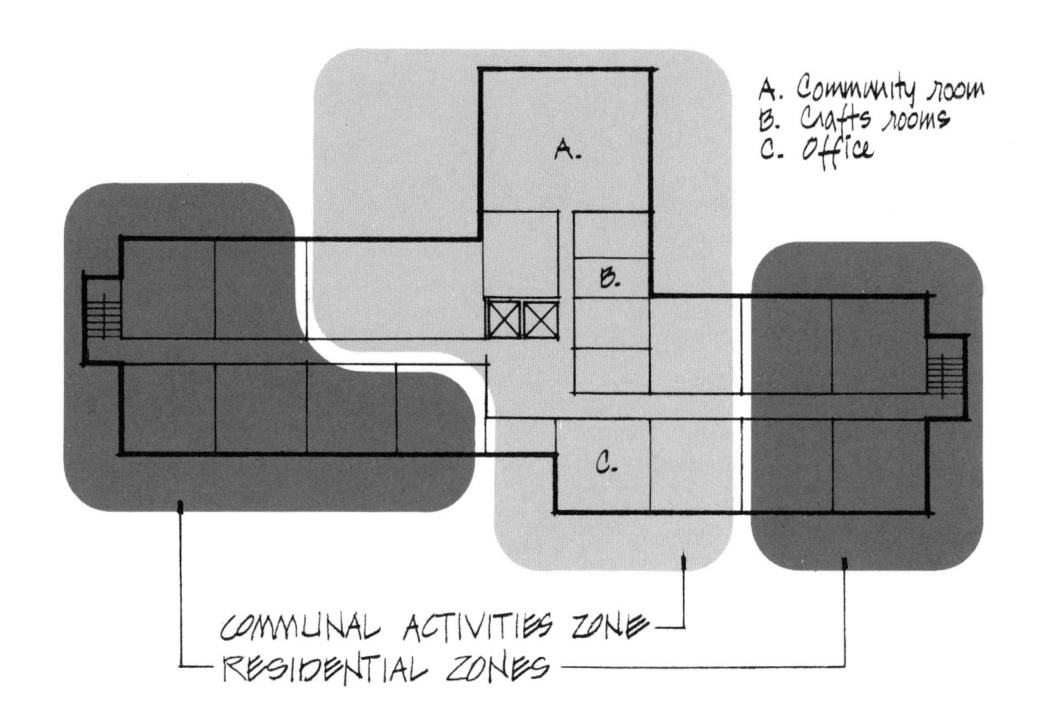

A. Community room
B. Crafts rooms
C. Office

COMMUNAL ACTIVITIES ZONE
RESIDENTIAL ZONES

The Residential Zone: This is the least public zone in a development. It is the home base, or miniature neighborhood, for the residents. It should not be a single zone but rather a series of similar zones, each of sufficiently limited scale so that individual residents can easily relate to them, much the same way that a person relates to the houses immediately around his own home in a single family situation. Without breaking down the scale somewhat, even a modest number of dwelling units, for example, 100 units, can become overpowering. Each of these zones should be easily identifiable.

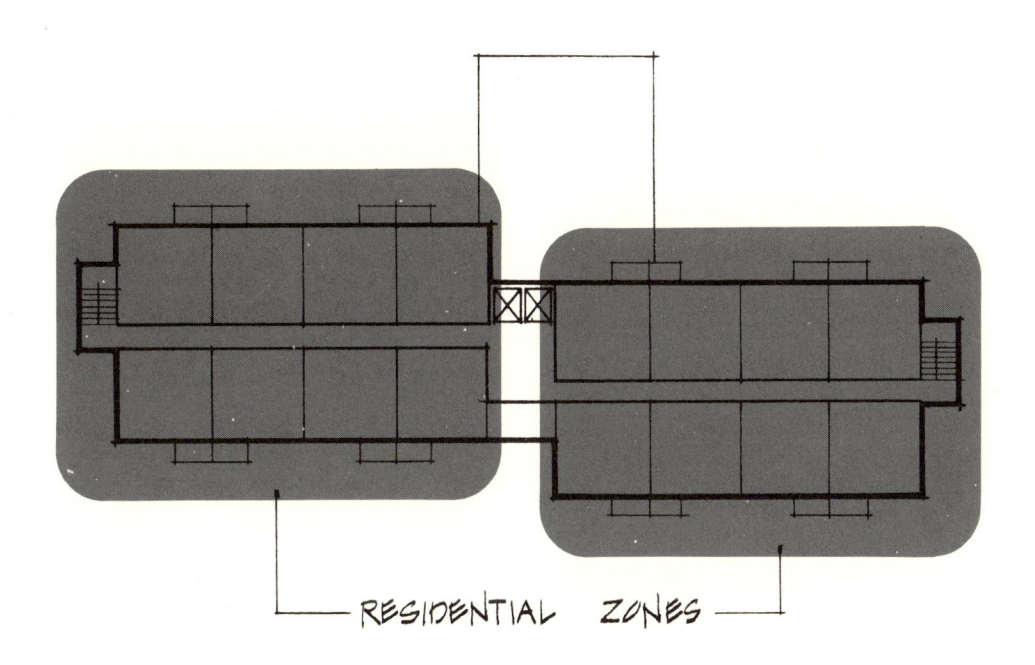

RESIDENTIAL ZONES

The activities provided within all five zones will vary for each development, depending on program and site characteristics. The intent and quality of each zone should, however, be consistently self-evident to the elderly residents. Each of the zones will be discussed in detail with emphasis on the following considerations:

Activities/Organization
Spatial character
Circulation and spatial sequence
Supporting development

The building types under consideration here include high- and medium-rise apartments, low-rise apartments, and townhouses. The site types discussed, however, are for high- and medium-rise apartment buildings. Design guidelines and standards for low-rise apartment and townhouse site settings can be found in *Townhouse Development Process.*[6]

[6] Michigan State Housing Development Authority, *Townhouse Development Process,* 1970.

The Neighborhood/Development Contact Zone

The obvious function of this zone is to link the development with the neighborhood and thus provide the residents with an entrance or so-called front door to the development. The functions in this zone are all directly related to circulation and spatial sequence. The overall zone contains the following elements:

1. The entrance drive and walk
2. The arrival or drop-off area
3. The parking area
4. The walkway from the parking area to the building
5. The service access system

The first two or four elements can be connected as a sequence or experience depending on whether one is walking or driving. There are many organizational alternatives for delineating the entrance and arrival sequence. There are four distinct options for this sequence:

The Axial Concept: This scheme envisions a very direct entrance drive-walkway approach path (1) to an arrival area (2). Parking (3) is to one or both sides of this entrance drive. A second entrance (4) is served by a connecting walkway system to the parking zone. Service is provided through the parking access drive.

The Indirect, Natural Concept: This scheme is often based on site determinants such as topography or meaningful stands of vegetation. The sequence of events is identical to that depicted in the concept above.

The Drive-by Concept: This scheme is typical for a smaller urban site where the building setback from the street right of way is less than 50 feet. The concept actually combines the entrance and arrival functions; however, the configuration still provides for potential separation of pedestrians and vehicles.

The Dual-Arrival Concept: The concept features two main entrances, one oriented to pedestrians and the urban streetscape and the other oriented to vehicles and parking. This organization would probably be best suited to an urban site where curb cuts would be difficult to obtain.

The concern here is not that the designer adopt one of these four concepts in his site plan, but rather that his design solution be easily comprehended by elderly residents. It must make sense as a physical design statement.

The entrance and arrival functions are extremely important to the development because they establish an image which can be a source of pride to the residents as well as a marketing tool for management.

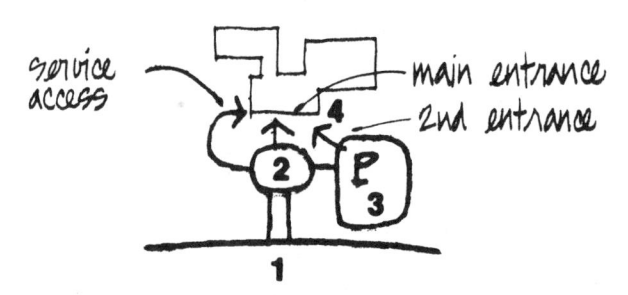

HEAD-ON AXIAL CONCEPT

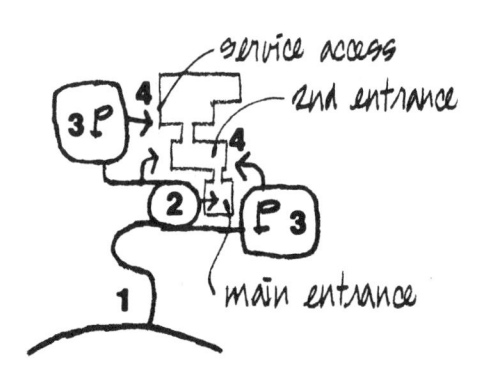

INDIRECT, NATURAL CONCEPT

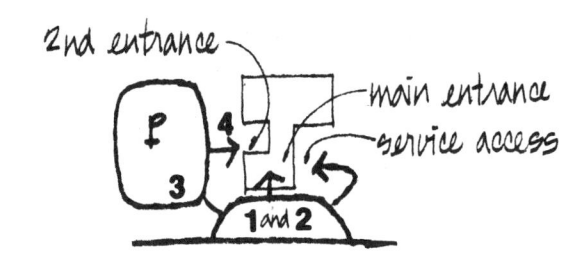

DRIVE-BY CONCEPT

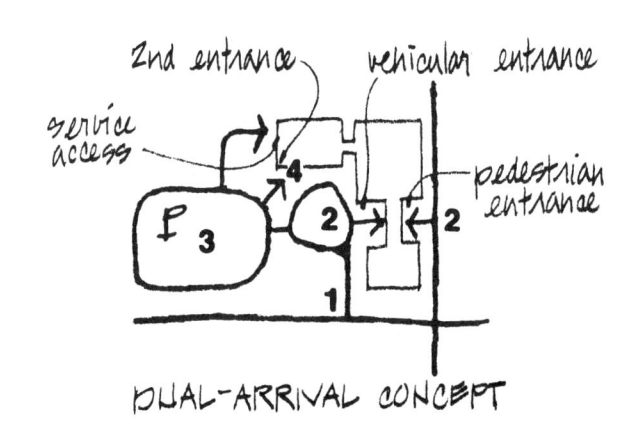

DUAL-ARRIVAL CONCEPT

High Rise Courtyard Development

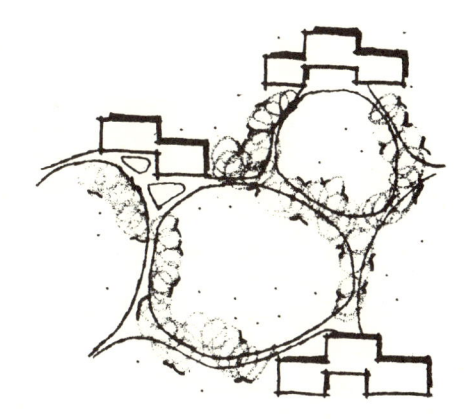

Low Rise Park Development

The Outdoor Common Area

There are two extremes in regard to the development of the outdoor common area. A small site begins to dictate a courtyard space very strongly related to the building or even a part of the building, that is, a roof deck, while a larger site begins to suggest a park-like organization of activities. An objective of primary importance is the containment of this space in order to provide a sense of security for residents. The area must be strongly separated from the neighborhood and the neighborhood/development contact zone. This area must not only be physically safe but it must also feel safe.

The outdoor common area includes three kinds of activities:

Passive Areas: These activities include places which permit solitude and those places which offer the opportunity to be a spectator of the activity of others.

Active Areas: These areas should offer a range of activities which should not be limited to rigorous athletic facilities but should also include a broad range of activities ranging from volleyball to pinochle.

Connecting Areas: These areas link other activities together and in this way become an activity area.

These activities are arranged within the outdoor common area as a complex of recreational attractions which have the potential for bringing elderly residents together. The external and internal site situations described on page 110, begin to indicate some design approaches to the overall organization of these three components.

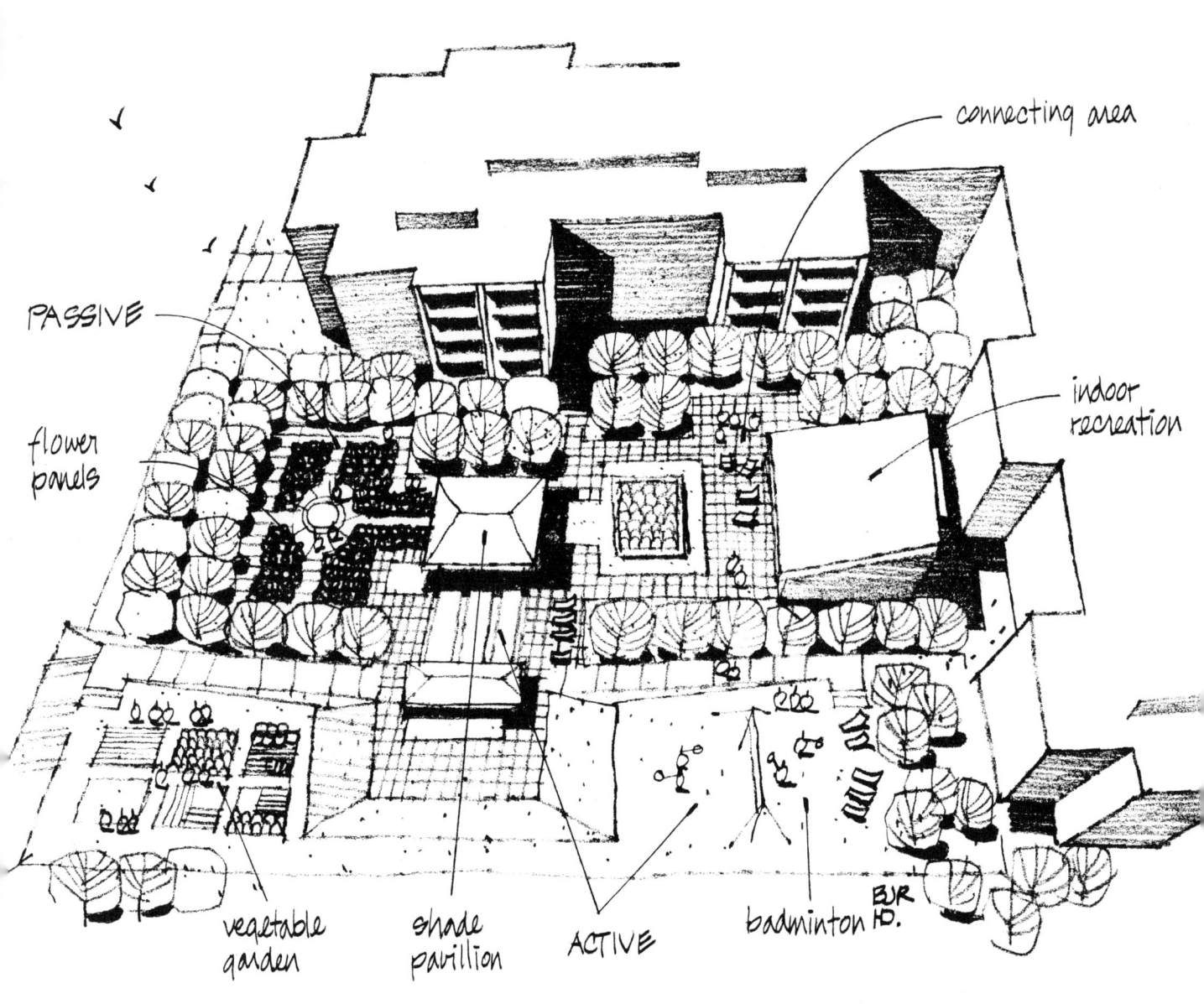

EXAMPLE OF MIDRISE OUTDOOR COMMON AREA

Since the external site begins to almost force a courtyard solution with the outdoor common area located directly adjacent to the building, it seems logical that a modular design might be most appropriate as a structuring device. Furthermore, with the potential for viewing these facilities downward from the upper floors, the idea of a strong modular pattern becomes even more valid. In the use of a modular design format, as with any other organizational device, it is important to consider the impact on the viewer at eye level. While the organization may be quite evident from a height of six stories, it must still make sense visually to the viewer using the facility on the ground. By creating a hierarchy of visual elements with a central visual focus, an organizational structure at eye level can be expressed. The expression of vertical elements on the ground plane is central to this objective. There should be a concept of point to point organization which gives the elderly resident a sense of where he is within the overall complex of facilities. The emphasis of a dominant center or focus aids in this process. Other activities or features within the outdoor common area should relate to this central focus, but always as subordinate elements.

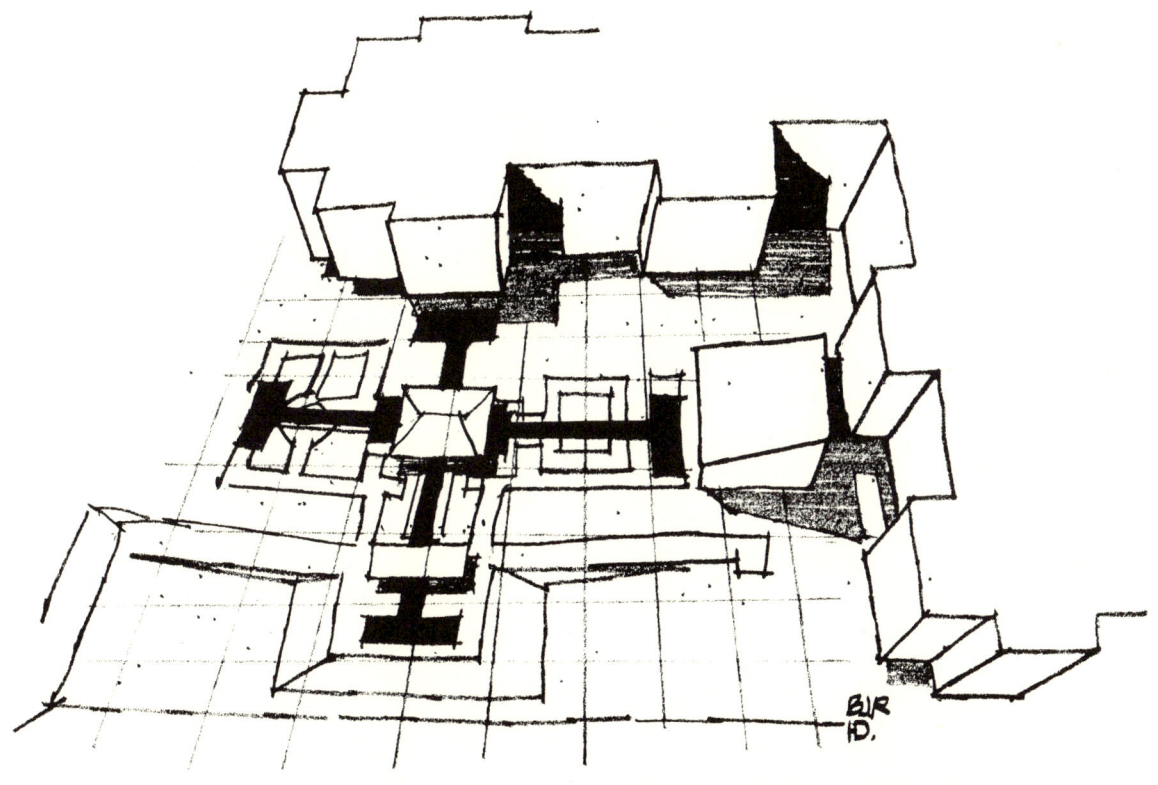

Example of Modular Design w/Point to Point Organization

The modular approach is not the only way to develop structural organization on a small site. A transition zone may be utilized between the building face and the edge of the outdoor common area. This device can permit the site designer to break with the architectural motif and develop a different, non-modular framework. As with other sections of these guidelines, the examples shown are not meant to limit a designer's imagination, but rather to encourage him to use his imagination.

The outdoor common area located within the internal site offers a broad range of organizational alternatives. The appropriate organizational concept is usually achieved by first evaluating the design determinants found on the site such as topography, vegetative cover, or other natural features. If no strong design directive is embodied in the site, the development program and the designer's imagination are the determinants of the site plan for the outdoor common area. A discussion of site determinants and how to respond to them is included in the section on buildings/site relationships, page 110. Organizational concepts that can be generated by the program are delineated below.

Axial Organization: This alternative concept envisions a more rigidly balanced organization. An axis demands at least two strong termini. For example, a community center can provide one terminus while a combination shade pavilion and picnic shelter can provide the other terminus.

Radial Organization: This concept involves a strong center from which activities radiate outward. The center is a focus and other facilities become subordinate to it.

The larger, internal site often involves the problem of too much openness. Large expanses of open lawn often communicate an overpowering institutional image. The concept of reinforcing the edges of the site can help to resolve this problem of openness and create a more residential image. How edges can be reinforced will be dealt with in the sections on planting and grading, pages 120 to 123.

As with the external site, emphasis of the vertical is important. In addition, the concept of a focus or center should be apparent to the elderly viewers as they use the facilities.

Although these two organizational motifs are somewhat arbitrary, they are easily understood at eye level and, if the site is lacking in design determinants, they can help to create a strong sense of place.

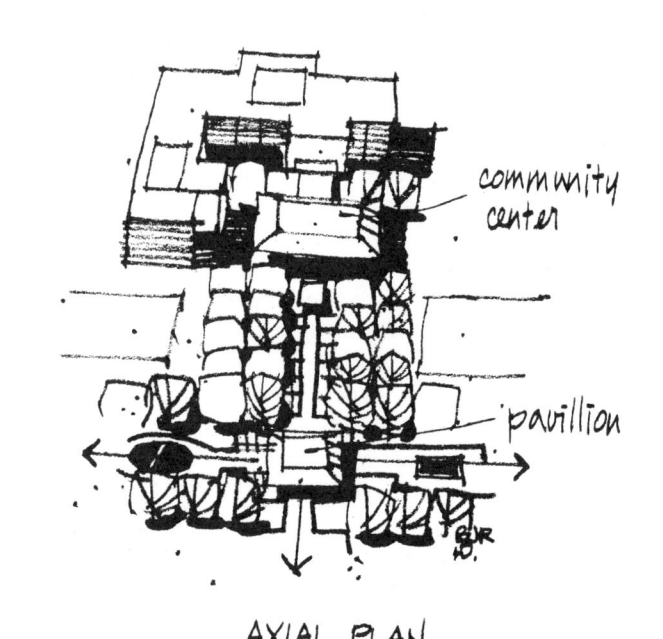

AXIAL PLAN

RADIAL PLAN

Indoor/Outdoor Contact Zone

The visual and functional relationships between interior and exterior spaces involve three distinct design concepts:

1. The interior space extended outdoors: This approach is usually expressed through the use of balconies on the dwelling units. The community center is often expressed this way, too, with a patio or deck combined with a glass wall. In some cases, a lobby might be visually extended out into the arrival or drop-off area.

DWELLING UNIT TO BALCONY

EXTENDING INDOOR SPACE OUTDOORS

2. The interior space with an adjacent window planting area: This concept permits the use of plant materials set against the windows, thus creating a framed view of a space or focal point some distance from the building.

PLANT MATERIALS SET AGAINST WINDOW

3. Indoor observation of outdoor security zone: With this approach the exits from the building are provided with a window which permits the resident to survey the zone and check for intruders before leaving the building. Another application of this concept involves the ability of the management office to carefully and unobtrusively monitor the arrival zone.

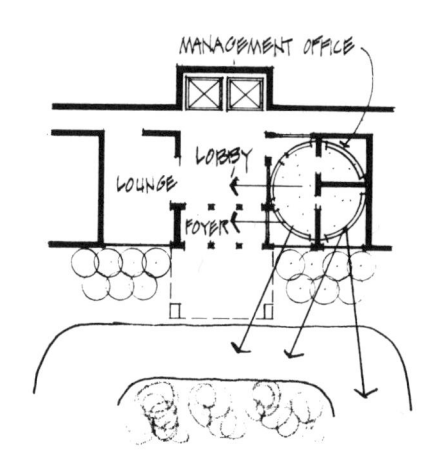

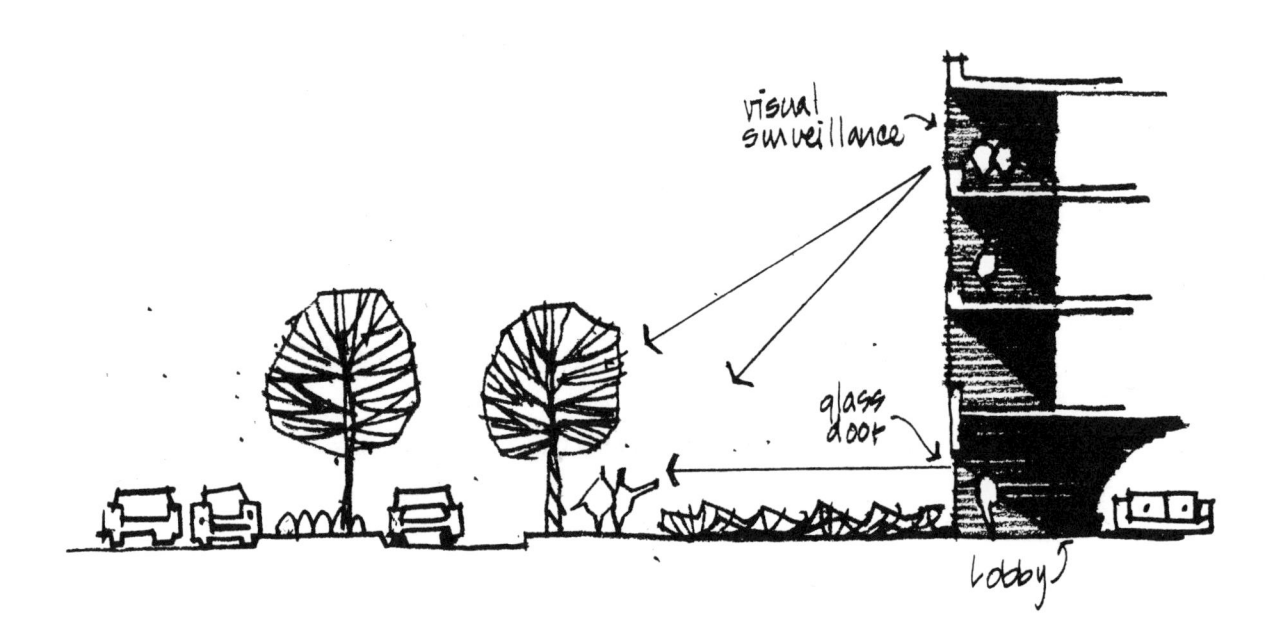

The building's orientation to the sun is a crucial factor to be considered in adapting the first two concepts to design. A beautiful view may no longer seem beautiful if the temperature is 90 degrees outside and the glare from the sun is intolerable. Connections between the indoors and outdoors should consider the angle of the sun. In some areas, it may be appropriate to use planting as a sun screen; awning and tinted glass are other options to be considered.

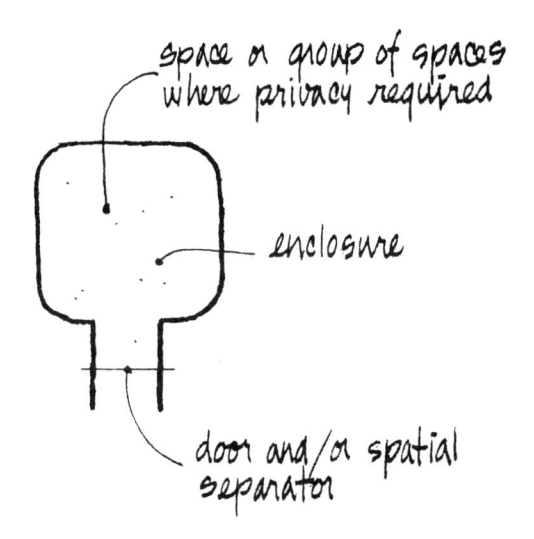

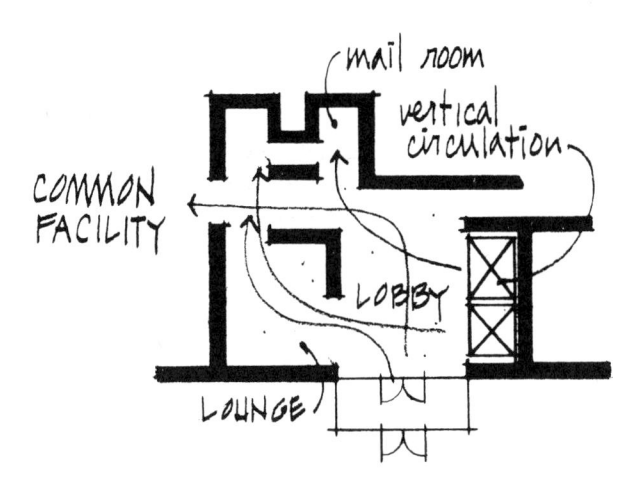

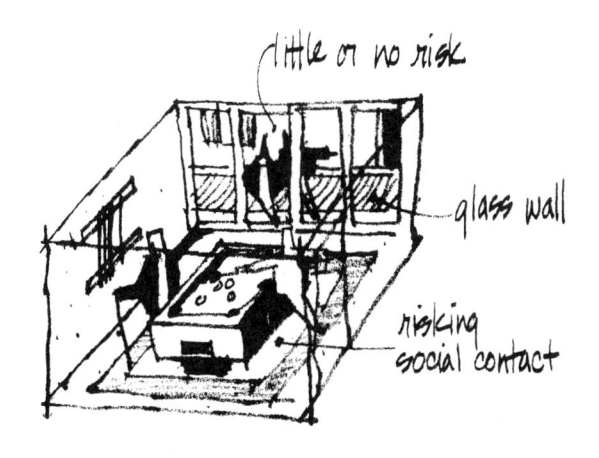

Indoor Communal Activities Zone

The indoor communal activities zone that is for development-wide activities exists most strongly in medium- and high-rise developments. In townhouse and low-rise elderly housing this zone is partly out of doors or is housed in a separate building (see *Townhouse Development Process*).[7] The discussion below therefore applies most directly to high- and medium-rise developments and to those low-rise developments where all facilities are connected internally.

This zone or zones is both the "front parlor" of a development and its utilitarian operating support. Some facilities, such as recreation rooms and lounges, are designed for specific social functions. Other facilities, including management offices, mail rooms, medical clinics, etc., are purely utilitarian in nature, but they can be conducive to natural social contact and can help to enhance the sense of home and the feeling that the development is a human place if properly designed.

These indoor facilities should be located according to the relative levels of privacy required for their successful operation. Where privacy is not mandatory, an appropriate choice between privacy and meeting people should always be afforded to the resident. Broadly, the following guidelines should be followed:

1. The management office, mail pick-up, and vertical circulation functions should be grouped around the primary entrance and lounge.

2. All facilities should be accessible without passing directly through the lounge.

3. Medical, social service, and central dining facilities, if provided, should be grouped in close proximity to the main circulation or vertical circulation element, but in such a way that it is not necessary for a resident to pass through (across) the lobby or lounge to reach them. These facilities should be separated from recreational and social spaces and they should be given an intimate and personal character.

4. The main entry lounge should be treated as an indoor front porch, a place where it is comfortable to observe the comings and goings of people without feeling threatened.

---

[7] Michigan State Housing Development Authority, *Townhouse Development Process*, 1970.

5. Most social and recreational facilities should be grouped together to create a complex which offers many options for flexibility of use through the proximity of space. These facilities should be located adjacent to the main lobby so that they are inviting and easily reached by visitors; this will greatly enhance the psychological links between the development and the community.

6. Communal facilities should never be located in such a way that a residential zone must be penetrated to reach them. It should also not be necessary to pass through a communal zone to reach a residential zone.

7. Spatially, the lobby, recreational, and social areas should become a focal point for the development.

8. All service and maintenance facilities should be located as dictated by functional requirements but they should not call attention to themselves as a part of the zone.

In low-rise developments this zone should be located at the focal or central point of the development and be positioned so as to link the neighborhood/development contact zone to the outdoor activities zone.

In high- and medium-rise buildings the broad role of this zone should be the same. Within the zone each subcomponent should be easily identifiable by its spatial character and its relative position should make sense.

Two general concepts about physical location pertain to this zone, and each has advantages.

1. *Integral to the building:* With this approach it is assumed that the facilities are located on the first floor of the building and are integral to the main structure. This way of locating facilities can offer substantial construction efficiency. On small sites, especially where the building mass is itself horizontally and vertically articulated, this approach offers efficiency of land utilization. As shown in the accompanying diagrams, potential organizations can either be linear or nucleated.

2. *Extra to the building:* With this approach it is assumed that some or all of this zone is housed in a low single story structure attached to the main structure. When such a building is used the entrance to the main building may be located in the link between the facilities and the main building. This approach can result in an appropriate stepping down to grade (scale articulation) when residential buildings are a total entity in a simple form. The relative freedom that this design scheme affords in building shape manipulation may also enhance the ease and probability of achieving a desirable relationship between building and site activity zones. As shown in the accompanying diagrams of possible desirable organization, this approach tends to produce several activity nuclei.

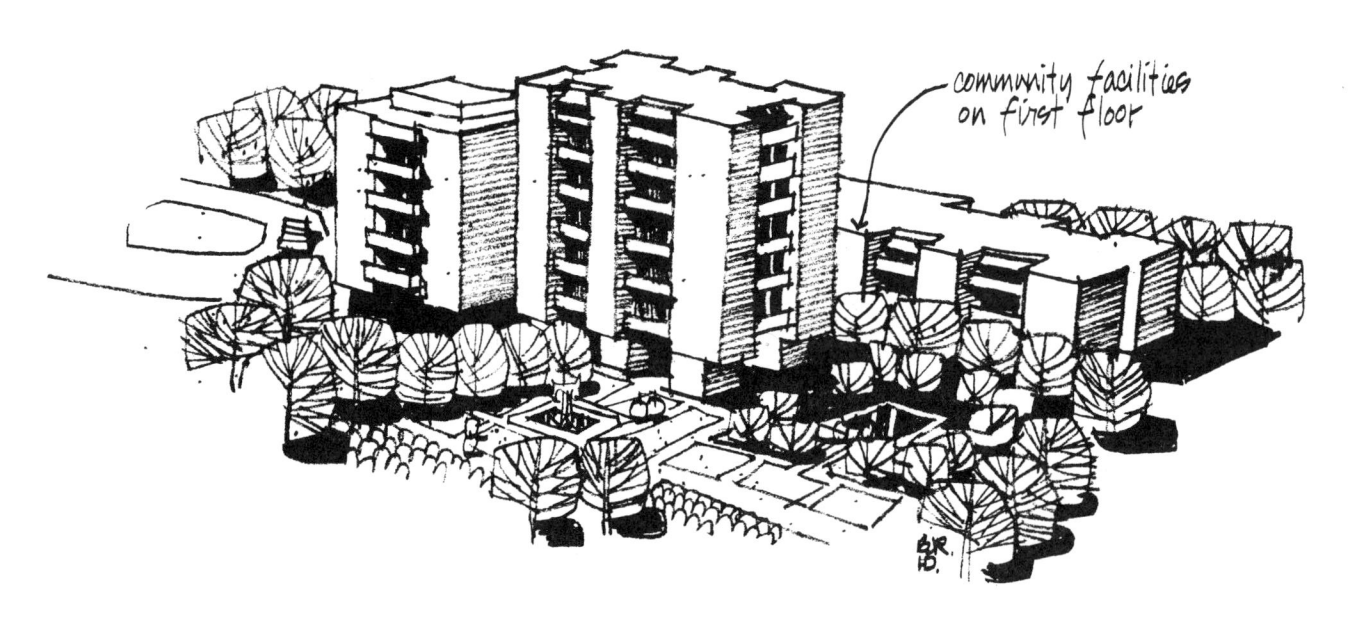

EXAMPLE OF INTEGRAL COMMUNITY FACILITIES

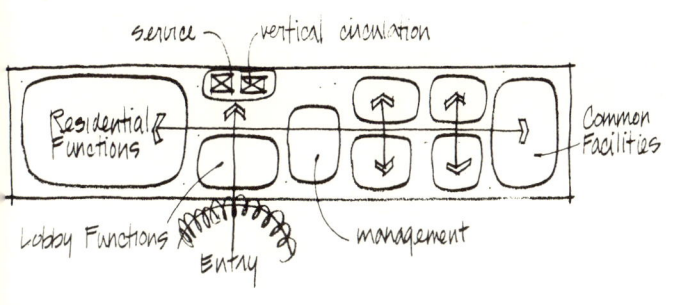

EXAMPLE WITHIN BUILDING LINEAR

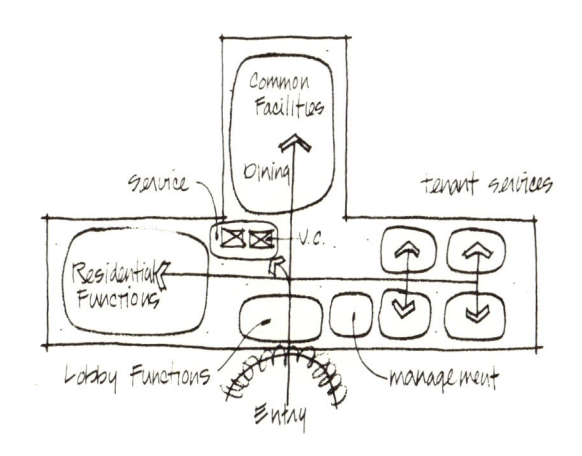

EXAMPLE WITHIN BUILDING NUCLEATED

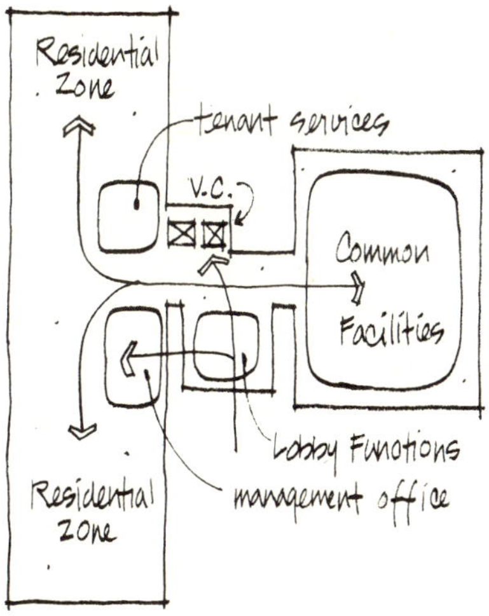

EXAMPLE TO THE BUILDING SEVERAL NUCLEI

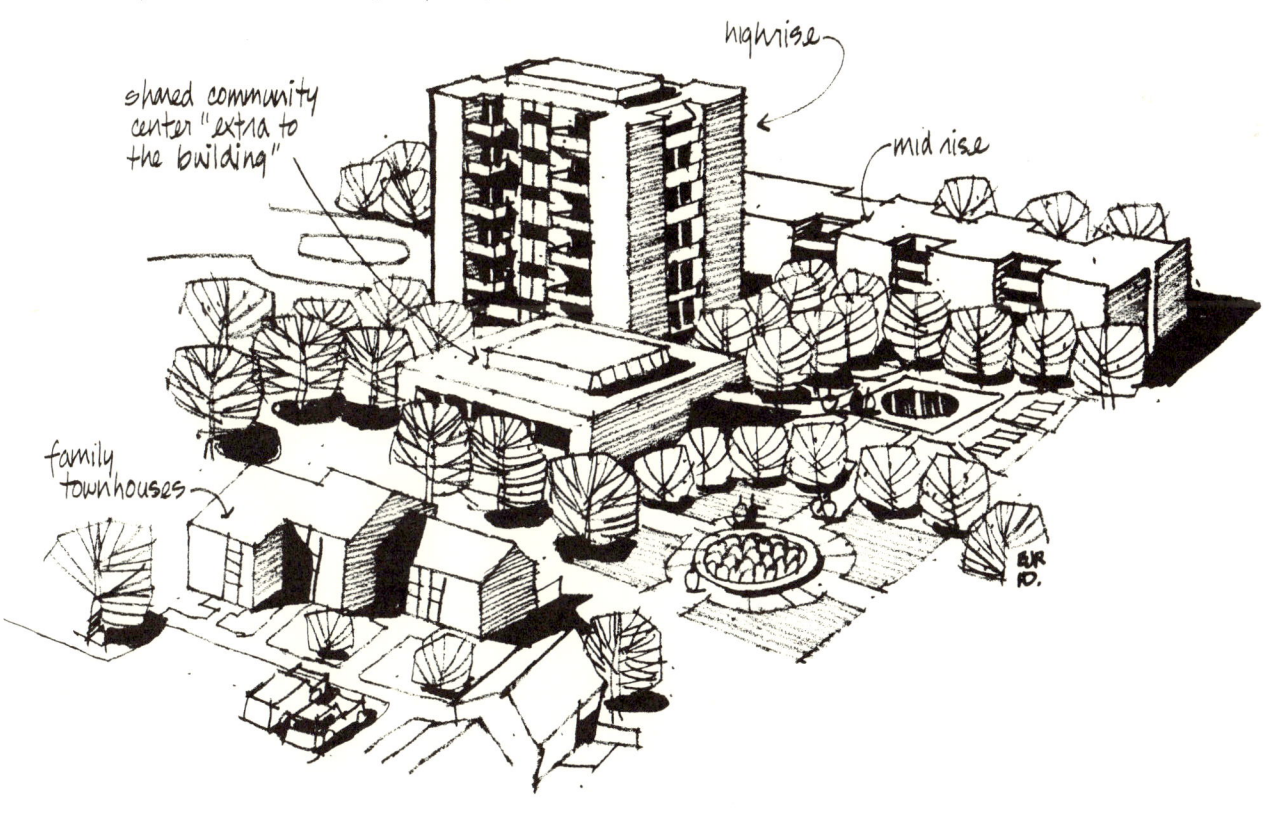

EXAMPLE OF ELDERLY and FAMILY MIXED WITH SHARED COMMUNITY FACILITIES

Sometimes the designer may wish to locate some of the functions of this zone on the top floor of a high-rise building. This should be done only if a specific advantage is gained, for example, capturing an outstanding view. Generally, however, such a location tends to introvert a building and its residents. Dissasociation from the ground reduces desirable community contacts. Basements should only be used for supplemental recreation facilities, storage, and service functions.

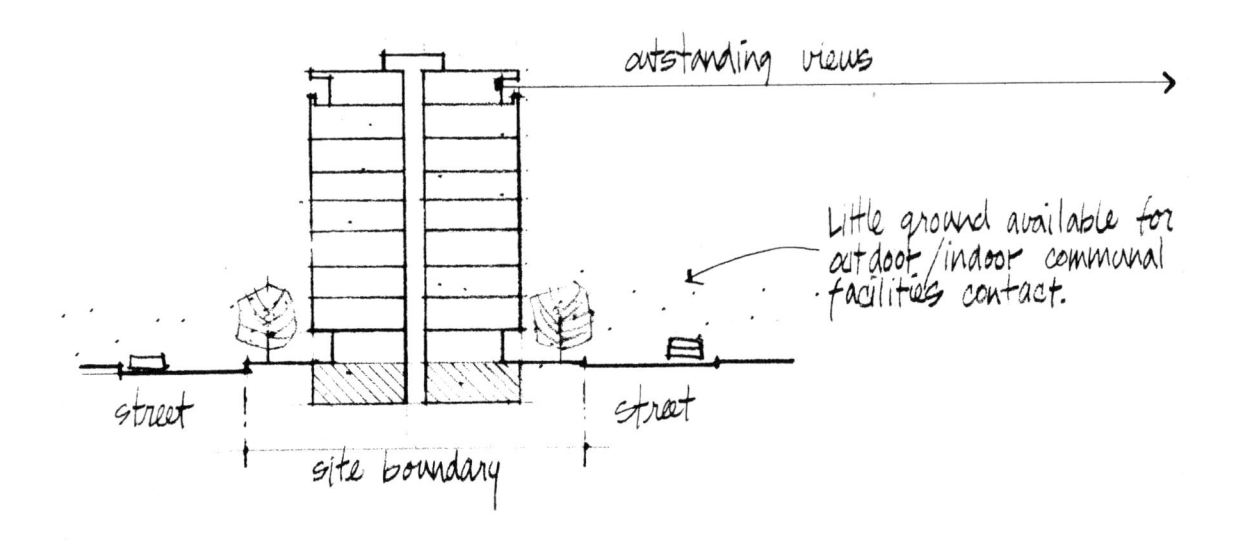

Residential Zones

The obvious function in each of these zones is the specific provision of places to live (dwelling units) and the supporting facilities necessary for daily life. Groups of dwelling units are clustered around or along a circulation path leading to a circulation node which either connects to a vertical circulation element or (in single story units) to the outdoors. The circulation node will generally serve more than one residential zone and it should be the next step on the scale of spatial sequence leading from the most private to the most public areas of a development. These nodal points (elevator lobbies or entry halls) are logical places to locate laundry rooms, central tenant storage (if this is not provided in the unit), communal balconies, lounges, etc.

In clustering dwelling units to create individual residential zones, size and form or organization will, of course, be a product of the individual development program and type of site. As a general rule, however, such zones should not contain less than six or more than fourteen dwelling units. Zones containing substantially more than fourteen units will probably have definite disassociation and dehumanizing effects upon residents.

When organizing units, care should be exercised to insure the privacy of each individual dwelling. One unit that directly overlooks another should be avoided at all costs. In no case should one dwelling unit look directly into another from a distance of less than 60 feet. A corner relationship at right angles between two units is especially undesirable for achieving privacy.

Small groups of units establish a proprietory sense in residents which enhances both security and pride in home.

PRIVACY LOSS FROM FACING UNIT - DISTANCE TOO SMALL

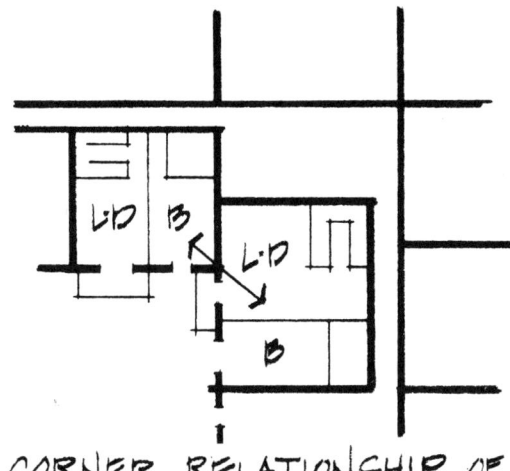

CORNER RELATIONSHIP OF UNITS CAUSES PRIVACY LOSS

RESIDENTIAL ZONE 6-14 UNITS DESIRABLE

SEMI-PRIVATE COMMUNAL ZONE
- *VERT. CIRC.*
- *LAUNDRY/LOUNGE*
- *STORAGE*

Many organizational alternatives exist for creating a residential zone, the two listed below, however, are the most common and offer the most opportunities for design:

Double or single loaded corridor
Cluster formed around a circulation place

As the designer explores various possibilities, he should keep the following parameters in mind:

1. Perception studies of the reaction of people indicate a negative response to corridors which are long and narrow.[8] Ideally, corridor or circulation path segments should not be more than 75 to 100 feet in length. Beyond these distances the path should be broken by staggering, widening, or angling off, complemented by color/texture changes. This parameter may be waived for developments where, for reasons of safety, full view from the circulation node to each dwelling unit is required.

2. Widening of corridors or the creation of circulation places for the purpose of creating seating areas or miniature lounges in the circulation path is not encouraged, especially if this means the resident cannot come and go from his apartment in privacy. Social contact is desirable but it should be a matter of choice.

3. Circulation paths should be seen as links to the outside world and they should therefore make sense visually and physically.

4. Dwelling unit entry doors which are immediately adjacent or which face one another across a narrow space are not encouraged because they may force unwanted social contact. The sense or feeling of a development for a resident is greatly improved if the circulation nodal point, at which a zone terminates, is spatially differentiated from the path leading to it. A small seating/waiting area may be appropriate here. It is very desirable if people are able to see the outdoors from this space, especially if there is a chance that, because of size, the resident perceives that he is lost or buried in the building. Without this view out, disorientation can occur rather rapidly.

5. A view out is also desirable from the circulation path of the zone.

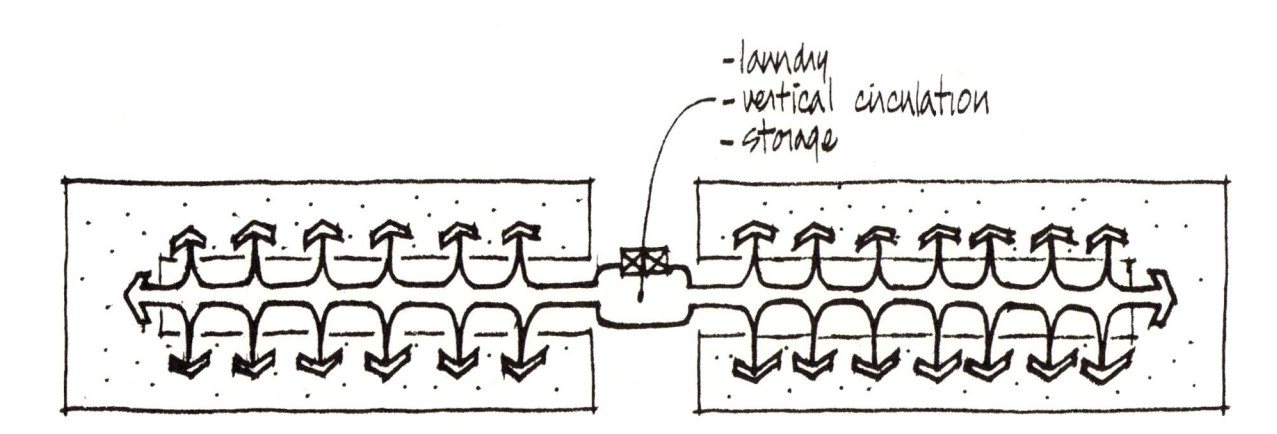

NOT DESIRABLE - OVERLY LONG CORRIDOR - TO MANY UNITS PER ZONE - CORRIDORS STRAIGHT

---

[8] Nils Larsson, *Housing the Elderly*, 2nd ed. (Ottawa: Central Mortgage and Housing Corp., 1972), page 20.

It should always be remembered that no matter how successful the dwelling unit design, each residential zone must continue to have a home-like image for the resident if an institutional environment is to be avoided.

It should also be remembered that in large developments, especially with high-rise units, sheer physical size, if unarticulated, can undo the best efforts to avoid an institutional atmosphere that will overpower the residents. For this reason, the specific expression of groups of zones in the massing of buildings reduces scale and enhances the individual's ability to relate to his place in the whole.

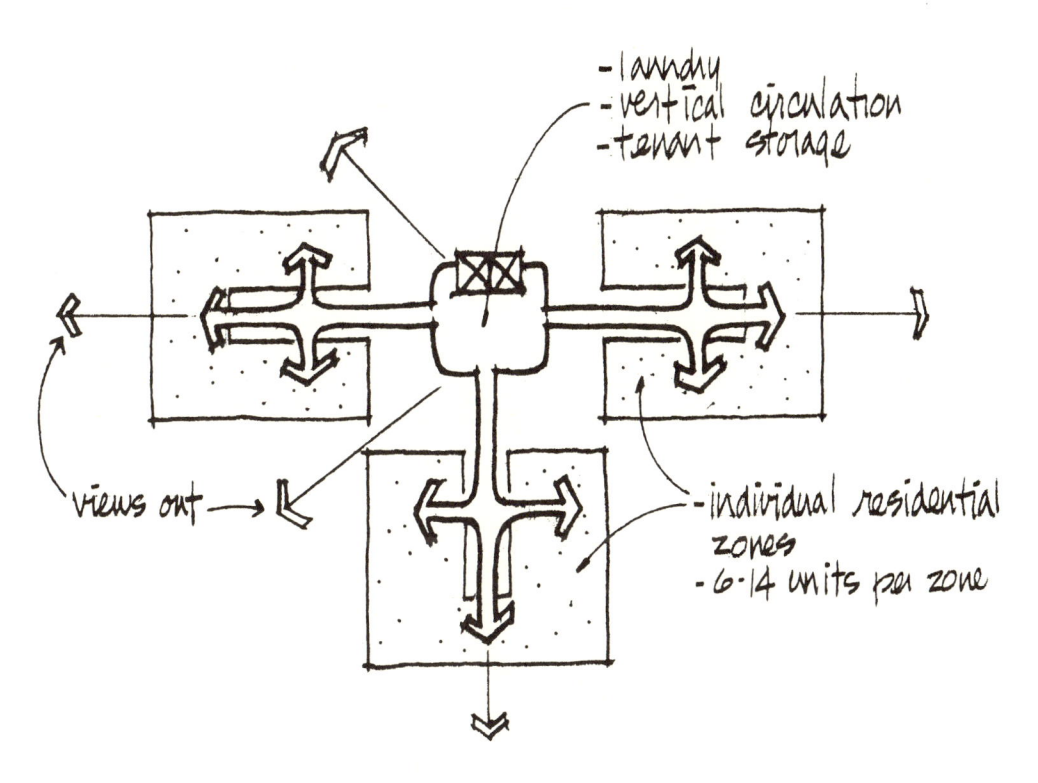

- laundry
- vertical circulation
- tenant storage

- views out

- individual residential zones
- 6-14 units per zone

DESIRABLE - FLOOR SUBDIVIDED INTO REASONABLE ZONES

DEVELOPMENT DESIGN

This division of the section on the design of housing for the elderly is concerned with the design of the building and site. After having investigated all of the required development activities, gained a thorough understanding of their functional and spatial requirements, and explored overall functional organization and design, it is appropriate to address the physical product which is the housing and its design expression.

The broad context of these explorations and the guidelines they generate are conducted within the framework of the behavioral factors discussed earlier in this section. In this context it is necessary to recognize and respect the rights of the elderly to be masters of their own homes. This philosophic concept can be translated into design terms. The individual unit within a housing development together with the sum total of amenities and services must become a home to the occupant. The right to privacy and the right to decide on the extent of voluntary participation in communal activities are attributes of ordinary home life which should be achieved. The internal and external appearance have a bearing on the sense of home, and the problems of minimizing or erasing the image of the institutional environment must be overcome.

The development design investigation is in three parts:

1. Design Determinants—Site Types, Building Types
2. Design Expression—Building Massing and Character, Landscape Development
3. Building Efficiency Guidelines

These parts must be viewed and read as a continuum.

The design examples given in this section are used only to illustrate the guidelines, and should not be construed as definitive answers. They are not intended to preclude other solutions.

DESIGN DETERMINANTS

Every development design will be strongly influenced by the nature of the site on which it will be located and by the characteristics of the building type or types used. Before design can begin, these must be carefully analyzed and understood.

Site Types

In order to achieve stated design goals, the building's design must spring from an understanding of, and sympathy with, its physical context. It is therefore appropriate to briefly analyze the design of housing for the elderly in terms of some broad generalizations which can be drawn about sites.

Although housing developments for the elderly have been constructed on all kinds of sites and in many different settings, broad analysis indicates that sites can be divided into two general categories by the nature of the setting. The first category can be classified as the external site; that is, the context of the site is so strong that the building and the development of the site should be shaped in response to the external pressures and characteristics within which it will exist. The following general design objectives are applicable to external sites. The site should:

...respond to and complement neighborhood scale, texture, and social contour.
...maintain and enhance the streetscape.
...blend the building(s) into the environment.
...relate functional components directly to their external counterparts.

The sites and buildings which can be said to be externally influenced are generally those which exist in highly developed settings either in an urban, suburban, or small town environment. Often, such sites are small and costly, and developments for the elderly on these sites will, of necessity, be very intensive. Generally, it is necessary that developments on these sites achieve their own identity without appearing to be, or, in fact, being separate from their surroundings. If the site and building design were to create the impression of separateness, then the broader objectives regarding non-isolation of the elderly would be violated. In addition, the sort of disruption of the urban continuum that can occur is both socially and visually undesirable, regardless of the nature of the development. Housing developments for the elderly have often been so large that they have become the dominant visual feature in the environment and, in these cases, even greater attention must be paid to appropriate responses to external influences.

DEVELOPMENT/NEIGHBORHOOD SCALE RELATIONSHIP

RESPONDING TO TOPOGRAPHY

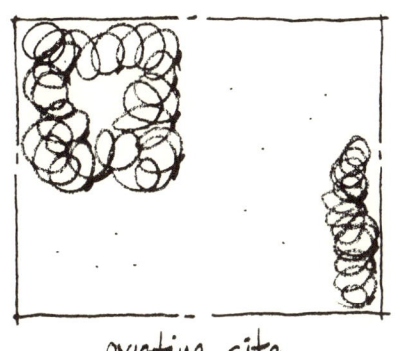

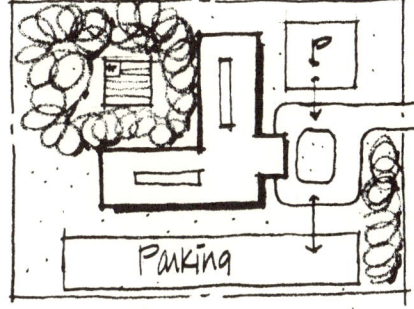

existing site / site development

RESPONDING TO VEGETATION

The second category of site can be classified as internally influenced; that is, the sites are so situated that either by virtue of extreme site size, or the absence of surrounding development, they do not have strong external factors other than orientation and circulation influencing them. On such sites the issue is not one of finding a sympathetic fit for a development but rather to create and establish a sense of place; that is, to fix the development in time and place so that a residential environment will exist. Often, where sites are in undeveloped or underdeveloped areas, their design will set the mood and pattern for future development. Many housing developments for the elderly built on internal sites have not recognized the need or the problem. These developments have been designed as large objects floating in space and the net result has been to create an institutional rather than a residential appearance.

The determinants of building to site relationships can be categorized into three groups:

1. On-site determinants (characteristics which give directives to building siting and land use organization):

    a. Topography and soils
    b. Vegetative cover
    c. Natural features (rock outcropping, ponds, etc.)
    d. Underground utility and sewer systems or easements

2. Off-site determinants:

    a. Sun orientation
    b. Views
    c. Neighborhood security problems
    d. Adjacent land uses and building massing
    e. Vehicular/pedestrian access
    f. Utilities and sewer systems
    g. Local zoning ordinances or codes

3. Development program — The list of needs to be accommodated on the site and expressed as facilities (see section on programming, page 23)

With an almost infinite number of potential sites, it becomes impossible to document all the specific responses that the designer might make to hypothetical situations. Therefore, two extremes are discussed, the large and almost park-like site and the small urban site. Each of these extremes begins to generate recognizable trends for design determinants which define the appropriate site/building relationships.

In general, the small urban site usually involves more determinants from the off-site grouping than from the other categories. For example, certain objectives become apparent with the urban site. Typical design responses to off-site determinants follow:

1. The building should blend well with the surrounding buildings.

2. The urban streetscape should be recognized and related to the development.

3. The development should not duplicate recreational facilities found on adjacent properties.

The emphasis of the site analysis is actually directed more at the adjacent, off-site determinants than at the site itself. The major concern is to blend and relate with the neighborhood. This blending insures that the development will not be isolated from the neighborhood and community.

The large, internal site, on the other hand, is usually characterized by design determinants found on the site. In most cases the challenge is to either respond to some overriding determinant such as vegetation or to develop a sense of place in a very open area. Typical design responses to on-site determinants follow:

1. The building siting should preserve existing, mature vegetation (heavily wooded site).

2. The building functions should be arranged to enclose a space (very open site).

On-site determinants must be analyzed, documented, and responded to. In many cases poor living environments have resulted from the failure to recognize some unique quality or deficiency in the site.

Building Types

It is essential that the designer understand the potentials and limitations of the most common building configurations when they are used for housing for the elderly, especially because no one type can be regarded as the correct solution for all situations.

High- and Medium-Rise Apartment Buildings (three or more stories): These building types have become the customary solution for housing for the elderly. There are many reasons why this has happened but four factors seem to stand above the rest. First, the density of development possible effectively reduces the land cost per unit where premium cost urban or suburban land is concerned. Second, studies indicate that while the building construction cost per unit is higher in high- and medium-rise buildings (as contrasted to low-rise, light-frame construction), the higher land and site development costs per unit for low-rise buildings substantially reduce or eliminate the apparent cost disadvantage of the high-rise building. Third, where high levels of social, recreational, and safety services are to be provided (as in most elderly developments), the compact building configuration facilitates the delivery of these services and greatly reduces operating costs. Fourth, because it is not desirable to isolate the elderly from the mainstream of community activity, the most desirable sites are those close to shopping, transportation, community facilities, etc. These sites are generally found in developed areas where frequently only smaller sites are available and low density, low-rise construction would seriously limit the number of elderly tenants accommodated.

It cannot be said that high- and medium-rise buildings are the first choice of elderly people accustomed to living at ground level with easy access to the street. More often than not, the marketing success of a high-rise development can be attributed to the tremendous housing needs of the elderly segment of the population rather than to a desire to live in a high-rise residence. The elderly tend to worry about using the elevator, being trapped on an upper floor during a fire, personal confusion arising from corridors and doors that look alike, or the distance required to carry laundry or shopping.

Nonetheless, a well-located high- or medium-rise building can offer real compensations as noted above in terms of physical and contextual proximity to both on- and off-site facilities and services. This type of building insures fully sheltered access to on-site facilities. Some methods of overcoming high-rise design problems are discussed in the subsection on building massing and character, page 116.

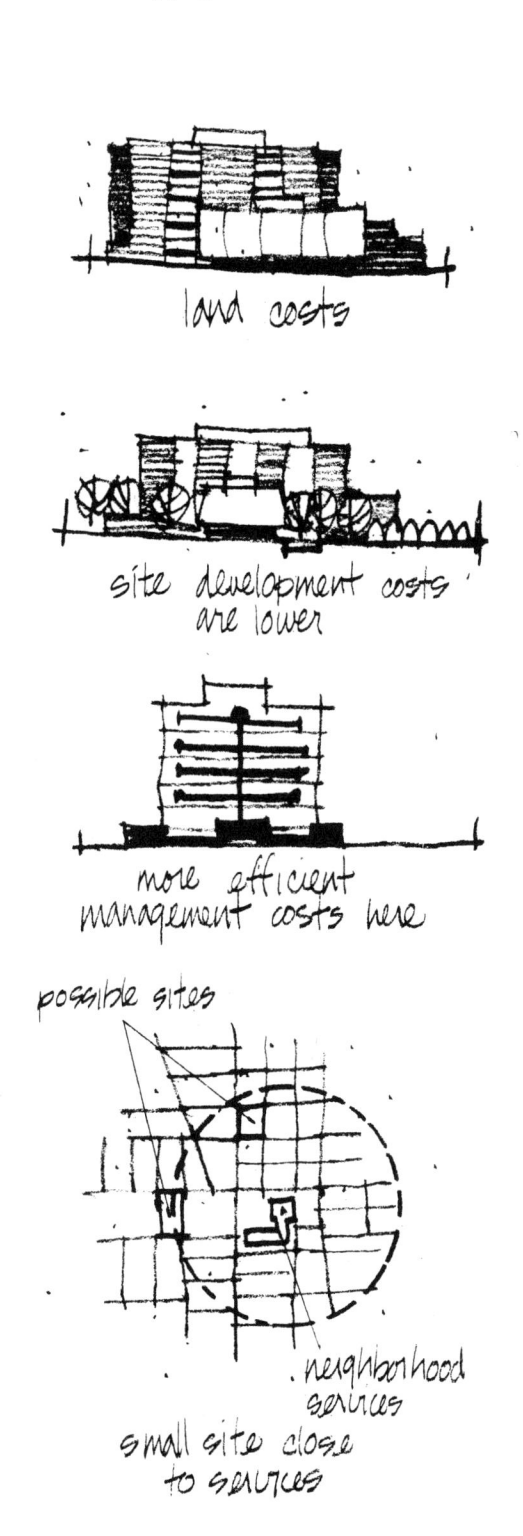

Low-Rise Apartment Buildings: The two-story garden apartment is probably the most common form of multiple housing today. For many housing users it provides sufficient access to the outdoors and single family residential scale without the cost associated with single family housing. It has a high level of construction efficiency and offers great potential for achieving necessary development density.

Adoption of this building type for the elderly generates several problems:

1. Because there are many separate buildings, common facilities need to be centralized for the entire project, resulting in excessive unsheltered walking distances and attendant inconveniences.

2. These buildings are rarely served by elevators because the cost of elevators is difficult to justify because of the small number of units served. The absence of elevators would mean that the second floor apartments must be reached by stairs. This is unacceptable, and it automatically precludes occupancy by some elderly people. Perhaps worse, this situation could result in forcing those elderly persons who were mobile at the time of initial occupancy to move when they begin to lose mobility.

3. The use of the dwelling units on the lower floor by elderly people and those on the upper floor by non-elderly people is frequently not advisable because of the interpersonal problems which can arise through the loss of acoustic privacy as well as general conflicts in lifestyles.

The single story garden apartment building offers advantages as housing for the elderly. It combines the benefits of the apartment building with some of those of the single family house. A central corridor could provide sheltered access to all dwelling unit doors and provides added entrance safety. Each dwelling unit can also have a fully private door leading to a private garden or semi-private outdoor space.

Because of the low development densities achieved with this type of building, it could prove uneconomical to build on costly urban or suburban land that is well located for the elderly. This type of building is therefore probably not suitable for an entire development. Its greatest potential use would seem to be as one of the building types in an elderly development where independent elderly housing is mixed with family housing.

Its greatest functional disadvantage is that of sprawl. This is especially critical in the functional relationship between dwelling units and common facilities, such as walking distance, safety, social services, etc.

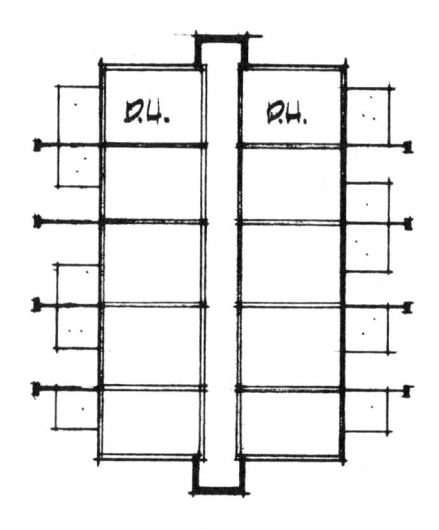

PLAN SINGLE STORY APARTMENT BUILDING

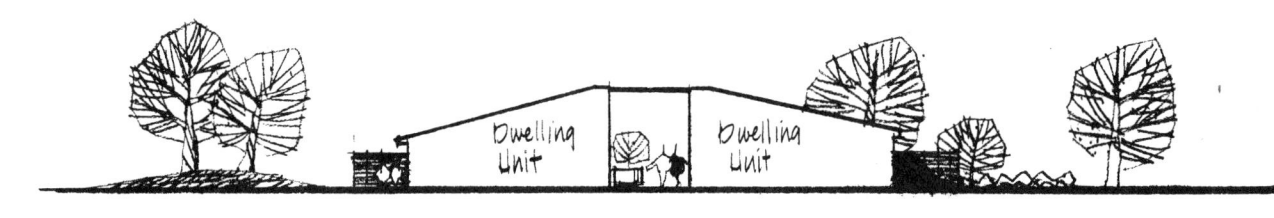

SECTION THROUGH LOW RISE DEVELOPMENT

Townhouses: This type of building has many of the characteristics of the single story garden apartment. The most significant difference is the lack of sheltered access to the dwelling unit entrances. Beyond this, its advantages and disadvantages for the elderly are the same as those of the single story apartment. Because of its unsheltered access, this type of building is probably best suited for elderly residents in a location with a temperate climate without severe weather conditions. As a type of building its greatest utility would seem to be in mixed family and elderly developments. It should be noted that townhouse units for the elderly should always be of single story design. While basements may be included, the unit should be so designed that the occupant can carry on all everyday activities including general storage without using the basement.

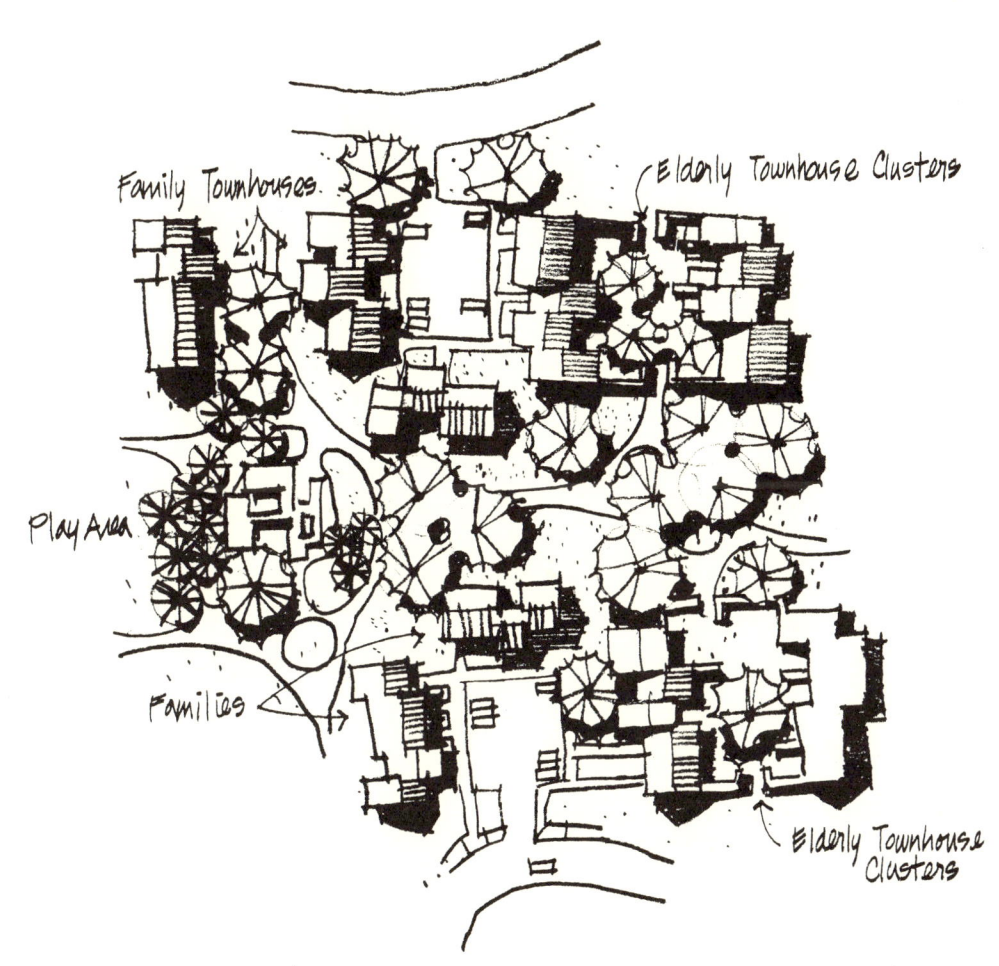

ONE OPTION FOR MIXING FAMILY and ELDERLY TOWNHOUSES

DESIGN EXPRESSION

The delineation of any functional organization concept is strongly dependent on a harmonious expression of the following design elements:

The Building: its massing and character
The Site: its landscape development

These two elements are discussed in terms of their implications for reinforcing functional concepts and establishing the development's image.

Building Massing and Character

The design of the building and the site development must always be carried on as a single activity. Components of the site must be related to their counterparts within the building and these components should seek their needed spatial definition from the natural warp and woof of the building form. Conversely, the building form must be manipulated in response to the organizational structure of the site.

As a general rule, multi-story simple rectangular, square, or round building forms, although economically efficient, are undesirable because they are identified with hospitals, motels, and similar institutions. The specific building form should evolve, of course, from the particular building program and the type and location of the site. The basic framework of the design must develop, however, from a recognition that massive scale is antithetical to a residential environment. The building scale should be broken down, by its massing and articulation, into component parts.

In general a single uniform building height is visually undesirable unless vertical surfaces are highly modulated. A more feasible and visually effective solution may be the vertical modulation of the mass while still maintaining simple straight walls and straightforward detailing.

There is a pervasive public preference for low-rise housing, and for housing which relates directly to human scale. Stepping a building up from grade in multi-story increments represents a reasonable compromise between human scale and the need for large building mass.

This method should not only be used to bring a building down to people, but it should also result in a building form which creates visual interest and aids the residents in making sense out of the environment.

On small urban sites or those sites which have powerful external physical influences at work, the manipulation of height affords the opportunity to align building elements to surrounding scale. On the small external site building shape and mass will be extensively influenced by site requirements and should therefore take on a very plastic system of organization.

On large sites or on those sites with minimal surrounding development, the building mass should be manipulated both horizontally and vertically to achieve the following:

General definition of place
Definition of arrival/departure zone
Transition up from grade
Adaptation to unique site contour or vegetation patterns
Definition and containment of outdoor activity zone

A BUILDING IN SPACE

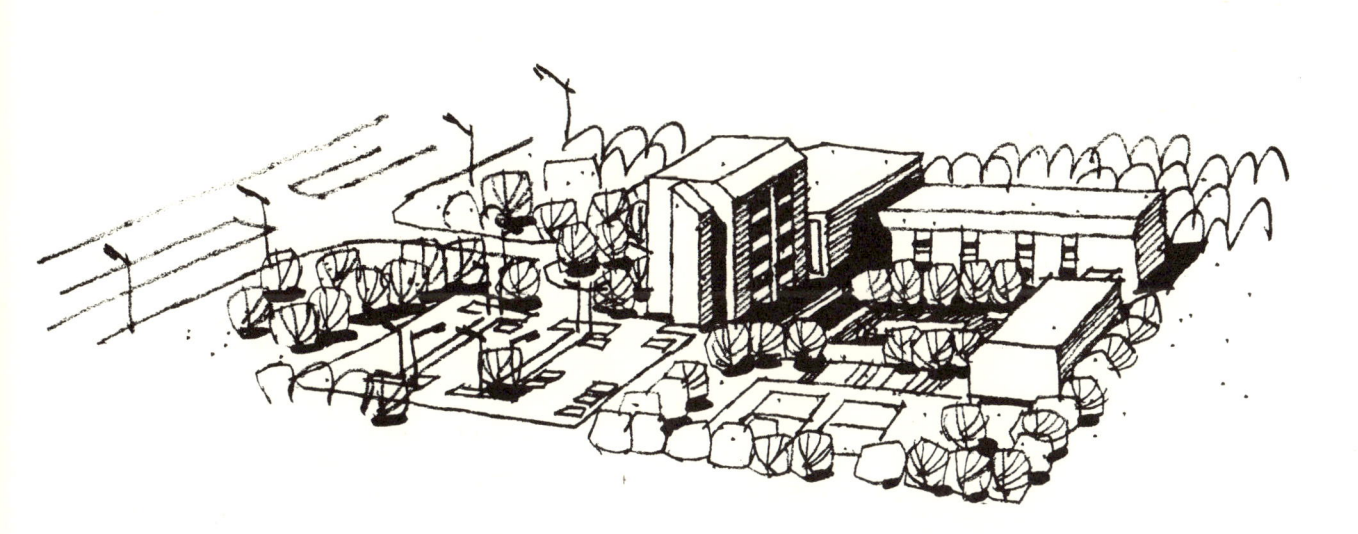

BUILDING MASSING WHICH CREATES A SENSE OF PLACE

In urban areas building mass can be effectively used to establish a strong street edge. Or where the edge is already too strong, it can provide spatial relief by being held back from the street.

The massing of residential buildings must reflect functional organization and give substantive visual cues to the resident and the visitor as to how it works. Further, the massing of buildings should establish an appropriate visual fit with their surroundings. To accomplish this, the following guides should be applied:

1. The organization of windows on a facade can clearly identify individual units and the residential zone. Care should be exercised to avoid uniform patterns which become monotonous and which offer no strong wall modulation.

2. Exterior materials as well as their color and texture should be selected for their logical relationship to the structural and overall enclosure system. They should also be selected for their ability to enhance and carry out the concept of relating a development to its surroundings. In general this means selecting materials which are consistent with those of the surrounding development — not necessarily the same material, but one which through color, texture, and form blends the development into an established environment or successfully establishes a residential character of its own where none exists. Usually, it is undesirable to make a visual issue out of a building for the elderly, setting it apart from the rest of the community.

3. In shaping the massing of large high- and medium-rise buildings it is helpful under some circumstances to use the block of common facilities space as one of the elements establishing a transitional building height. This can be accomplished by treating this space as a separate building block, one or two stories in height, which is linked either directly or through a connecting arrival lobby to the residential blocks. Use of this technique should not preclude manipulation of the residential blocks in the same building.

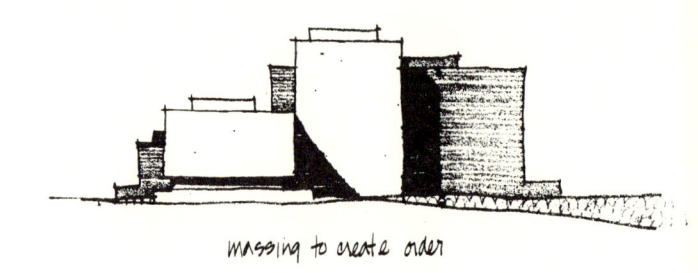

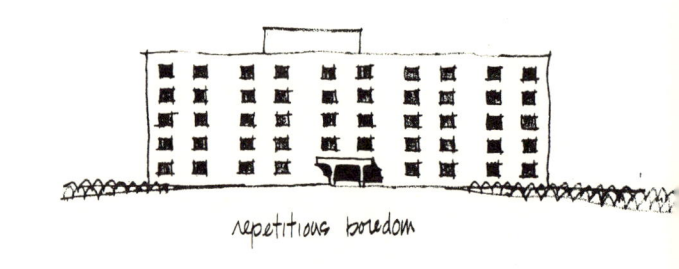

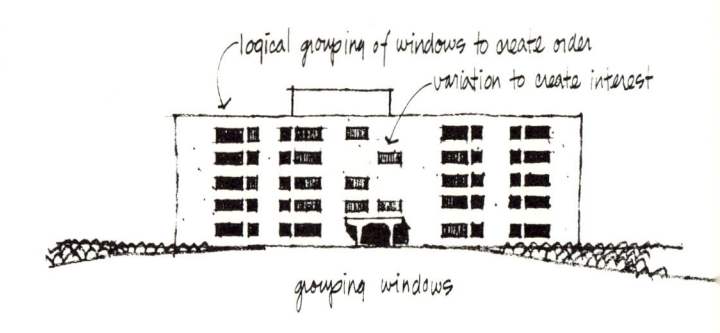

massing to create order

fenestration to create interest

repetitious boredom

logical grouping of windows to create order
variation to create interest

grouping windows

4. The tops of buildings are sometimes a serious visual problem; first, because rooftop equipment and penthouses have not been adequately accounted for in the building design, and second, because there is rarely adequate attention paid to the manner in which the building elevation is stopped or ended at the roof. Both factors must be dealt with. Buildings must stop gracefully and with conviction. They cannot end arbitrarily if they are to be visually appealing. Treating the rooftop elements and parapets as a capping element is the simplest method. This method will only succeed if the cap is a substantive change from the vertical rhythm of the facade and is of a scale sufficient to firmly establish its presence.

Another way to resolve the top of a high rise building

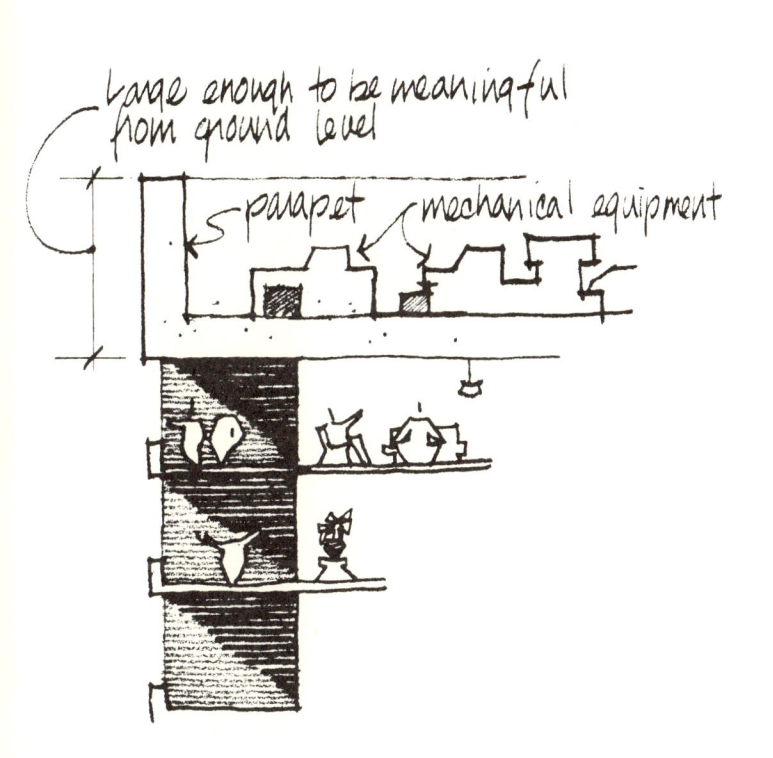

Large enough to be meaningful from ground level

parapet — mechanical equipment

The Landscape Development

Not only must the component activity zones involve a strong and readable organization of activities and space, but their organization should also be supported and enriched by the landscape development. Rather than reapply the same design principles to each zone repetitively, a general discussion is provided concerning each supporting subconcept such as planting, grading, etc. After each specific discussion, typical examples will be provided to illustrate how the principles can be applied. It must be kept in mind that these landscape development elements must be integrated into a harmonious system which reinforces the overall spatial concept. They appear as separate entities here only for illustrative purposes.

Planting: Planting is one of the key elements available to the designer. It can be used to reinforce his overall organizational and spatial concept. Planting is a multi-valued element in the landscape.

Planting has the following potentials for visually structuring a development. Planting can:

...direct a viewer's eye to a desired point in space.
...serve as a visual focus.
...unify divergent forms.
...define and separate views.
...frame a view.
...provide color.

Planting has the following potentials for functionally organizing a development. Planting can:

...provide shade.
...form a physical barrier.
...reduce noise levels.
...reduce soil erosion.

Along with these many positive uses of planting, there are two negative concerns which must be kept in mind.

  Planting can provide concealment for potential assailants.
  Planting requires maintenance.

In analyzing these two considerations, it should be recognized that planting can be categorized into five height classifications.

1. Lawn or grass areas (2 to 3 inches)
2. Low ground covers (6 to 12 inches)
3. Low shrubs (2 to 3 feet)
4. Intermediate trees and shrubs (4 to 20 feet with branches to the ground)
5. Canopy trees (12 feet and taller with high branches)

ENFRAMEMENT

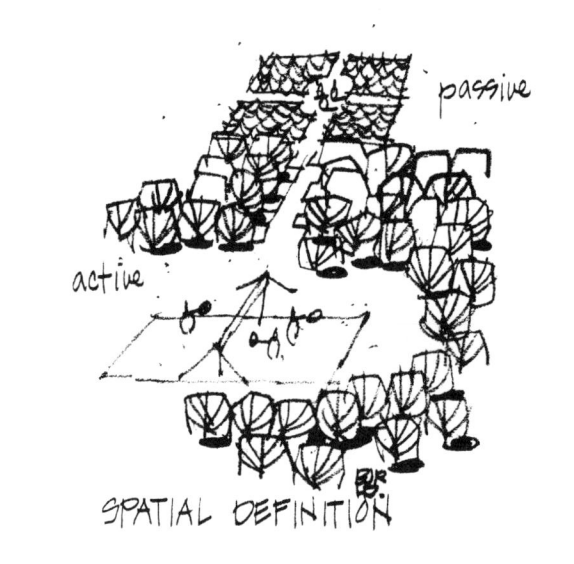

SPATIAL DEFINITION

CLASSIFICATION BY HEIGHT

Generally, planting in the lower height classifications tends to require more maintenance while low branching intermediate trees and shrubs provide the best opportunities for concealment. The establishment of maintenance zones throughout the development is one way of limiting the amount of area to be mowed or otherwise maintained, thus reducing maintenance costs. A second goal in regard to maintenance is to establish definitive edges between areas that are to receive different levels or kinds of maintenance. It is along the edges of planting areas that most of the time consuming maintenance and maintenance dollars are spent. By establishing obvious maintenance zones and carefully delineating simple and easily maintained edges, the development stands a better chance of receiving maintenance and the maintenance it does receive should cost less.

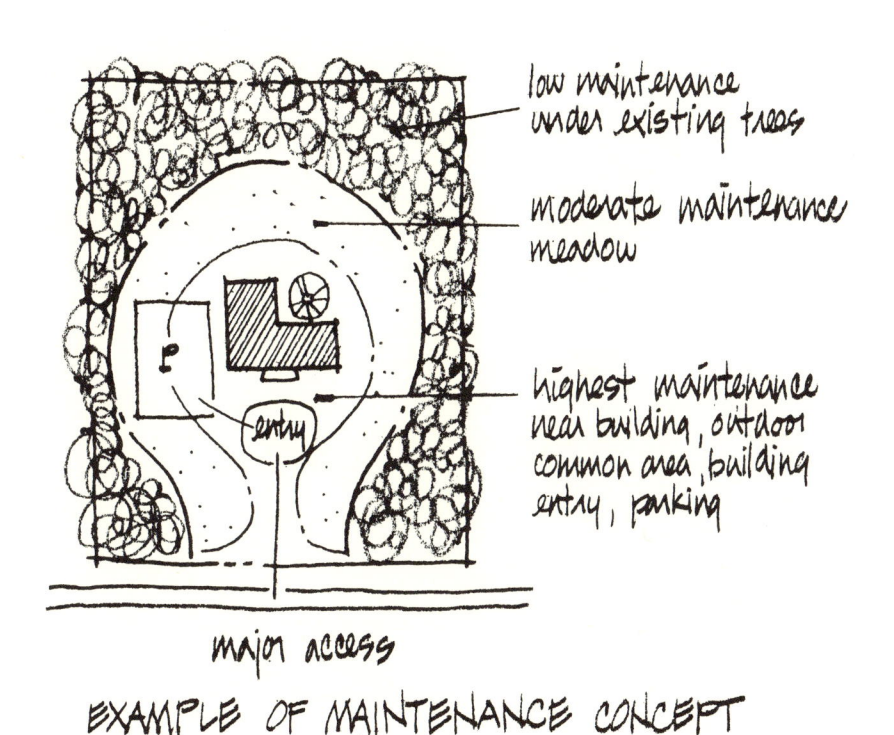

EXAMPLE OF MAINTENANCE CONCEPT

- low maintenance under existing trees
- moderate maintenance meadow
- highest maintenance near building, outdoor common area, building entry, parking
- major access

The critical zone in regard to acts of violence is the neighborhood/development contact zone. Of special concern is the parking area and walkway to the building from the parking area. The area in the immediate vicinity of the main entrance is also an area of concern.

Planting within these special security zones should be selected carefully in regard to its potential for concealment. Intermediate trees and shrubs may be used to accent entrance area and other special areas. These plantings should be handled in such a way as to prevent possible places of concealment. Landscape lighting and pruning are two ways of helping to minimize concealment potential. Other categories of shrubbery and trees may be located freely within these zones, which can be more specifically designated as the area within 50 feet of a building entrance, parking area, or connecting walkways.

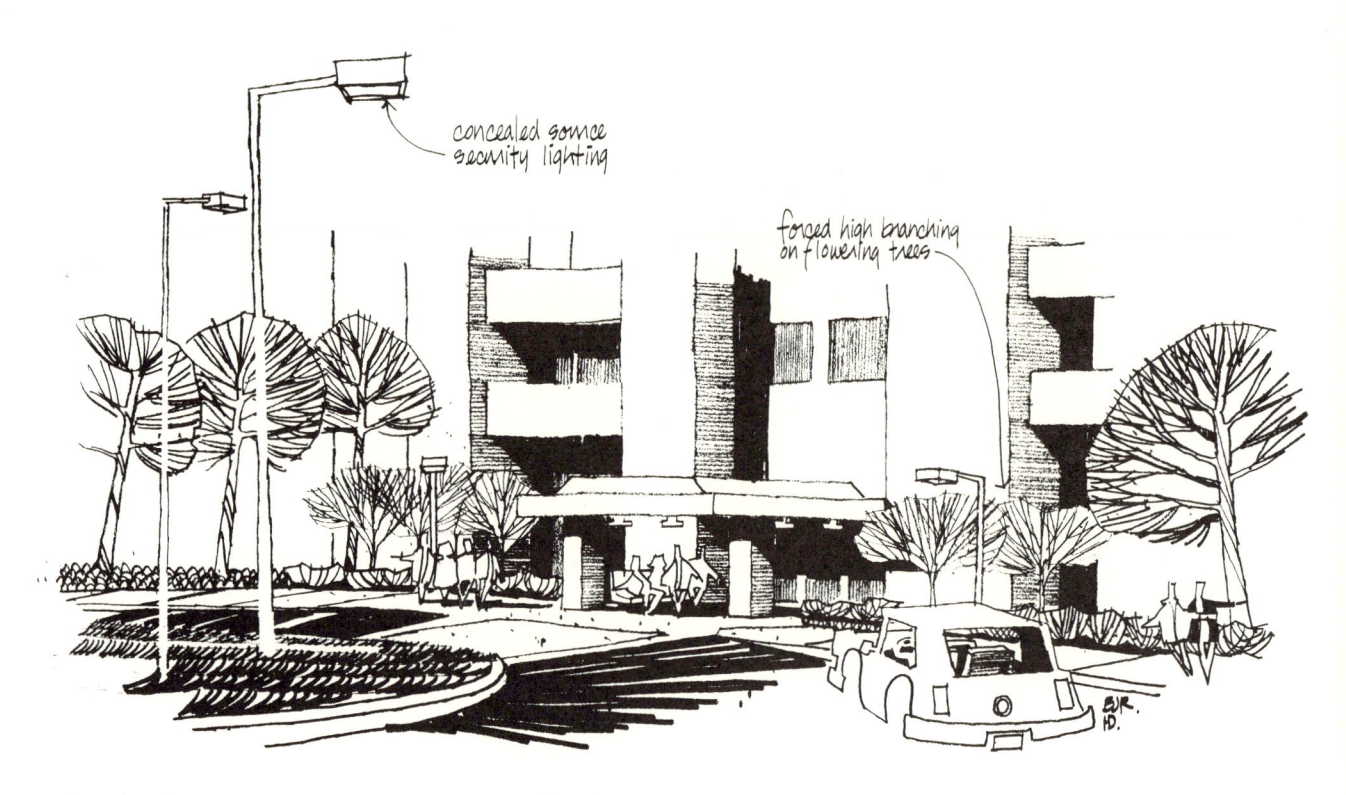

PLANTING and LIGHTING for SECURITY

Planting can be used to visually reinforce an organizational concept of the site plan and thus help the elderly resident to make sense out of the environment. It can also create visual interest. The site thus invites the viewer to explore and experience the landscape. Through its functional qualities (providing shade, etc.) it can offer many options for using the site and its facilities. The site as a whole should be considered when locating masses of planting with the details for each specific area or zone to be considered later.

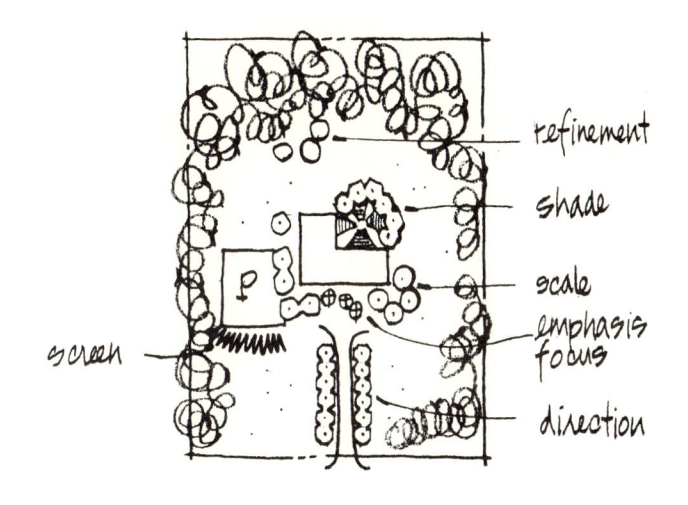

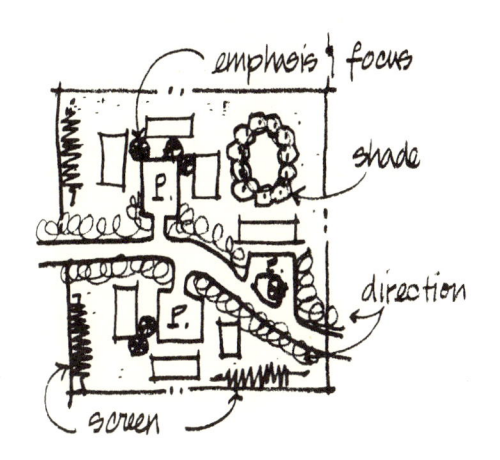

Grading: The development's grading can be thought of as another opportunity to reinforce and articulate an overall site organization and circulation concept. Too often grading is only thought of as a way of making sure surface water does not drain into buildings and the real potential of the ground plane as a structuring device is completely overlooked. Some of the visual and functional uses of grading are listed below. Grading can:

...direct a viewer's eye to a desired point in space.
...serve as a visual focus.
...unify divergent forms.
...separate visually incompatible land uses.
...form a physical barrier.
...form a windbreak.
...reduce noise levels.
...reduce erosion.

Many of these uses are similar to those described for planting. This is indicative of the strong relationship between planting and grading. The two elements should be designed together as a system because, when they are designed separately, there is the possibility that the two may be in opposition, creating confusion and diluting the overall organizational concept.

GRADING CAN REINFORCE SITE PLAN ORGANIZATION

Lighting: A lighting concept should also support the overall concept of the site organization. Outdoor lighting can be used in the following ways. Lighting can:

...accentuate an area or object in space.
...define an area or the edge of an area.
...provide a sense of personal security.

The neighborhood/development contact zone and the outdoor common area have different lighting needs in regard to provisions for security. The outdoor common area, for security reasons, should not be used at night by solitary individuals. The need in this area is to provide adequate lighting for social and recreational activities without special attention to security. The neighborhood/development contact zone, on the other hand, requires special security precautions to help prevent criminal acts. This zone also needs special delineation in order to form a visual context for the entrance-arrival area.

The parking area and the walkway from the parking area to the building should have a higher density of security lighting than areas elsewhere on the site. The lighting in this area should light the entire security zone defined in the section on planting, page 122.

Lighting can define the site's organizational structure thus giving residents, as in the case of grading and planting, another cue as to how the site plan works. It can also create visual interest by accentuating certain objects or areas. Finally, it can provide the elderly resident with a sense of personal security.

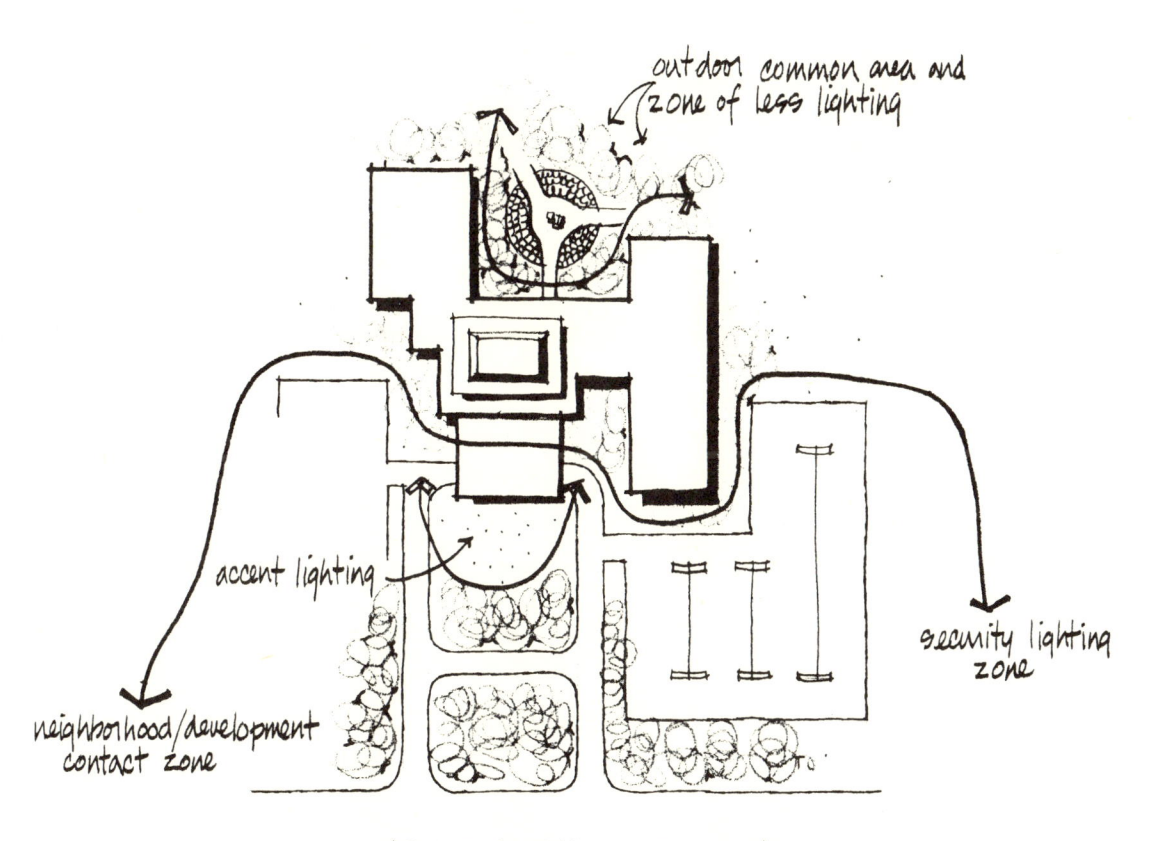

LIGHTING EMPHASIS BY ZONES

Signing: The implementation of a coordinated signing concept has three strong benefits:

Signing provides information.
Signing can help to unify diverse areas and facilities.
Signing can add visual interest.

Signs can be classified into two categories; those which identify objects, areas, or facilities and those which direct people to objects, areas, or facilities. Simplicity and clarity are two key criteria to be kept in mind while developing a sign concept. Furthermore, it is desirable to keep the number of signs to a minimum. One indication of a weak site organization concept is the need for many signs.

Outdoor Furniture: Outdoor furniture as discussed here includes seating, tables, and trash receptacles. The neighborhood/development contact zone and the outdoor common area involve different considerations in regard to outdoor furniture.

Vandalism and the possibility of theft must be considered in the neighborhood/development contact zone. For this reason, the furniture used in this zone should be relatively immovable or fixed in place. For an urban site, the character of the street furniture should blend or match the character of the streetscape in the community.

Outdoor furniture provided in the outdoor common area can be more portable. The use of fixed benches for outdoor seating is discouraged in favor of lighter, portable aluminum and fabric lawn furniture. Portable furniture of this type permits a choice for the elderly resident as to where and with whom he will sit, whereas fixed furniture tends to limit these kinds of choices. A storage facility for this furniture should be provided in close proximity to the areas in which it is to be used.

Special Details: Special needs of the elderly for site detailing can also be categorized into two groups:

1. Those details which make an environment barrier-free for handicapped people: Within this context barrier-free should not be limited to provisions for wheelchairs, but should also include provisions for those with impaired vision or hearing losses.

2. Those details which have the quality of making a development more home-like than an institution: For example, the edge of planting beds can be designed the way they might have been detailed around an elderly person's home during his or her years of living as a family instead of using a more contemporary detail. This requires some field research but it can make a difference in the overall effect of the total site development. Local colloquial and folk customs should be acknowledged in the design process. The question to ask is, is this what I like, or is this what future residents might like?

Flexibility: It is important to design flexible use options into the outdoor spaces organized on the site. To force the elderly to participate and engage in an activity in a fixed way will tend to limit the appeal and use of the outdoor facilities. People must be able to choose where and in what capacity they will participate in activities. Some specific examples of the flexible activity space are illustrated here.

Places should provide degrees of risk for their users. Generally, locations along the outside edges of places tend to be areas of lower risk than the centers of spaces which tend to involve higher risks. People are either doing something in a place or they are watching someone else do something. The possibility for observation encourages the observer to become a participant. Few people want to be first, and precedent is very comforting. The implications of this behavioral knowledge to physical design are to provide the residents with a network of observation points and activities to observe. This network can be the impetus to join in.

BUILDING EFFICIENCY GUIDELINES

To evaluate the cost effectiveness of a given building design proposal, it is necessary to make several measurements, called efficiency ratios, which relate usable versus non-usable floor area. These ratios can serve as a valuable guide for the development team.

When any or all of these ratios in a given development exceed the parameters indicated below, there is reason to believe that an excessive amount of building floor area is being devoted to certain building components which, while necessary, do not, by becoming larger, substantively improve the quality of life for the residents. Elimination of such excesses will result in either reduced building area (and thus construction cost) and/or the possibility of increasing the size of dwelling units or common facilities. The definitions of area terms begin on page 6 of the section on programming.

Building Efficiency Ratios

These ratios are used to evaluate the various major components of buildings against each other. They apply to all apartment buildings and are based upon the assumption that the total development is for the independent elderly. Where applicable a second ratio is shown to illustrate a total development for the dependent elderly where space for congregate facilities is achieved by reducing dwelling unit areas. The third type is mixed independent and dependent elderly housing. Because ratios in this case will vary for each development as the mix varies, no guideline ratios can be determined.

Dwelling Unit Efficiency Ratio

The sum of the floor areas of all required activity spaces or rooms divided by the Dwelling Unit Area equals the Dwelling Unit Efficiency Ratio. Balconies should not be included in this calculation.

Required activity spaces or rooms are:

- Sleeping
- Living
- Dining
- Food preparation
- Personal hygiene (baths)
- Closets

The following should not be included in the floor area for required activity spaces:

- Stairs within dwelling units
- Halls, foyers, etc.
- Basements associated with individual dwelling units
- Mechanical, general storage, and laundry areas contained within individual dwelling units

The Dwelling Unit Efficiency Ratio should not be less than:

0.70 for townhouses or maisonettes
0.80 for apartments

BUILDING EFFICIENCY RATIO

	Independent	Congregate
$\dfrac{\text{Residential Gross Area}}{\text{Building Gross Area}} =$	0.75 (mid- and high-rise) 0.80 (1 and 2 story)	0.80 Not applicable
$\dfrac{\text{Circulation Gross Area}}{\text{Building Gross Area}} =$	0.25	0.35
$\dfrac{\text{Common Facilities Gross Area}}{\text{Residential Gross Area}} =$	0.10	0.15

5
technical standards

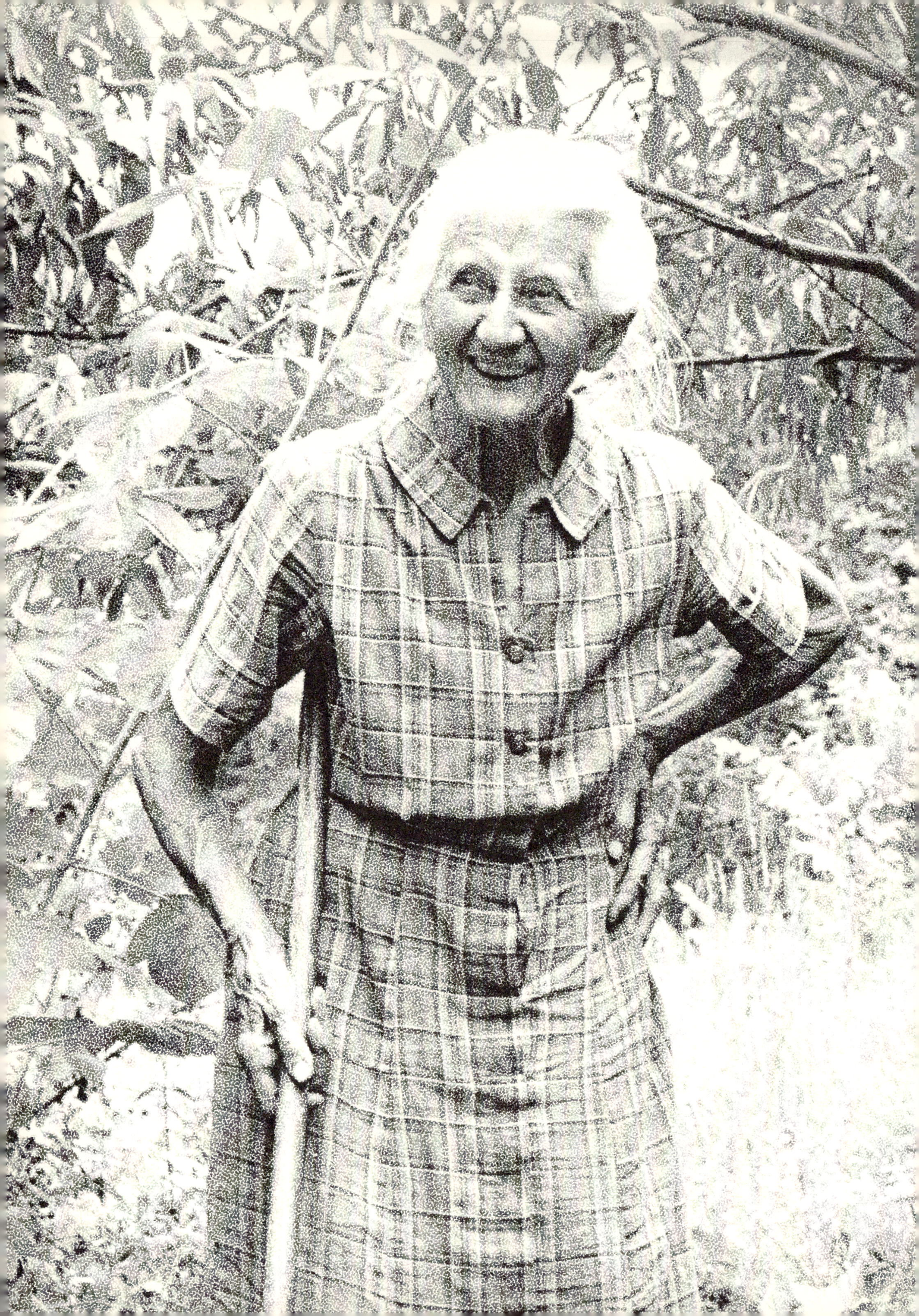

technical standards

INTENT

This section sets forth specific technical standards for various physical components of a development such as mechanical-electrical equipment, roads and walks, hardware, planting, etc. These standards deal with such concerns as physical dimension, material, construction method and performance, and are intended to be used as a reference manual by the development team. For example, if the design criteria call for a door in a particular location, reference to this section will tell the user what the recommended standards are for doors. Thus, the technical standards complement the section on design.

The development team should, as a first step, adopt as its technical standards base the standards set forth by the United States Department of Housing and Urban Development, Federal Housing Administration, contained in the latest editions of the Minimum Property Standards for Multifamily Housing (FHA-MPS-MF) and Housing for the Elderly (FHA-MPS-HE), and related bulletins published by the Federal Housing Administration (FHA). This section is a supplement to these standards and it both adds to and modifies them. It has become apparent that special consideration must be given to certain areas if housing of the desired quality is to be achieved. These additions and modifications can therefore be regarded as an extension of the aforesaid standards base.

The following is a detailed explanation of the components which are to be considered as part of the housing for the elderly development process.

SITE GRADING

Gradients: There should be no gradients greater than 5 percent or smaller than 1 percent on any area which will be walked on. In case slopes are greater than 5 percent, applicable handicap requirements must be complied with. There should be no gradients greater than 5 percent on any area which will be driven over. Parking areas should not have a cross slope gradient greater than 3 percent. The use of steps should be avoided.

Drainage: Drain inlets should be located so that water is not sheeted across major circulation paths. Drain inlets should be located in areas where flooding due to failure of the inlet will not result in any inconvenience to the elderly residents.

In conjunction with the gradient standards already discussed, there are several areas on the site which should be given special detailing.

Building Entrance in the Arrival Court Area: The use of curbs between the surface of the entrance drive and the door to the building is prohibited. The entrance should incorporate bollards or columns which support the overhead canopy to separate vehicles from pedestrians. These bollards or columns should be a minimum of 5 feet apart. The gradient from the door sill should be no more than 2.5 percent and no less than 1 percent.

Residents' Entrance to the Parking Lot Area: The curb defining the parking lot should receive special detailing to permit easy use of wheelchairs. Curbing should be made of concrete.

PAVING

Paving is divided into three categories: roads and drives, walks, and parking.

Roads and Drives: The entrance drive should be a minimum width of 24 feet for a single, two-way road curb to curb. In a boulevard system, each one-way drive should be 20 feet wide curb to curb and the median should be 15 feet wide for a total width of 55 feet.

The arrival court or drop-off zone should have a minimum interior curb radius of 33 feet and a minimum exterior curb radius of 57 feet.

Parking access or service drives should be a minimum of 20 feet wide and should be curbed.

Entrance drives and access drives should not crowd the building where dwelling units occupy the first floor. These drives should be located a minimum dimension of half the building height from the center line of the drive to the face of the building. For low-rise building types, these dimensions should conform to those specified in the *Townhouse Development Process.*[1]

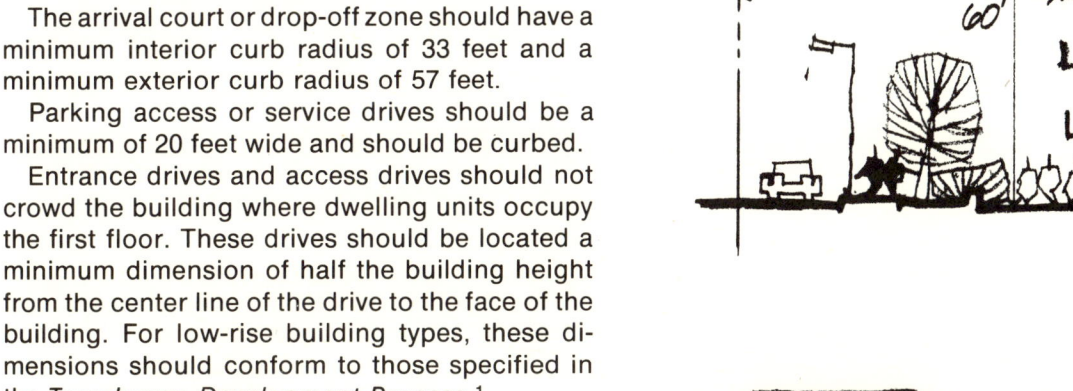

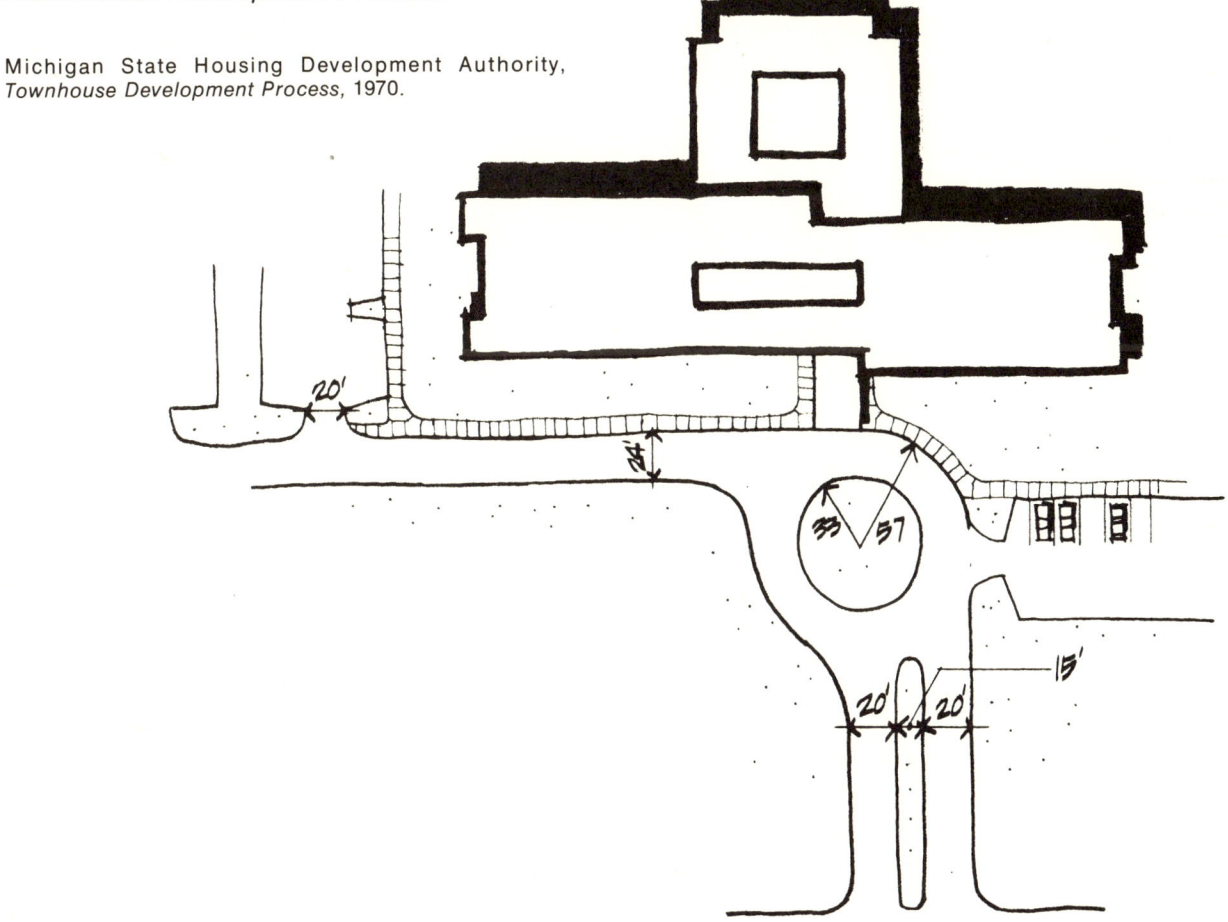

[1] Michigan State Housing Development Authority, *Townhouse Development Process,* 1970.

Walks: Walkways located within the neighborhood/development contact zone should be a minimum of 6 feet wide while walkways located in the outdoor common area should be a minimum of 5 feet wide. Walkway paving should be concrete with a broom finish, non-slip surface. A special band of textured, non-slip paving should be used on the entrances to the building.

Parking: Each space should be 10 feet wide and 20 feet deep with 24 feet of aisle space, resulting in a double loaded parking lot with a dimension of 64 feet. Five percent of the total number of parking spaces should be 12 feet wide and designated for handicapped residents.

Double Loaded   Single Loaded

Parking must be bituminous or concrete to meet local standards.

PLANTING

One of the most often criticized aspects of planting in regard to tall buildings (eight to twelve stories) is that the planting is insignificant. A common rationalization is "we will just have to wait until the trees mature." In order to make planting effective, there must be sufficient planting that is large enough to have a visual impact. The following table has been established as a general guide for determining the quantity and size of trees to be planted. This table is for sites of average density and size with few existing trees that can be saved. On sites of higher density and small acreage, for example, planting requirements may be adjusted. An intensely developed urban site of small acreage resulting in minimum common open space may require fewer trees and portions of the site may be limited to streetscape-type planting. In such a case, quantity may be reduced and the size may be increased to compensate. On sites that are wooded and have major groups or specimen trees that can be retained, adjustments in tree planting requirements may also be permitted.

PLANTING/DWELLING UNIT RATIOS

Type	Size	Ratio
Major canopy trees	4" Cal.	1 tree per 3 units
Evergreen trees	6' Ht.	1 tree per 3 units
Flowering trees	6-7' Ht.	1 tree per 5 units

Plus accent shrubs and ground cover

LIGHTING

Evidence documented by the lighting industry indicates that light tends to reduce the incidence of crime. The table which follows indicates the minimum average level of illumination recommended for parking areas.

To minimize glare, light standards should be arranged to provide an overlap and thus avoid hot spots. Outdoor light fixtures should be chosen which minimize the light source to pedestrians and drivers. Globe fixtures should be avoided.

PARKING AREA LIGHTING

General parking lots	2 footcandles
High vandalism areas	10 footcandles
Vidicon television surveillance	25 footcandles
Minimum for television viewing of important interdiction areas	10 footcandles

Source: James F. Finn, Building Owners and Managers Associates Security Flood Lighting Seminar, Detroit Edison Company, Detroit, Michigan, 1973. Used with permission of the author.

RECREATION FACILITIES

The following is a description of the outdoor barbecue and patio area which should be a part of each development. This area should be located in the outdoor common area and should consist of an area paved in concrete, brick, or stone and equal to 20 percent of the area required for the outdoor common area. The area should be in 50 percent shade. This shaded area may be achieved architecturally or through the use of canopy trees. Light, portable tables and chairs are preferable to fixed furniture.

The following is a brief, but not all inclusive, list of recreation facilities that might be included in a development:

Shuffleboard, regulation size
Badminton, regulation size
Bocce ball, regulation size
Swimming pool, 16' x 34' mimimum
Resident's garden area, varies

OUTDOOR FURNITURE

The overriding criteria for the design of outdoor furniture is comfort. Seats or benches should have backs and should be made of soft material such as wood. Outdoor seating should not be lower than standard chair height. Outdoor tables should be designed with the underside of the top of table a minimum of 29 inches high to allow the arms of wheelchairs to fit under them. Fixed, table-bench combinations should be avoided.

TRASH REMOVAL AND SERVICE

Each development should be equipped with or serviced by an effective means of trash collection and disposal in addition to a garbage disposal in the kitchen sink of each dwelling unit.

In apartment developments of three stories or more, the means of garbage collection should include central deposit points on each floor occupied by tenants. At the present time the most desirable system is based on central trash compaction. In this system trash chutes are located at a central point on each floor which vent into a central trash compactor in a room on the first floor. The system design and the pick-up schedule should be scaled to accommodate at least 2 pounds of trash per occupant per day at 7.5 pounds per cubic foot before compaction. The trash compactor should feed a dumpster or other similar transfer device which should be stored within the building. Doors of sufficient width should be provided to allow free access to the outside so that the trash container may be moved to a pick-up vehicle.

At this time, incinerators or the transport of raw garbage and trash in the building for conventional pick-up are undesirable solutions.

An acceptable system should fulfill the following specifications:

1. A substantial round or rectangular vertical metal chute, not less than 24 inches nominal diameter of aluminized or stainless steel with not less than #16 U.S. gauge wall thickness for the first three floors and serving all floors
2. Fire-protected vertical shaft for chute installation with sprinklers in the chute at not less than every other floor and at the top of the building
3. Botton-hinged, safety-type, quiet self-closing hopper door of class B-UL fire rating on each floor, with nominal dimensions not less than 15 by 18 inches and not greater than 18 by 18 inches
4. Hopper doors on each floor located in a room or enclosure of at least 20 sq. ft. in area separated from the other parts of the building by wall, floor, ceiling assemblies, and a self-closing door of not less than 1-hour fire rating with the top of the hopper no greater than 3'-6" above the floor
5. No projections of any kind inside the free fall area of the chute below the top hopper door, and all joints ground smooth or overlapped to avoid resistance to normal trash flow
6. Remote control washing and disinfectant sprays at top of chute
7. Chute that discharges directly into a system which automatically compacts and loads the material into containers for removal from the building
8. System that is capable of withstanding impact of dense, heavy articles without loss of function
9. Trash compaction room of 1-hour fire rated construction, protected by sprinklers, equipped with rodent protection, readily cleanable, and equipped with grate protected floor drains
10. Bottom of trash chute should be equipped with a normally open, self-closing fire safety door[2]

Since compactor devices are to be used inside the buildings, loading docks should not be necessary on buildings which do not include congregate facilities. However, a service drive should connect the service/compactor area door with the vehicular circulation system. This drive should be a minimum of 12 feet wide and paved to withstand use by heavy trucks. Radii and maneuvering space should permit easy access.

For developments which provide congregate facilities, a service dock must be included at the service entrance. Dimensions for service doors and truck docks should be as per the latest FHA-MPS-MF.

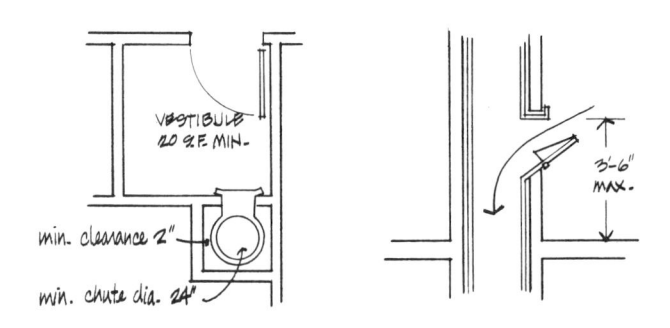

TYPICAL TRASH CHUTE FACILITIES FOR EACH FLOOR

[2] U.S. Department of Commerce, National Bureau of Standards, *Guide Criteria for the Design of Operation Breakthrough Housing Systems*, Vol. 2, "Multifamily Low Rise," September, 1970.

SIGNING

It is essential that residential facilities for the elderly make sense. They should be easily understood and not confusing. To a great extent achievement of this condition is dependent on the effective functional organization and appropriate spatial character of the facilities. There will be many instances, however, in which full comprehensibility can only be achieved through the use of a supplemental direct information system. Signing can be categorized into two systems, outdoor and indoor sign systems. General guidelines for the development and application of signs and signage systems are set forth below.

The difference between a successful and an unsuccessful signage and identification system is often determined by how the system responds to the following issues:

Pattern and hierarachy
Legibility
Location

The word "system" means that all signs should be related to each other and be part of a larger whole; therefore, part of the sign's success can be related to the consistency of the sign system that will cause people to look for information in particular and similar locations throughout the building. Signage should be consistent throughout a development; that is, it should generally be all of a similar design, color scheme, and pattern. All information to be communicated should be analyzed and organized into an ordered hierarchy ranging from the most general to the most specific information, that is, from such broad concerns as the existence and direction of common facilities to the names of individual public rooms or suite numbers. The design of the signage system should reflect this hierarchy. Similar categories of information should be communicated by similar signs in terms of size, color, typeface, type size, design, and location. It may also be desirable to vary the overall size of the signs in direct relation to the importance of the sign category, the distance from which they must be read, and the numbers of people who will be viewing them at any given time. If a variation in the size of the signs is used it should be used consistently.

Information about category, general location, or direction should be presented on the largest signs while room names and numbers should be presented on the smallest signs. When color is used as part of the system, the brightest and most vivid colors should be used for critical general and public information, while the most subdued colors should be used for semi-private areas and information such as suite numbers.

Usually, necessary information should not be presented in a typeface smaller than 1-1/4 inches high. It is better to present information on oversized rather than undersized signs to compensate for the losses in vision suffered by many older persons.

Wherever possible, symbols should be used in conjunction with information conveyed by words to insure comprehension.

Decisions about the size of the sign, symbol, and typeface should be guided by the following factors:

1. The maximum distance from which the sign must be read should be considered.

2. Typefaces which are stylized or extensively serifed should be avoided. Typefaces which are excessively condensed or extended should also be avoided. Typefaces such as helvetica, universe, folio, and futura are desirable.

3. A substantial level of contrast should be achieved between the letters and symbols and the field on which they are displayed. Generally, it is better to use light colored letters and symbols on a dark field such as white on black or dark blue than vice versa. Where dark letters and symbols are used on a light field, the field should not be white; it should be a neutral grey.

4. Signs should be made of durable materials.

5. The spacing of the typeface should be similar to that which is produced by a normal typewriter. Too much or too little space between the letters quickly destroys legibility.

OUTDOOR SIGNS

Various signing studies have concluded that the average human span of attention allows a person to recognize about six objects at a glance.[3] There are three ways that people might perceive a housing for the elderly development while out-of-doors:

Passersby: People might drive by the development and recognize it as one event among many along the road.

Site Entrance and Egress: People might drive onto the site or leave it and need directions as to how to use the site.

Building Entrance: As pedestrians, people need information as to how things work in a development. An example would be a sign on a door which reads "push."

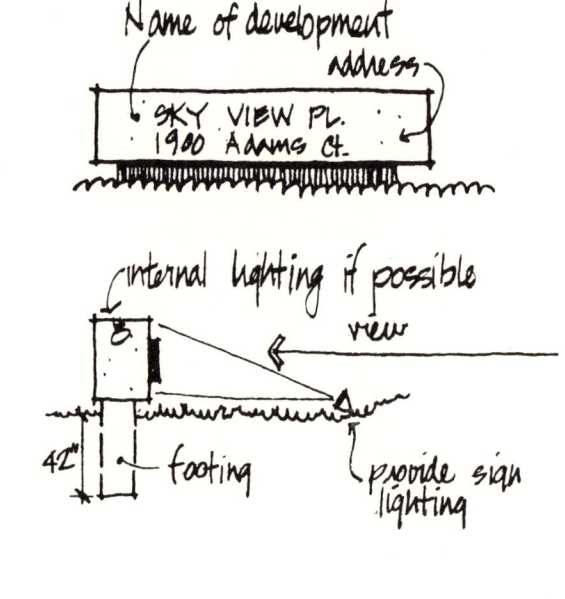

EXAMPLE OF ENTRANCE SIGN

SYMBOLIC TRAFFIC SIGNS

These three ways of viewing a site evoke different responses in regard to sign size, colors, and lettering styles.

The size of lettering and signs is dependent on the speed at which people are traveling when they view the sign in question. A range of acceptable sizes is documented below.

Signs at the pedestrian level should be sized as if they were being viewed from a car traveling 15 miles per hour.

The need for too many signs is an indication that the development site has been poorly planned.

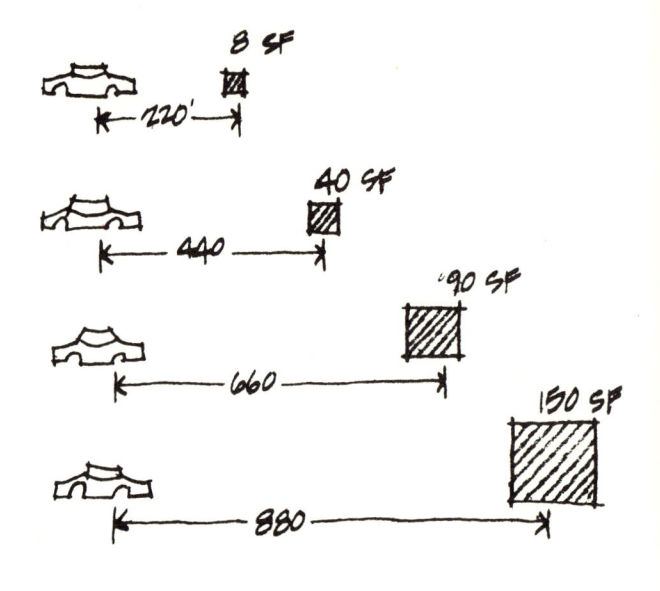

ENTRANCE SIGN SIZES

[3] William R. Ewald, Jr., and Daniel R. Mandelker, *Street Graphics: A Concept and a System* (McLean, Va.: The American Society of Landscape Architects, 1971), page 20.

INDOOR SIGNS

At circulation nodes, such as the main entrance lobby, elevator lobbies, etc., signs should be located to indicate the direction to facilities or groups of facilities. Signage should distinguish between public and private areas. On residential floors where several directions of travel are possible from either the stairs or elevator, dwelling unit designators should be used.

Where activities are grouped together the general sign indicating direction should be presented as a simple sign which first indicates the broad category into which the activities fall, for example, a category such as "Resident Services" might include medical, social, and management services; secondly, a smaller sign would indicate the individual activities to be found under the general heading.

The following are specific and detailed concerns about indoor signing which must be taken into account:

1. Suite identification signs should allow for the presentation of the resident's name if he or she should so desire.
2. All dwelling units should be clearly identified by a number or letter designator, or by a combination of a number and letter designator. All public rooms and other spaces should be designated by name.
3. All room and space identification signs should be a minimum of 1¼ inches high with raised letters and/or numbers mounted to the wall. The signs should be mounted above the floor in the range of 4 feet and 8 inches to 5 feet to the center line of the sign (in a horizontal line), and adjacent to the latch side of the door or entry opening.
4. All exits should be identified according to the requirements of the applicable fire code for the particular state.
5. All elevator locations and controls should be clearly indicated.
6. Signs should be provided to indicate the existence and location of facilities for the handicapped. Such information devices have the following purposes:
    a. To identify suitable entry/exit facilities
    b. To identify suitable vertical circulation facilities
    c. To identify suitable personal hygiene facilities
    d. To identify other facilities which are provided for the handicapped
7. Generally, it is better to locate a sign adjacent to the door rather than on the door itself so that it may be easily read when the door is open.
8. All signs should be readable at night.

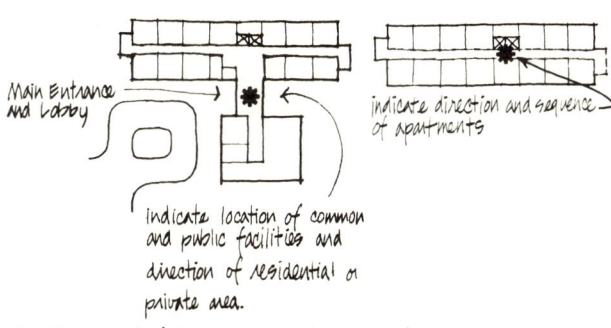

ILLUSTRATION OF POSSIBLE SIGN LOCATIONS

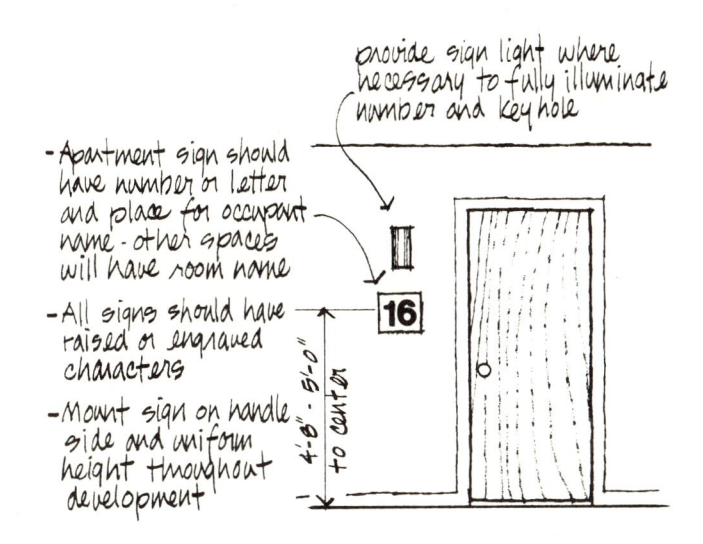

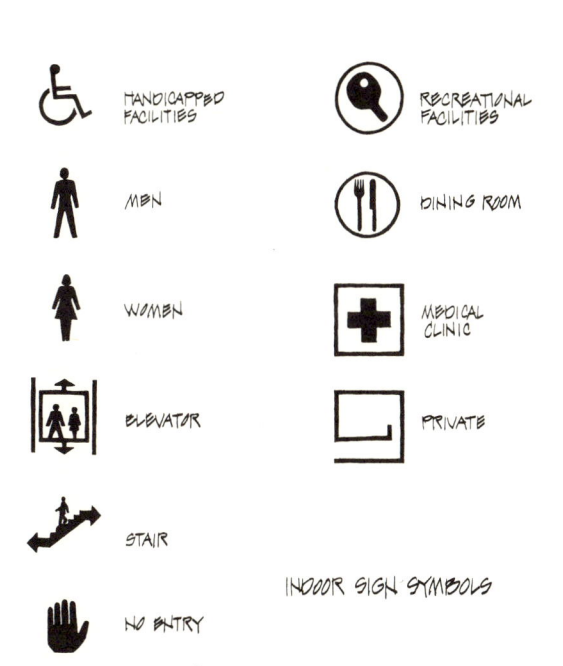

- Apartment sign should have number or letter and place for occupant name - other spaces will have room name
- All signs should have raised or engraved characters
- Mount sign on handle side and uniform height throughout development
- provide sign light where necessary to fully illuminate number and keyhole
- 4'-8" to 5'-0" to center

INDOOR SIGN SYMBOLS

- HANDICAPPED FACILITIES
- MEN
- WOMEN
- ELEVATOR
- STAIR
- NO ENTRY
- RECREATIONAL FACILITIES
- DINING ROOM
- MEDICAL CLINIC
- PRIVATE

CIRCULATION

CORRIDORS

Corridors must be carefully designed if they are to compensate for the physical and visual deterioration of the residents. Slip-resistant floors and high lighting levels are necessary features. Individual entrances boldly marked by colors, unit numbers, and lighting are desirable elements. All of these add cheer to the environment and help to identify private spaces.

An institutional atmosphere in the corridors must be softened through the use of color, the provision of outside views, and well-designed artificial lighting.

Perception studies of reactions of people indicate a negative emotional response to corridors which, for reasons of economy, tend to be long and narrow.[4] Ideally, therefore, corridor segments should not be more than 75 to 100 feet in length. Where this is impossible, lengthy corridors should be broken by staggering or changes of direction, and by variations in color and texture. Windows can provide natural light and visual interest and relief.

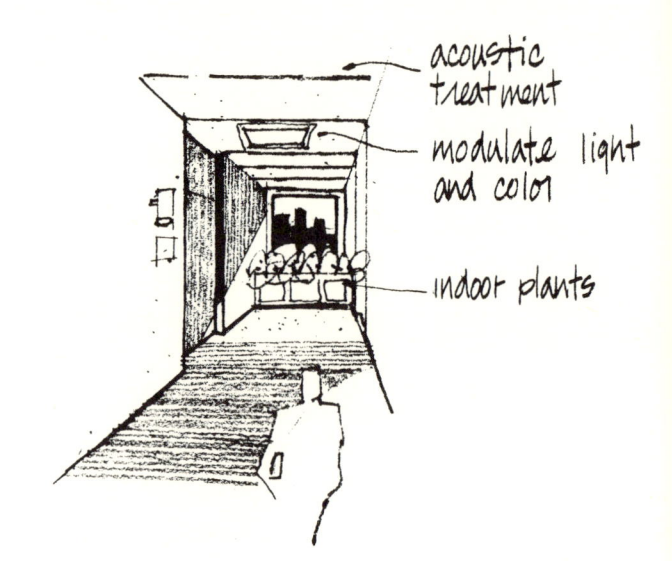

[4] Nils Larsson, *Housing the Elderly*, 2nd ed. (Ottawa: Central Mortgage and Housing Corp., 1972), page 20.

CORRIDOR WITH A VIEW OUT AND NATURAL LIGHT INTRODUCED

ELEVATOR LOBBY WITH A VIEW OUT ESTABLISHING CONNECTION WITH THE OUTDOORS

NOT DESIRABLE

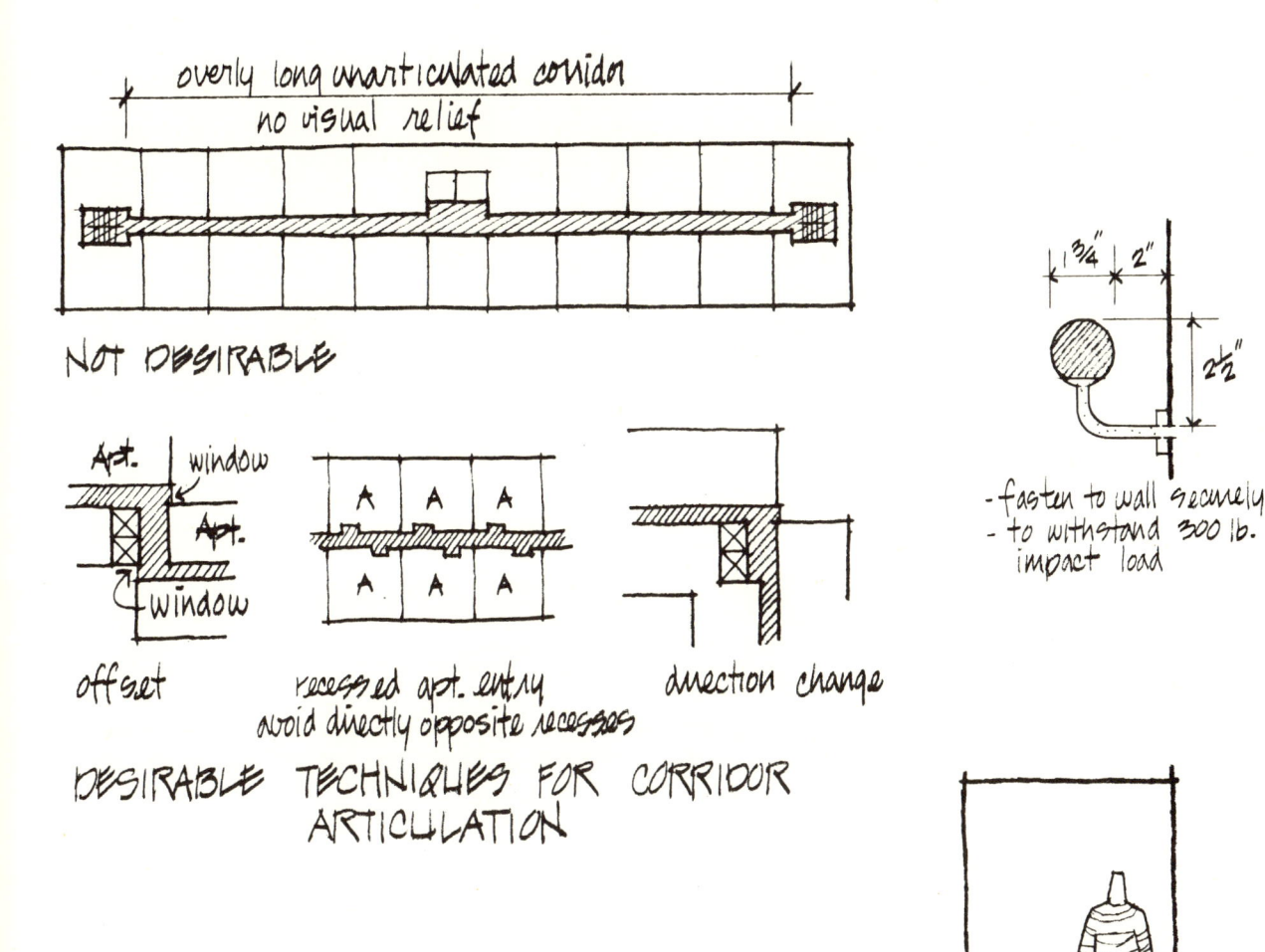

DESIRABLE TECHNIQUES FOR CORRIDOR ARTICULATION

Corridors should have a clear dimension of at least 5 feet wide. Where units are designated for use by the handicapped, handrails should be provided. Where handrails are provided, they are needed on both walls of the corridor so that an elderly person with a disabled right or left hand can use the support on either side. Handrails should be thick to insure a good grip. If tubular handrails are used, they should be at least 1-3/4 inches in diameter, and mounted at a height of 2 feet and 9 inches. When handrails are interrupted by a doorway or opening, they should return to the wall before being terminated or have some form of tactile warning about 6 inches from the ends.[5]

Where changes in level are necessary in corridors, the standards in the sections on ramps, page 140, and stairs, page 140, should be applied. The level of illumination should be higher than normal (see page 160 of this section) but should be modulated.

[5] Ibid., pages 19-20.

STAIRS

Despite the need to avoid changes in level as much as possible, stairs are inevitable in multi-story buildings. Stairs can be made more comfortable to use by careful design which recognizes user limitations.

Perception difficulties make it important to provide at least three risers per flight. Stairs should be designed with runs which are as straight and short as possible and with a maximum of ten risers between landings. Steps should have plain faces with integral non-projecting nosings. Open risers are unacceptable.

All staircases, including means of egress, should be designed with a maximum rise of 7 inches, a minimum run of 10-1/2 inches, and a minimum tread width of 11 inches. The product of rise and run shall not be less than 70, or more than 75.

Handrails should be provided on both sides of stairs at a height of 2 feet and 8 inches above nosing. Handrails should extend a minimum of 2 feet beyond the last step in a flight, and should be continuous around landings. Tubular handrails of at least 1-3/4 inches in diameter are recommended for ease of grip.[6]

[6] Ibid., pages 19-20.

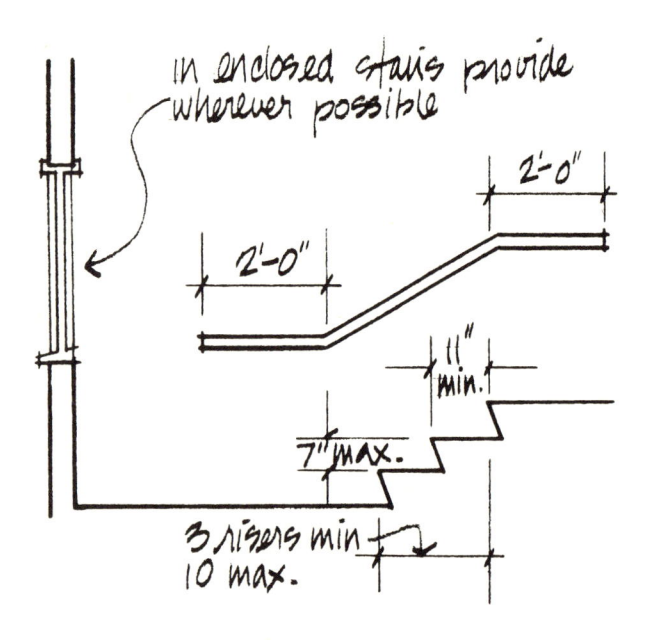

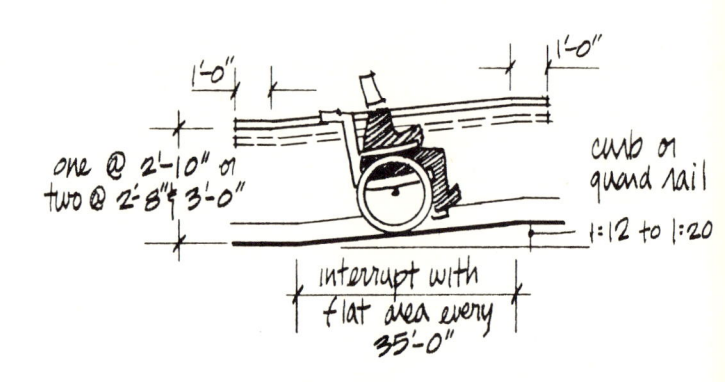

RAMPS

Ramps are not acceptable substitutes for stairs; rather, they are supplementary to them, especially where the handicapped user is involved. Ramps should have a clear dimension between handrails of at least 5 feet wide.

Ramps should conform to the requirements of the appropriate state or local code. In general, the following applies.

A curb 8 inches high or a guard rail mounted about 8 inches above the ramp deck should be provided to prevent wheelchairs from slipping over the edge.

If a change in level is necessary, a gradient of 1:20 is preferred but, in any case, it should not exceed 1:12. Ramps should be interrupted at least every 30 feet by a landing, free of door swings, as wide as the ramp, and at least 6 feet in length.

Ramps should be equipped with handrails to provide support for those who walk with difficulty, and to assist those in wheelchairs. Handrails placed on both sides of the ramp at a height of 2 feet and 8 inches may provide a satisfactory solution. But a far better design is to have two sets of handrails on both sides, one at a height of 3 feet, and the other at a height of 2 feet and 6 inches for wheelchair use.

Handrails should extend a minimum of 1 foot beyond ramp terminals. Tubular handrails are recommended and should be 1-3/4 inches in diameter to assure a firm grip. Ramps should have non-slip surfaces.[7]

[7] Ibid., pages 19-20.

ELEVATORS

Elevators are a mandatory element in multi-story buildings to compensate for the loss of mobility experienced by elderly people. Even a two-story building without an elevator eliminates itself as a housing option for some elderly people.

Buildings having two or more stories should be equipped with at least one elevator. Elevators should serve every distinct floor level within a building; minor changes in floor level will not be considered as two distinct floor levels. A resident must be able to reach the elevator from his dwelling unit without traversing a ramp or stairway.

Buildings having four or more stories with more than 100 dwelling units should be equipped with two elevators.

Control buttons should be arranged horizontally not higher than 4 feet and 8 inches above the cab floor to permit their use from a wheelchair. As a general rule safety and reliability are more important than speed.

At least one elevator should have a minimum interior cab size of 5 by 7 feet to accommodate a stretcher or furniture moving.

At least one elevator should have relatively direct access to the building service entrance to facilitate the moving of furniture in and out of the elevator.

Handrails shall be provided on all sides of the cab at a height of 2 feet and 8 inches above the floor. A shelf for packages should be provided in the cab, as well as in each elevator lobby. The shelf should be at least 8 inches wide by 1 foot 4 inches long, mounted at a height of about 2 feet and 6 inches. Doors should open and close slowly and have a reopening sensor that responds very quickly when pressed.

A manual elevator lowering device which can be safely operated by building maintenance personnel should be incorporated into the elevator design. The elevator call and floor selection control system should not be of the heat-activated type. A voice intercom system should connect the elevator cab with a receiver located in the manager's office or in the lobby.[8]

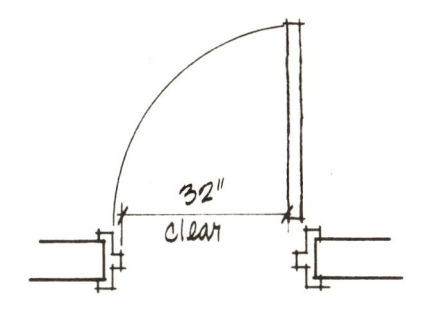

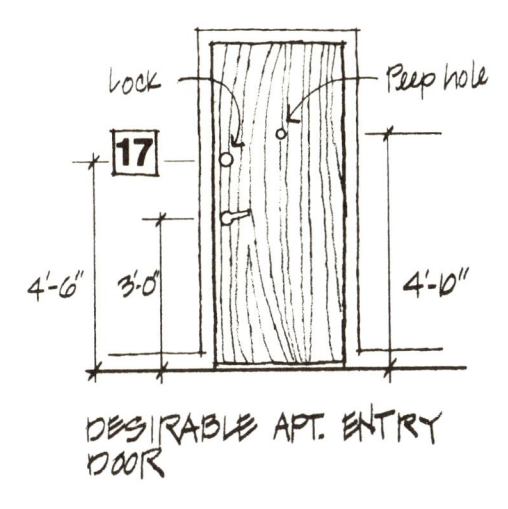

DOORS AND ACCESS OPENINGS

Door design, opening, and placement should reflect the limited muscular strength and poor eyesight of old people, and the confinement of some to wheelchairs.

All door openings should allow for someone who is in a wheelchair or for someone who is using a mechanical walking aid to pass easily. Therefore, all door openings should have a minimum clear opening of 32 inches. Primary building and dwelling unit entrance doors should have a minimum clear opening of 34 inches. At least 39 inches of clear approach space should be provided on each side of primary doors.

Good lighting outside of the front door should be provided so that it is easy for residents to find the keyhole and dwelling unit designator; visitors will also be illuminated when viewed through the peephole. The peephole should be between 54 and 58 inches above the floor. Raised door sills or a step at doors, including public and private entrance doors, are considered unacceptable.

[8] Ibid., page 18.

A master key to all front doors should be provided. Automatic door closers are not recommended but, when used, they must have a check action with a delay of 4 to 6 seconds. The pressure required to push such a door should not exceed 5 pounds. Doors with a double swing should be avoided. Revolving doors are not desirable, especially where the handicapped are involved. If revolving doors are used, a swing door should be provided as well. Door handles of the level type are recommended as they can more easily be used by persons with arthritic hands. The mounting height for keyed locks should be about 4 feet and 6 inches to ease the difficulty of stooping to see and reach the keyhole. Locks should be of the dead bolt type.[9]

---

[9] Ibid., page 33.

SURFACES

FLOORS AND FLOORING

The elderly tend to be less agile of foot than the young, and thus great care must be taken in the design of floors and the selection of flooring material to eliminate hazards and to minimize the chances of an accidental slip or stumble.

1. Floors must be flat and changes in level must not occur in unexpected places.

2. Where changes in level are required or unavoidable, they should be clearly marked, occur at logical locations, and conform to the requirements for either stairs or ramps or both as applicable.

3. Flooring materials should be resilient, non-skid, waterproof, greaseproof, alkaliproof, etc. The materials must be durable, have good maintenance characteristics, and be appropriate for the specific location. Above all, flooring materials should be warm in appearance and residential in character.

4. Suggested general floor finishes are:
    a. Wall to wall, short pile carpeting
    b. Vinyl tile or sheet
    c. Linolium
    d. Vinyl asbestos

5. Unglazed, non-slip ceramic tile is strongly recommended for bathrooms.

6. Raised sills and thresholds must be avoided at interior doors and should be kept to a minimum at exterior doors. The joints between unlike materials should be smooth with no raised edge strips or moldings.

7. Strong patterns should be avoided. Floor colors in dwelling units should allow for the widest possibility of tenant choice and decoration. It should also be remembered that light colors tend to expand space while dark colors may have the opposite effect.

WALLS AND CEILINGS

Kitchens, bathrooms, and woodwork should be painted with a high- or semi-gloss finish for easy cleaning; the rest of the wall areas may be painted with a durable, washable matte finish.

Colors that give a warm and cheerful environment should be used for all areas, including floors, sanitary fittings, and tiles. Light colors should be used for counter tops.

Strong colors inside the units should be avoided because the residents will use their own drapes and furniture and cannot be expected to match them to extreme colors. In addition, in small apartments the heavier colors tend to dominate and close in the spaces.

Different colors can be used for the convenience and safety of residents to pick out handrails, stairs and stair treads, fire exits, washrooms, etc. Strong color can be used effectively in halls, lobbies, and communal areas both for spatial modulation and ease of comprehension.

White or light colors should be used around windows to reduce glare, which can be physically painful for the elderly, especially where non-glare (grey or bronze) glass is used.

Easily maintained wall finishes in public and private areas should be provided. Rough textures may be physical hazards unless care in location and choice is exercised.

FOOD PREPARATION EQUIPMENT

This section deals with equipment and facilities in the food preparation area of the dwelling unit in terms of quantities, sizes, and detailed location. The question of the functional organization of the food preparation area and its relationship to other areas of the dwelling unit is discussed in the section on design, page 73. The discussion here is divided into two parts. The first deals directly with the minimum standards against which all proposed developments should be measured and to which all should comply. The second begins with the minimum standards as a base and develops optimum standards for the various components of the food preparation area where appropriate. These optimum standards are desirable, but the achievement of some may not be economically feasible within the context of low and moderate income housing programs. Optimum standards are offered, however, as a guide where a higher amenity level is affordable and as a direction for product improvement.

MINIMUM STANDARDS

Refrigerator: The refrigerator should be an upright freestanding model with integral freezing compartment. The minimum acceptable sizes are 10 cubic feet for a one-bedroom unit and 12 cubic feet for a two-bedroom unit. The freezer compartment should be located at the top or the side of the refrigerator. Refrigerators of the undercounter type are unacceptable because of the excessive stooping required in their use.

The refrigerator should be of the self-defrosting type. (This is a designated amenity.)

The general storage shelves of the refrigerator should pull out on roller guides and should be removable for ease in cleaning.

Cooking Unit and Oven: The cooking unit and oven should be electric; they should be both approved and listed by the Underwriter Laboratories (UL) in their publication, *Electric Appliance and Utilization Equipment List.* Gas cooking devices are not recommended because the elderly often have a poor sense of smell and are forgetful, thus becoming vulnerable to the hazards of fire and explosion.

Cooking devices should have pilot lights to visually indicate when they are on. A master cutoff switch should be provided if possible. The controls on cooking devices should be easily read by sight; controls should be located at the front of the device to eliminate the necessity of reaching over hot cooking surfaces.

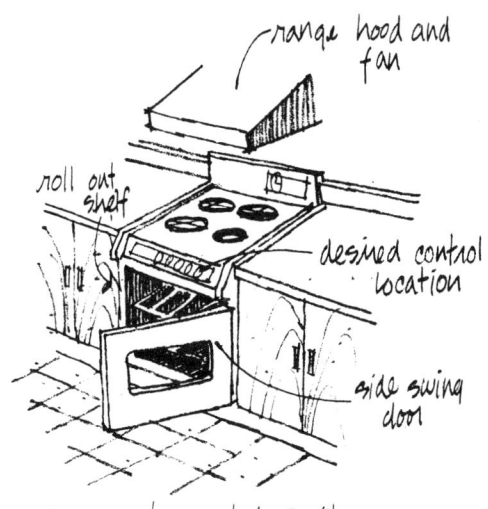

Where an integral cook top and oven unit (stove) are used, the oven should be located below the cook top. Stoves with ovens that are overhead or at eye level are not acceptable because of the reaching required. The door on the oven should be hung on the side and swing out if such units are available. This type of oven door is safer and also allows the oven to be used by someone sitting in a wheelchair.

All cook tops should have a hood and exhaust fan mounted directly above the cooking surface. Ceiling mounted exhaust fans are considered unacceptable. The cook top should have four burners and have a minimum width of 24 inches.

Sink: The kitchen sink should be of stainless steel and mounted on the counter top. The minimum overall dimensions are 24 inches by 21 inches. Where counter top area permits, a sink with a double compartment equal to the capacity of a sink with a single compartment is preferred.

Cabinets, Shelves, Counters, and Closets: Each kitchen or kitchenette should have:

1. Accessible storage space for food and cooking and eating utensils
2. Sufficient space for average kitchen accessories
3. Sufficient storage space for those items of household equipment normally used and for which storage is not provided elsewhere such as brooms, mops, soap, etc.

DESIRABLE KNEE SPACE AT KITCHEN SINK

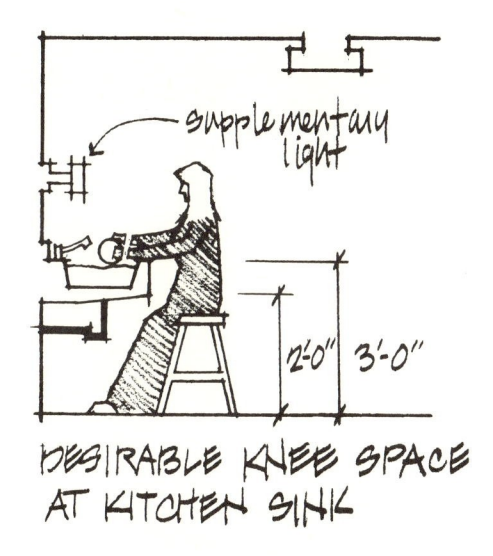

4. Sufficient work surface area for the preparation and serving of food and the cleanup of cooking and eating utensils

Kitchen storage should be provided in the form of wall and base cabinets as follows:

Shelving: 40 sq. ft.
Drawers: 7 sq. ft.

Kitchen storage should be designed to satisfy the following requirements:

1. Usable storage space in or under stoves, or under wall ovens, when provided in the form of shelves or drawers that roll out, may be included in the minimum shelf area.

2. Conventional base cabinets over counter tops should not be deeper than 12 inches and the highest shelf should be no more than 66 inches from the floor.

3. No cabinet or shelf space should be located above refrigerators.

4. The minimum clearance between counter tops and wall shelves should be 24 inches at the sink and 15 inches in other locations.

5. At least 80 percent of all shelving should be enclosed by cabinetry or a pantry. Cabinet doors should have rounded edges.

No less than 10 square feet of counter top work surface should be provided in kitchens. Counter tops should be approximately 24 inches deep and no higher than 36 inches above the floor. In calculating the length of the counter top, the length occupied by sinks and cook tops may not be counted. Counter tops should have rounded leading edges. Where possible, supplementary counter top space should be provided at table top height so that a resident can use this space for food preparation and for eating light meals. In apartments designed for the handicapped, half of the required counter space should be at work table height.

Storage of household equipment should be provided by a broom closet of at least 3 square feet in floor area. These closets should have shelves for the storage of cleaning materials and they should have a clear area of sufficient height to accommodate an upright vacuum cleaner and brooms.

A separate compartment with a door should be provided in each kitchen for a garbage and trash container.

Garbage Disposal: All kitchen sinks should be equipped with garbage disposals that are fully insulated for sound.

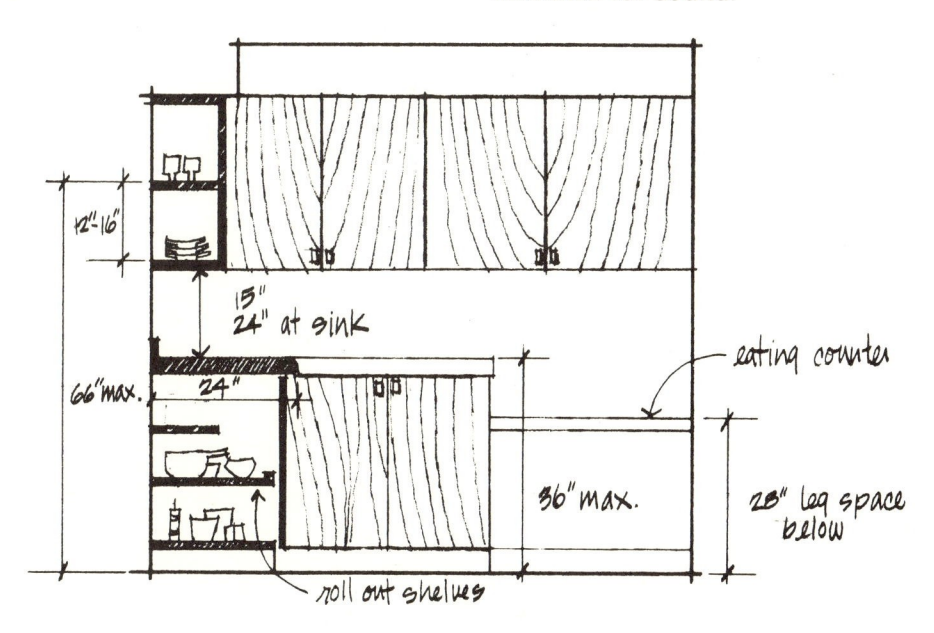

OPTIMUM STANDARDS

The following modifications can be made to optimize kitchen facilities.

Refrigerator: A horizontally shaped refrigerator that is hung on the wall and mounted in the range of 34 to 72 inches greatly improves usability by eliminating stooping.

Cooking Unit and Oven: A separate cook top mounted on the counter and an oven mounted on the wall greatly increase flexibility of placement and enhance functional organization and usability. The cook top should be mounted no higher than 34 inches above the floor, while the oven should be mounted at waist level (that is, the bottom of the oven should be 27 inches above the floor).

Sinks: Sinks should be mounted 34 inches above the floor.

Cabinets, Shelves, Counters, and Closets: Many elderly people tend to develop a stoop and are, consequently, shorter than the average adult. As noted earlier, they also have trouble bending and reaching. Therefore, while maintaining the storage requirement of the minimum standards and increasing the work surface area to 12 square feet, the following changes in location and configuration should be made to optimize storage and work surface facilities.

1. Counter tops should be located 34 inches above the floor. This counter area should be supplemented by some counter area at table height to accommodate light dining and food preparation from a sitting position (4 to 6 square feet). Pull-out counters could provide for this need.

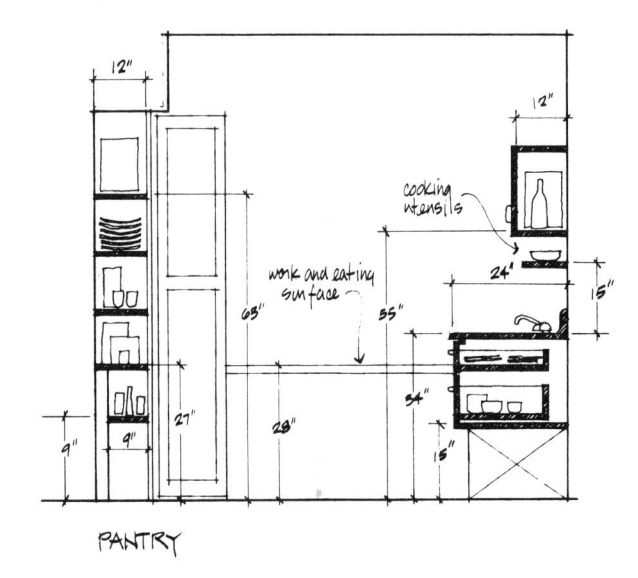

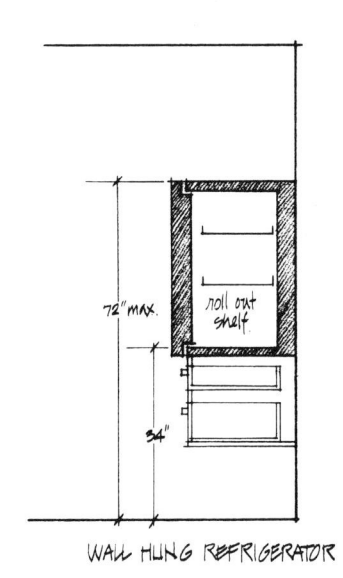

2. Shelves 12 inches or deeper should not be mounted higher than 55 inches above the floor when the shelf is above a counter, or 63 inches above the floor when no counter interferes. Shelves of this depth should not be located lower than 27 inches above the floor.

3. Approximately 50 percent of the kitchen storage space should be provided by pantry cupboards or a closet. Shallow pantry shelves (less than 12 inches) may be mounted as low as 21 inches above the floor.

4. Storage space under counters should be in the form of deep drawers on roller guides rather than cabinets with shelves.

5. Sliding cabinet doors will be substituted for doors of the swing type in the optimally designed kitchen. Where cabinet doors cannot be avoided on cabinets that are 34 inches or higher above the floor, they should be limited to no more than 15 inches in width.

6. All sharp corners and edges will be rounded off cabinet doors.

7. Wall mounted hanging devices for cooking utensils such as pots, pans, large spoons, etc., should be provided at convenient locations.

PERSONAL HYGIENE EQUIPMENT

The following requirements are the minimum equipment specifications for elderly developments; they are also applicable for adoption for use by the handicapped. Each requirement is accompanied by locational and size parameters.

The Lavatory Basin: Each bathroom or lavatory should have a lavatory basin firmly supported to withstand pulling or leaning loads of up to 300 pounds. Vanity cabinets are not recommended as they require excessive stooping and leaning to be used. Vanity counter tops are desirable. Provision for storage should be made in wall hung cabinetry where necessary.

Basins should be of the cantilever type, either wall mounted on chair hangers or mounted in a vanity top. An installation of this kind is more easily used by someone in a wheelchair. The most desirable mounting height for basins will provide a minimum clear dimension below the basin and/or vanity top of 2 feet and 2 inches and place the top of the basin and/or counter 2 feet and 9 inches above the floor. Water taps on basins should be low profile with cross shaped or lever handles. Round knobs should not be used.

The Water Closet: Each bathroom or lavatory should have a water closet with a seat height of 17 inches (the elderly have difficulty with seating and standing motions). If users in wheelchairs are anticipated, the seat height should be 20 inches. Where economically feasible, the water closet should be of the wall hung type for convenience in floor cleaning. The toilet-paper holder should be located in front of or directly at the side of the water closet, in a position where leaning or twisting is not required to use it.

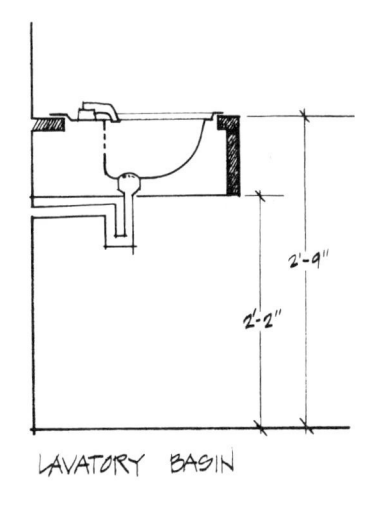

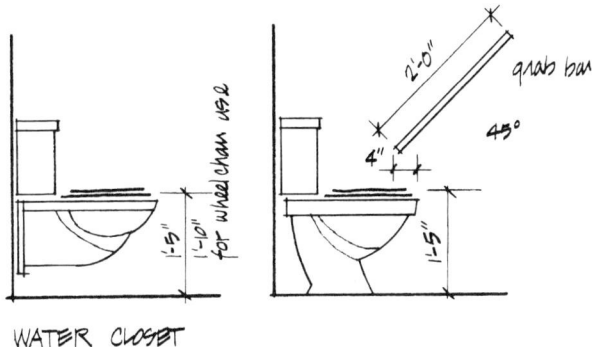

Bath and Shower: The question of whether a bathtub or shower is more desirable has been debated at length. It has been fairly well established that showers are both cleaner and safer than bathtubs, and showers seem to better meet the goal of extending the span of independent living for the elderly. Many elderly persons, however, enjoy and need the therapeutic benefits of a sitz bath. The situation could easily be resolved by providing both a shower and a bathtub in separate installations; however, this is not economically feasible. It seems, therefore, that a compromise is required, that is, a specially manufactured tub/shower combination. This compromise is the recommended solution, although showers will be considered where central bathtubs are provided on each occupied floor (one tub for twenty dwelling units).

Bathtubs should have controls that are easily operated from outside of the tub without excessive leaning or stretching and should include an automatic mixing valve with an upper temperature limit of 120 degrees F. Tubs should have a flat bottom with a non-slip surface. Abrasive tapes and heavy, sharp textures should be avoided. The sides of the bathtub should not be higher than 15 inches and the lengthwise dimensions should not be less than 60 inches.

Soap dishes and similar attachments should be recessed. Water controls should be placed so that they are not a hazard either in normal usage or when the bather slips.

Bathtubs should be equipped with shower heads. The shower head should be adjustable in height and, preferably, detachable with a flexible head. There should be several wall positions for the head to fix it at various heights. Bathtubs should be equipped with a detachable seat which allows the bather to shower sitting down. A grab bar and soap dish, placed at a high level about 51 inches from the bottom of the tub will avoid the necessity to bend down for soap or to use the shower curtain for support when taking a shower. Glass enclosures instead of shower curtains are not advisable as they further restrict getting in and out of the tub.

Where showers are provided instead of bathtubs (that is, where centralized bathtubs are available), they should be of sufficient size to allow the bather to stand or sit outside of the area of the spray while soaping his body. The shower enclosure should be equipped with a folding seat as sitting showers prolong independence for those who either require assistance in standing or who are completely infirm. As mentioned above, the shower head should be variable in height and preferably of the detachable type with a flexible head. The highest shower head position should not exceed 60 inches.

Shower controls should be easily reachable from outside the shower stall and should include both an automatic mixing valve limiting the maximum water temperature at the head to 120 degrees F., and a water temperature testing spout to be used by the bather before entering the shower. The soap dish and grab bar should be conveniently located 51 inches above the floor of the shower. Where technically feasible, the raised entrance curb should be eliminated. If glass is used in the shower enclosure, it should be tempered for safety.

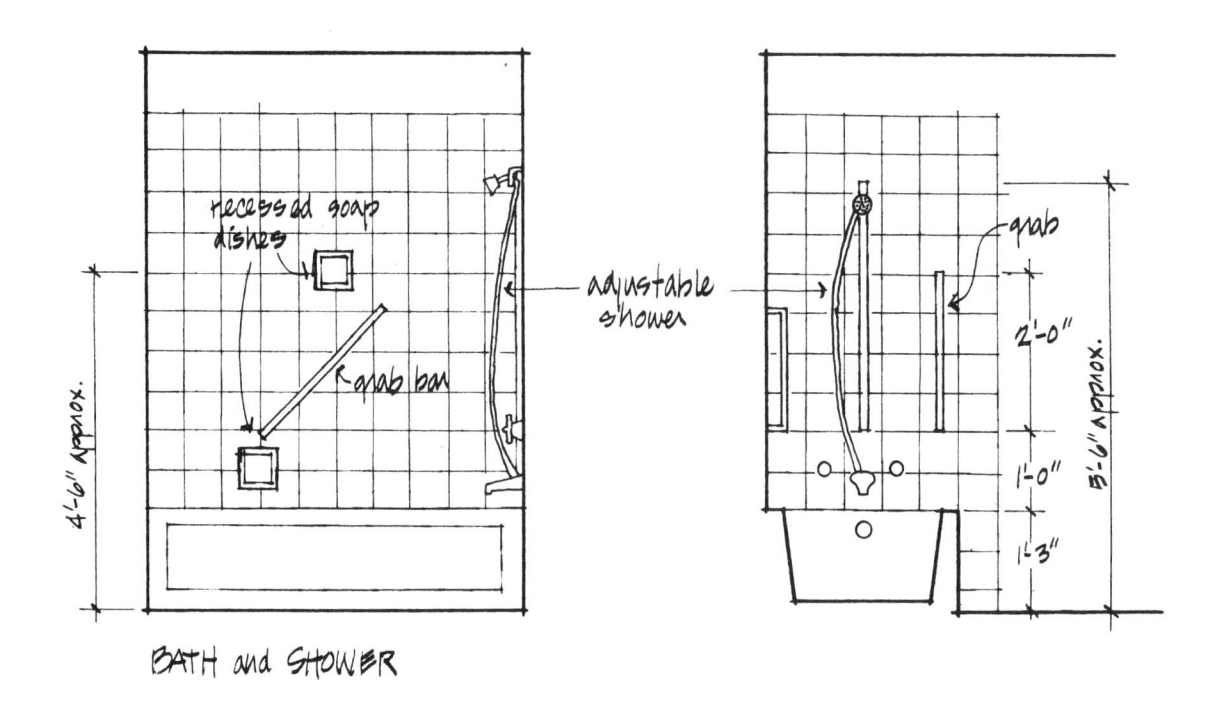

BATH and SHOWER

Grab Bars: Grab bars are generally overused and sometimes bear little relationship to the anatomy of the human body. If improperly located, they not only fail to serve the user but they can also become a hazard if someone should slip. Grab bars should be used judiciously and wherever possible located to serve more than one bathroom position. Bars should be approximately 1 inch in diameter, be capable of withstanding a pulling or hanging load of 300 pounds, and be fixed to structure members rather than to wall finishes or materials. There should be at least one grab bar at the water closet and another in the bathtub or shower, located and in the configuration shown in the accompanying diagram.

Storage and Mirror: The preferred provision for storage needs is a large mirror behind the lavatory (not a medicine cabinet/mirror combination) and a separate storage unit built into a wall large enough to hold both medicine/toiletries and towels. The storage unit should be located so that reaching across counter tops is not required. If towel storage is located externally in a linen closet, the bathroom should have a mirror behind the lavatory and a separate medicine cabinet which is convenient to the lavatory but placed so that excessive reaching is not required.

Electric Outlets: A convenient duplex outlet should be located adjacent to the mirror and lavatory approximately 6 inches above the height of the lavatory and positioned so that reaching across the lavatory or counter top is not required.

MAIL EQUIPMENT

Mailboxes should be large enough to receive magazines, newspapers, and packages of a similar dimension. Mailboxes and their installation should conform to all applicable requirements and standards of the United States Postal Service.

Groups of boxes should not be lower than 30 inches or higher than 56 inches above the floor measured from the bottom of the lowest box to the top of the highest box, respectively.

Each box should be clearly identified for reading both by sight and by touch, with the same identifier (number and/or letter) as the dwelling unit it services. It should also have a slot for a name plate.

Locks on mailboxes should not be of the combination type as the elderly are often forgetful. Wherever economically feasible, mailboxes should be designed to be opened by the dwelling unit key.

EMERGENCY SYSTEMS

Fire alarm equipment bearing the certification of the appropriate agencies should be provided in all residential developments for the elderly. Detailed requirements for alarm equipment are discussed on page 162 of this section.

In addition to the required means of egress as specified by the local fire and building codes, all floors of every building of three or more stories on which some or all of the dwelling units do not have private balconies should be provided with appropriate common balconies placed at central locations and reached from circulation nodes. Balconies have provided an effective means to offset smoke inhalation and suffocation, the single largest cause of death in fire.

All dwelling units should be equipped with emergency call/alarm devices. The minimum acceptable provision is for an alarm button in the bathroom, although another alarm at the side of the bed is also very desirable. If an alarm at the side of the bed is not feasible, placing the telephone at the side of the bed should be the minimum requirement.

Depending upon the type of accommodation and the particular development, the alarm button should be used for one or all of the following purposes.

1. Sounding an alarm in the management office and the manager's apartment or in another such location where staff assistance may be available

2. Activating a light signal outside of the front door of the apartment (buzzers should not be used because they may create havoc)

3. Unlocking the dwelling unit access door (desirable but not mandatory)

All signaling devices based upon sound should emit both low and high frequency sounds.

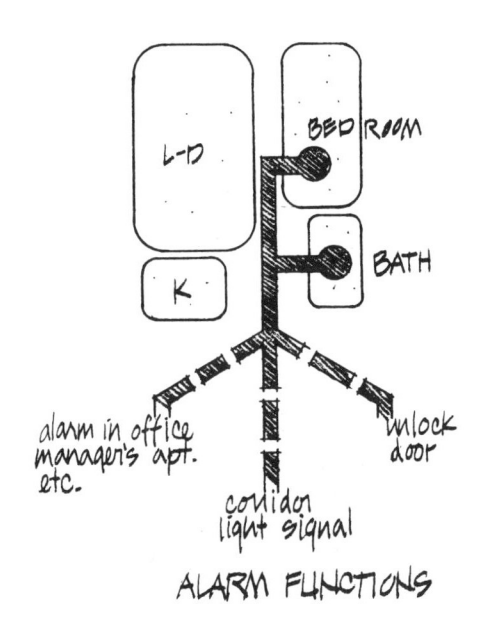

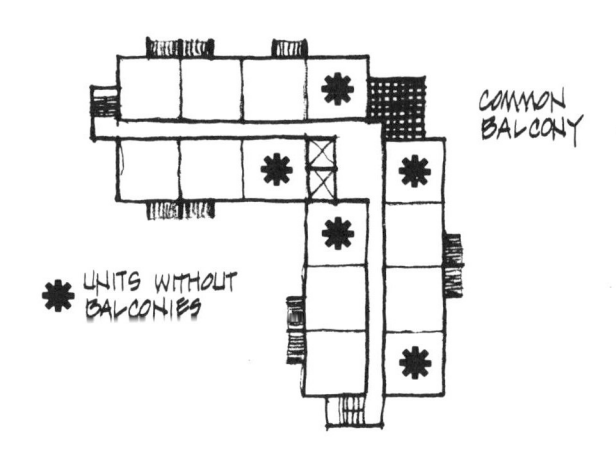

MECHANICAL SYSTEMS

The objectives of this subsection are to outline requirements for mechanical systems, and to prescribe guidelines that will minimize the possibility that an unacceptable system will be installed. The intent is to provide mechanical equipment which is appropriate for the type, size, plan, and construction of the development and to insure that it is designed and installed to assure safety of operation; protection from moisture, corrosion, or other destructive elements; of reasonable durability, economy of maintenance; proper capacity and quality for its intended use; and free from objectionable sound.

This subsection includes by reference the most current recommendations of the American Society of Heating, Refrigerating and Air Conditioning Engineers (ASHRAE), whether specifically stated or not. All other local and state requirements should also be met.

All mechanical equipment should be installed so that maintenance and replacement can be performed without the removal of other equipment. Clearance around boilers, pumps, and other equipment should be provided for operation, maintenance, repair, replacement, and removal from premises. Clearance should not be less than that recommended by the manufacturer. Piping connections to equipment should be made with the valves, unions, or flange fittings necessary to permit their repair or removal without causing damage to piping or equipment.

PLUMBING

Water piping should be sized to eliminate noises in the piping. Piping should be sized to eliminate scalding at showers. Temperature and pressure compensating shower valves are recommended. A down feed water supply system for buildings requiring a water booster pressure system is recommended, although it is recognized that this must be coordinated with the "rent-up" plan for the development. Lower levels should be up fed from city main pressure. Hot and cold water shut off valves for each living unit should be provided so that the piping within each unit can be isolated without affecting the supply to other units. A "look see" access panel to all pipe spaces should be provided. All cold water piping and horizontal portions of rain conductors should be insulated. Expansion loops in hot water piping should be provided. Expansion joints should be avoided.

FIRE PROTECTION

The requirements for fire alarm systems in buildings are discussed on page 162 of this section. In addition to a fire alarm system, the entire building may be provided with an automatic sprinkler system.

Where portions of a building are to be used for the storage of, or contain a workshop involving, highly combustible and flammable materials, a one-source sprinkler system should be provided.

Public and private garages located within or partly within buildings having living units on the floor above should be equipped with an automatic sprinkler system.

Automatic sprinklers are recommended in all areas of egress.

An automatic sprinkler system should be of a standard approved type and installed to provide complete coverage of all portions of the building being protected. The installation should conform to the standards of the National Fire Protection Association as set forth in NFPA No. 13, *Standards for the Installation of Sprinkler Systems.*

HEATING

Unless otherwise indicated, calculations of heat loss shall be made in accordance with the data and procedures contained in the *ASHRAE Guide and Data Book.*

Where boilers are used, a heating system serving twenty or more living units should be supplied by not less than two parallel, connected boilers. Each of the two boilers should have a net capacity of not less than 70 percent of the connected load. When three boilers are provided, each should have a net capacity of not less than 35 percent of the total connected load. When four or more boilers are provided, each should have a net capacity directly proportionate to its equal share of the total connected load. When the heating system is the source of domestic hot water, multiple boilers should be provided.

All heating systems should be designed so that each living unit has at least one thermostat to control space temperature.

Heating systems should be provided with a heating control system designed to vary the amount of heat provided to maintain indoor temperatures at design conditions in response to fluctuations of outdoor temperatures.

Heating systems should be designed to assure freedom from drafts when the outside air design temperature is less than 40°. Systems should be designed to introduce heat low at the exterior walls.

Perimeter radiation, low wall, sill, or floor supply air registers are recommended. Low wall, sill, or floor returns are considered acceptable.

Stacked fan coil systems and vertical furnaces with high supplies should be located at outside walls between two rooms. Return air registers should be located low to draw air from each room. Perimeter radiation may be required if a third room with an outside wall is served by the same fan or furnace unit. Perimeter radiation may be electric and may be a future consideration providing the electrical systems are designed so that the radiation can be installed without additional electrical work.

Horizontal fan coil systems located away from the outside wall and supplying air overhead will require perimeter radiation as outlined above for stacked fan coil and furnace systems.

VENTILATION

When mechanical ventilation to assure air movement for summer comfort is provided in lieu of through or cross ventilation, 10 changes per hour of supply or exhaust air for the living unit should be provided.

1. The system design should be such that air supplied to or exhausted from each room should move across the room to provide air circulation between an open window and the room air inlet or outlet.

2. The system may be (1) individual, serving each living unit, (2) group, serving a group of living units, (3) central, serving all the living units.

3. The system, whether individual, group, or central, should be such that air supplied or exhausted from each living unit is controlled by the occupant by means of a readily accessible and operable damper or switch.

4. Dust filters for all air supply systems should be provided.

5. Screened weatherproof louvers should be provided for all vent openings in exterior walls and similarly exposed locations.

The volume of air removed from a living unit by exhaust ventilation should be replaced by at least an equal amount of fresh air. Replacement air should be filtered, heated, and, when summer air conditioning is provided, it should be cooled.

The following requirements apply to systems that are designed to allow make-up air via infiltration and from the corridor through a normally fitted door:

1. Ductless kitchen exhaust hoods should be used instead of a central exhaust fan.

2. Individual toilet exhaust fans should be used instead of a central exhaust fan.

3. Make-up air from the corridor through a normally fitted door should be a maximum of 30 CPM. This air should be 100 percent outside air, filtered, heated, and, when summer air conditioning is provided, it should be cooled.

4. Make-up air via infiltration together with make-up air through a normally fitted corridor door should equal the quantity of air exhausted from the toilets. Sufficient operating sashes and/or doorwalls should be provided to insure adequacy of make-up air. Calculations should be based on normally fitted doors and windows. Living unit heating and cooling calculations should include infiltration loads.

Make-up air may be supplied to and through a smoke tight ceiling space above the corridor with transfer to living spaces through fire dampered corridor wall openings.

If the ceiling space above the corridor is used for make-up air, care should be taken to eliminate sound transfer from living space to living space on the opposite side of the corridor and living space to corridor.

The minimum air volume requirements for rooms or spaces to be provided with mechanical ventilation should be as follows:

1. Kitchen—8 air changes per hour of exhaust ventilation for hood type exhaust and 12 air changes per hour for ceiling and wall exhaust fans or registers

2. Bathrooms—8 air changes per hour of exhaust ventilation

3. Public entrance spaces—4 air changes per hour of supply ventilation

4. Public corridors—4 air changes per hour of supply ventilation (exhaust ventilation may be through rooms such as janitor closets, laundry room, etc.)

Corridors should not be used as supply or return air plenums for apartment ventilation except when make-up air for living units is allowed to pass from corridor to living unit through a normally fitted door.

Central exhaust fans should be selected for quiet operation and mounted on a sound attenuating curb. Sound curb may be eliminated if 10'-0" minimum acoustically lined ductwork plus two acoustically lined elbows are installed between the fan connection and all exhaust registers. Exhaust shafts and ducts must be sized and arranged to allow for easy air balancing. Individual ceiling or wall exhaust fans should be selected for quiet operation and should be top of the line quality for living units. Exhaust ductwork should be carefully sized to suit fan capacity at rated static pressure. Exhaust terminated at outside wall louver should be approved if the louvers are located away from balconies, doors, and operating sash. Wall louvers should be equipped with a back draft damper. Exhaust, if routed to a vertical shaft, should be arranged to eliminate sound transmission from unit to unit.

AIR CONDITIONING

All common spaces such as lounges, meeting rooms, game rooms, and associated corridors should be air conditioned. All other occupied spaces, if not air conditioned, should be designed to allow for the easy addition of air conditioning in the future.

Although living unit air conditioning may not be a project requirement, the mechanical and electrical equipment should be sized for the addition of air conditioning in the future. All equipment such as condensate drain pans and piping, capped and valved pipe connections, and future equipment space allowance should be provided. The following requirements pertain to peak load calculations.

The design temperatures used should be:
1. The inside design temperature for dwelling units and occupied ancillary and common spaces should be 75 degrees F.
2. The outside design temperature should be 95 degrees F.

Acceptable System Types

1. System No. 1 uses perimeter radiation for heating and through the wall electric air conditioning units. Through the wall air conditioning units should be arranged to supply no more than two rooms with the addition of ductwork.

The following should be provided if through the wall units are planned for air conditioning in the future:

a. Wall sleeves for future air conditioning units should be provided.

b. Drain piping for air conditioning unit pan drainage should be provided.

c. The electrical system should be designed with space and spare capacity for future air conditioning with an outlet near the through the wall unit for easy connection.

2. System No. 2 uses gas, oil, or electric furnace/air conditioner (all air) with sheet metal ductwork to the floor, wall, or ceiling air outlets.

The following should be provided if individual furnaces are used and the addition of condensing units is planned for air conditioning in the future:

a. The electrical system should be designed with space and spare capacity for future air conditioning with an outlet near the furnace for easy connection.

b. The furnace should be sized for future air conditioning with provisions for the easy addition of a condensing section.

c. Drain piping for the pan drainage of the air conditioning unit should be provided.

3. System No. 3 uses two-pipe stacked fan coil units with summer to winter change over control and sheet metal ductwork to the floor, wall, or ceiling air outlets. A four-pipe system is preferable, however.

The following should be provided if fan coil systems are used and future air conditioning is to be provided by remote refrigeration equipment:

a. Insulated water distribution piping should be provided.

b. Fan coil units sized for air conditioning should be provided.

c. An air conditioning unit pan drainage system should be provided.

d. All supply ductwork should be insulated and should include a vapor barrier as required for future air conditioning.

e. Areas should be designated for future refrigeration equipment such as chillers, pumps, cooling towers, etc.

f. The mechanical equipment room and structure should be sized to accommodate the future equipment.

g. The design of the electrical system should include provisions for spare capacity and space in the mechanical room for the addition of central air conditioning equipment in the future.

h. The design of the electrical system should provide spare capacity in branch circuit panels and outlets located to accommodate fan coil units in the future.

4. System No. 4 is an electro-hydronic system with sheet metal ductwork to floor, wall, or ceiling air outlets. The system should be complete with a boiler or a heat exchanger and a closed circuit cooler to provide tempering of the heating/cooling medium. Only the cooler may be deleted from this system when air conditioning is not part of the initial construction.

5. Heat pump systems may be used where applicable.

General Conditions

1. One watt per square foot minimum allowance should be provided for lighting, cooking, and equipment loads.

2. Cooling equipment should be selected to satisfy sensible cooling requirements.

3. Credits may be taken for drapes, venetian blinds, etc., when they are included in the building design.

4. Storage affect may be considered.

5. Subcooling to 70 degrees F. may be considered.

6. Infiltration and make-up air should be considered.

7. Heating and air conditioning systems that are able to take advantage of diversity factors such as east-west solar variations and internal load swing are recommended.

When air conditioning is a project requirement, the capacity of the air conditioning equipment should be full size.

All air conditioning systems should be designed in conformance with the criteria contained in the *ASHRAE Guide and Data Book.*

The capacity of equipment should not be less than the calculated heat gain under indoor and outdoor design conditions.

Calculation of heat gain should be made in accordance with the *ASHRAE Guide and Data Book,* standards of the Air Conditioning and Refrigeration Institute (ACRI), or other recognized and acceptable methods.

ELECTRICAL SYSTEMS

The objective of this subsection is to outline requirements for the electrical systems and to prescribe guidelines that will minimize the possibility that an inadequate system will be installed. The intent is to provide electrical service which is essential and appropriate for the type, size, and construction of the development and which is designed and installed to assure safety of operation; reasonable durability, economy of maintenance; and adequate illumination for efficient operation of appliances and equipment as well as adequate capacity and utility for its intended use.

All recommendations herein include the National Electric Code (NEC), Occupational Safety and Health Administration (OSHA) — United States Department of Labor, state fire marshal, and state health department whether specifically stated or not.

ELECTRICAL

Installation should comply with the requirements of the National Electric Code.

A spare circuit capacity of 25 percent over the calculated load for service entrance conductors and electrical equipment should be provided.

No electrical equipment, lighting panels, cabinets, etc., should be located in bath, wash or toilet rooms, clothes or linen closets.

LIGHTING OUTLETS

Public stairways and public hallways should be evenly illuminated to provide a minimum of six footcandles "maintained," and doubled at building and stair entrances or change of floor level or at slopes.

Parking areas, walkways, and yard spaces should be evenly illuminated to provide a minimum of one footcandle "maintained." Outdoor lighting is discussed on page 133 of this section.

Permanent lighting fixtures, wall switch controlled, should be installed in kitchen ceilings (150 watt minimum) and over sinks (100 watt minimum), dining areas (200 watt minimum), bathrooms (150 watt minimum), private halls (75 watt minimum), passageways and stairways (100 watt minimum). Lighting should be placed in corridors so that room or unit doors, signs, keyholes, etc., are clearly illuminated.

All permanent lighting fixtures for exterior doorways, balconies, and patios should have a minimum capacity of 100 watts. If a receptacle is installed on a patio or a balcony in lieu of a lighting fixture it should be provided with ground fault protection.

Multiple switch control should be provided at main levels for all stair lighting, basements, second levels, and attics. These lighting outlets are not to be counted as comprising any of the required outlets in these areas.

Permanent lighting fixtures should be installed in utility rooms, public recreation rooms, community rooms, and other areas requiring general illumination, wall switch controlled, with a minimum of one lighting fixture in each 200 square feet or major fraction of this area.

Permanent lighting fixtures should be installed in garages and basements with a minimum of one lighting fixture in each 200 square feet or major fraction of this area for general illumination.

Permanent lighting fixtures should be installed in laundry rooms, wall switch controlled, with a minimum of one lighting fixture in each 200 square feet or major fraction of this area. A separate permanent lighting fixture, pull chain controlled, should be provided to illuminate laundry trays or appliances when provided.

A permanent, flush-mounted night lighting fixture located between the bed and the bathroom, switched at the door, should be provided. Night lights should be mounted no more than 2 feet above the floor.

In all medium- and high-rise buildings, when insufficient natural sunlight is available in main and elevator lobbies to sustain indoor plant life, artificial grow lights should be installed. In main lobbies such installations should cover at least 30 square feet of floor area. In elevator lobbies at least 10 square feet of floor area should be served. These lights should be located to serve plants located at both the floor plane and at table top height.

EXIT SIGNS AND EMERGENCY LIGHTING

All buildings should have exit signs provided in accordance with the requirements of the state fire marshal.

Access to exits should be marked in all cases where they are not immediately visible to the occupants. Every exit sign should have the word "EXIT" in plain, legible letters not less than 6 inches high, with the principal strokes of letters not less than three-quarters of an inch wide and should be illuminated with not less than 5 footcandles.

Any building with more than 25 living units should have emergency exit lighting for every public space, corridor, stairway, and other means of egress. Emergency exit lighting should be provided in accordance with the standards of the National Fire Protection Association as set forth in NFPA No. 101.

The emergency exit lighting system should be arranged to provide the required illumination automatically in the event of any interruption of normal lighting such as public utility or other outside electrical power supply failure, opening of a circuit breaker or fuse, or any manual acts, including the accidental opening of a switch controlling normal lighting facilities.

RECEPTACLES

In bathrooms a duplex receptacle should be installed adjacent to the mirror or wash basin, not less than 30 inches and not more than 60 inches above the floor and rated 15 amperes, 125 volts.

Basements, utility rooms, laundry rooms, and attics should have at least one duplex receptacle installed. This receptacle is not to be counted as comprising any of the required outlets such as for washing machines, furnaces, etc.

Unfinished attic space adaptable for living which is accessible by permanent stairs should be provided with at least one duplex receptacle which should be wired on an independent circuit.

Halls, corridors, passageways, etc., should have at least one duplex receptacle for each 50 linear feet of hall length.

Kitchens should have at least one of the required duplex receptacles installed not less than 30 inches or more than 60 inches above the floor, rated 15 amperes, 125 volts.

In housing for the elderly, receptacles should be mounted not less than 2 feet above the floor.

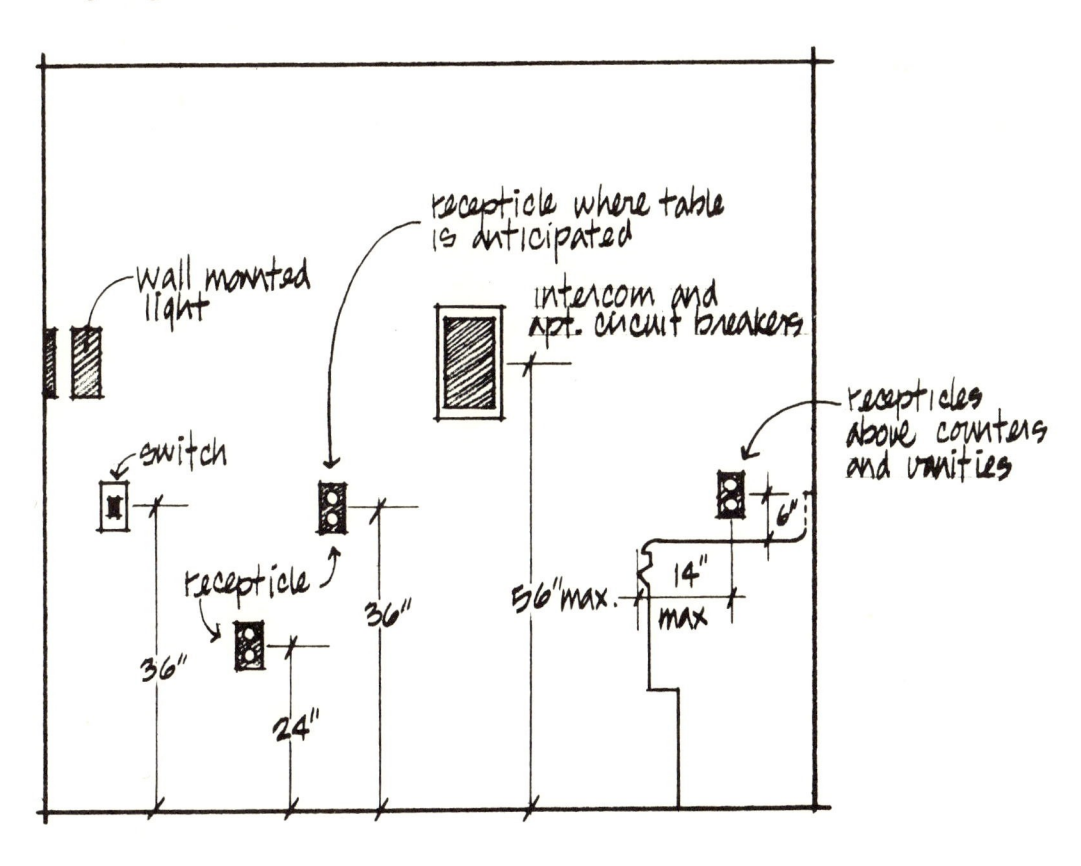

BRANCH CIRCUITS

No branch circuits should be connected to serve more than one apartment.

Maximum allowable wattage per branch circuit for residential aplication only should be 1,320 watts on No. 14 AWG and 1,800 watts on No. 12 AWG.

At least two 20 ampere circuits should be provided to serve the receptacle outlets in kitchen and dining room areas. At least three of the required kitchen receptacle outlets should be readily accessible. These receptacles should be divided on the small appliance circuits.

Circuits supplying fixed or stationary appliances or motors of 1/3 HP or 600 watts rating, or greater, should supply only such motors or appliances.

At least one 20 ampere branch circuit should be provided for laundry receptacle(s). This includes situations where laundry facilities are within the dwelling unit.

At least one individual branch circuit of not less than 15 ampere capacity should be installed for heating units in dwelling units. A disconnect switch should be mounted on the exterior of the furnace or on a surface adjacent to the furnace.

Kitchens should be provided with a receptacle outlet under the sink with an independent disconnect switch mounted in the wall adjacent to the sink for the use of garbage disposals.

DOOR ENTRANCE INTERCOM SYSTEM

Each building should be provided with a door entrance intercom system. The main door directory should include name slots, push buttons for each living unit, and a speaker or telephone handset.

Living unit speakers should have talk, listen, and door release push button controls.

ELECTRIC PROVISIONS FOR AIR CONDITIONING

When a fan coil system is used and central air conditioning is to be provided in the future by remote refrigeration, spare capacity in electrical panels and wired outlets to accommodate future fan coil units should be provided. Space provisions and spare capacity in the electrical panels designated for the addition of central air conditioning equipment should be made.

When furnaces are used and the addition of condensing units is planned for air conditioning in the future, the space and spare capacity in the electrical panel should be provided.

When through the wall units are planned for the addition of air conditioning in the future, space and spare capacity in the branch circuit panel and a wired outlet near the unit should be provided.

FIRE ALARM SYSTEMS

All buildings should have fire protection systems provided in accordance with the requirements of the state fire marshal.

Every building of eight or more living units, in which each unit does not have direct access to the exterior at grade level, should be equipped with a manual fire alarm system. Each floor should have at least one or more manual fire alarm boxes and sounding devices at visible points in the natural paths of escape from fire and near each exit from a fire compartment.

Buildings of four or more stories should have an alarm system which transmits an alarm automatically to either the fire department or to a 24 hour monitoring service. An annunciator which indicates the fire floor should be located at a central point within the building.

Buildings of eight or more stories should have a zoned, non-coded alarm system that sounds an alarm on the fire floor, the floor below the fire floor, and the floor above the fire floor, and provisions at the central monitoring point to activate a general fire alarm.

Buildings containing more than eight living units per floor should be divided into at least two fire compartments by a one-hour fire rated wall containing a three-quarter-hour fire door with a closure and holder activated by a smoke detector.

All fire alarm systems should be electrically supervised and fed from the building emergency service.

Not less than one automatic smoke detector, which may be a single-station alarm device, should be installed in each living unit near the sleeping areas.

All smoke detectors that control fire doors should automatically initiate a general fire alarm when activated.

Fire alarms, smoke detectors, and extinguishing equipment should be listed by a nationally recognized testing laboratory that maintains periodic inspection of production of listed equipment, and whose listing states either that the equipment meets nationally recognized standards or has been tested and found suitable for use in a specified manner.

Smoke detectors should comply with Underwriters Laboratories (UL) No. 168 for photoelectric type detectors and UL No. 167 for ionization type detectors.

All smoke detectors should be permanently mounted to a standard electrical outlet box on or adjacent to the ceiling. Those which activate fire doors may be incorporated in the door closer.

Installation of fire alarm and extinguishing systems should be in accordance with the standards of the National Fire Protection Association as set forth in NFPA No. 72A for fire alarm systems and NFPA No. 13 for sprinkler systems.

STRUCTURAL SYSTEMS

Such factors as initial cost economy, maintenance costs over the useful life of the structure, durability, fire resistance, flexibility of occupant usage, and appearance also must be considered in the selection of the structural system. There are presently a myriad of structural systems available to designers, most of which offer various advantages. Designers must always strive to obtain a system which offers the optimum solution to the specific engineering problem, particularly for larger or higher structures. A suggested approach to system evaluation is provided here.

SELECTION OF SYSTEMS

The table below represents a systems analysis procedure.

The structural systems which may be suitable for use on any particular project are to be entered across the top of the table. Obviously, many systems may be immediately rejected for various reasons and only those systems which offer a possible usage should be considered.

A partial list of factors which may influence the selection of the structural system is tabulated down the side of the table. This list attempts to define the structural systems in terms of the project function, size, location, and the specific requirements thereof under which the system must perform.

By consideration of the various factors, many systems may be immediately rejected as unsuitable for use. Many of the factors listed are satisfied by several systems with varying degrees of suitability.

It is suggested that the systems which appear to have merit after an initial review and rejection of unsuitable systems be ranked on a numerical comparison basis to assist the designer in his final selection of the structural system.

The structural designer should at all times consider his system relative to the overall project. The most economical structure does not always result in the most economical project. Items 7e and 7f are intended to cause the effective consideration of the structure relative to all other building trades. For example, will the most economical floor system used create hardships on the mechanical system or cause increased floor to floor dimensions, thereby causing a large increase in the cost of mechanical and architectural trades?

FACTORS TO BE CONSIDERED IN THE SELECTION OF THE STRUCTURAL SYSTEM

Factors to be considered \ Structural System							
1. Usage of structure (housing, storage, etc.)							
2. Structure area							
3. Number of stories							
4. Applicable local codes							
5. Soil conditions							
a. Are heavy dead loads problem?							
b. Is soil of variable type requiring rigid or flexible structure?							
c. Water table elevations							
1. Are basements problem?							
2. Construction difficulties?							
6. Site conditions							
a. Rolling site - are structures stable to resist one sided soil surcharges?							
b. Are soil washouts possible?							
7. Construction phase							
a. Availability of structural materials?							
b. Availability of skilled labor?							
c. Speed and ease of construction							
d. Initial construction cost							
e. Interface with other construction materials							
f. Interface with other systems							
8. Service phase							
a. Anticipated useful life							
b. Fire resistance							
1. Code requirements							
2. Judgement							
c. Insect and rot resistance							
d. Resistance to thermal stresses							
e. Resistance to shrinkage							
f. Resistance to vibration							
g. Resistance to sound							
h. Maintenance costs							
i. Insurance rates							
9. Structural red lights							
a. Has progressive collapse been considered?							
b. Has snowdrift in roof valleys and at adjacent roof elevations been considered?							
c. Have stresses at all stages of construction been accounted for?							
10. Other specific factors							
a.							
b.							
c.							
d.							

6
resources

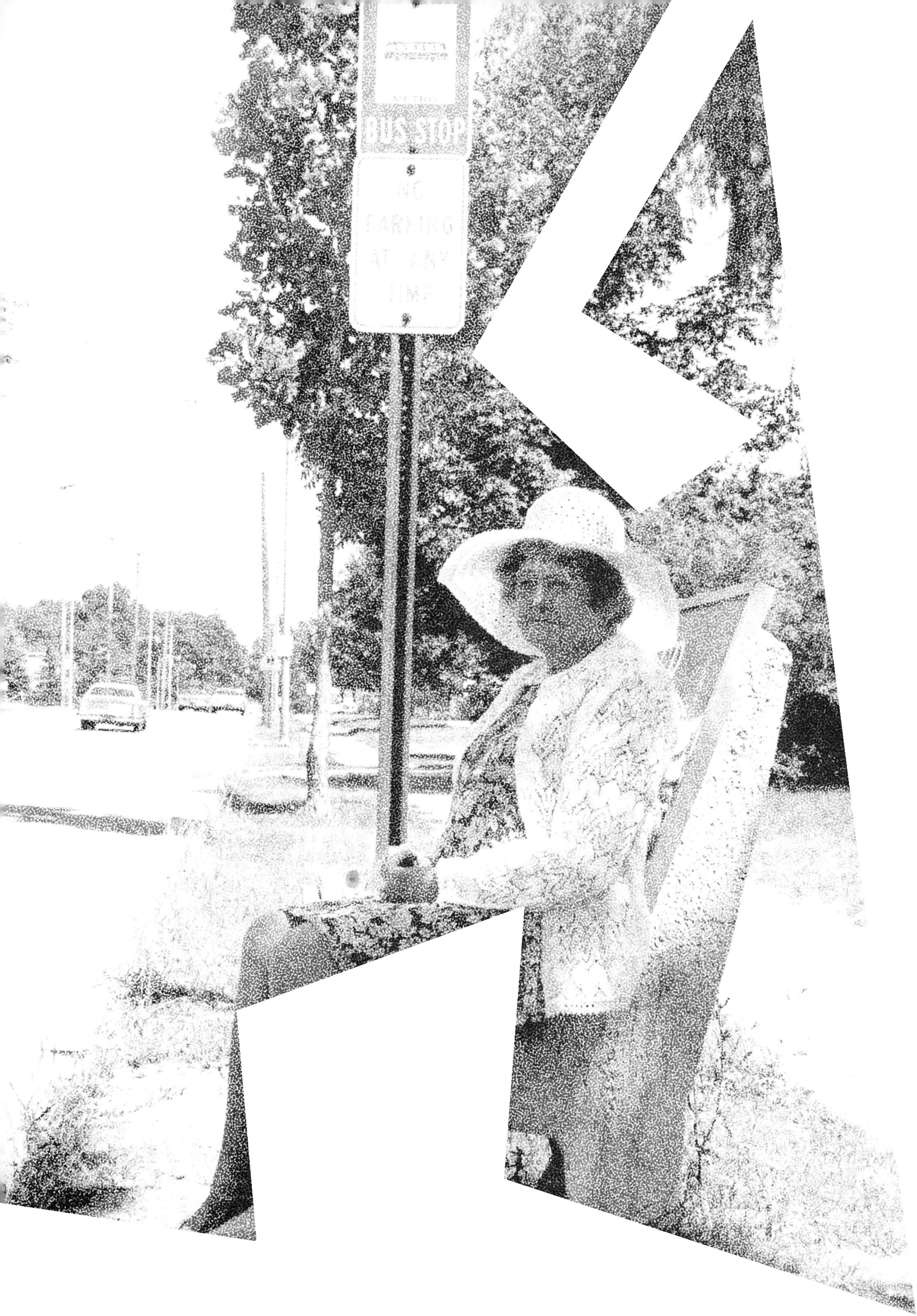
BUS STOP
NO PARKING AT ANY TIME

resources

BIBLIOGRAPHY

Adams, Michael J. *The Elderly and Their Environment: A Pilot Inquiry into Senior Citizens' Housing Satisfaction.* Ottawa: Central Mortgage and Housing Corp., April 1972.

"Alternatives to Fear." *Progressive Architecture,* October 1972, p. 92.

Ashley / Meyer / Smith, Architects / Planners. *Housing for the Elderly, Research and Study.* Cambridge, Mass.: Fall 1971.

ASHRAE Guide and Data Book: Applications, 1971. New York: American Society of Heating, Refrigerating and Air-Conditioning Engineers, 1971.

ASHRAE Guide and Data Book: Equipment, 1972. New York: American Society of Heating, Refrigerating and Air-Conditioning Engineers, 1972.

ASHRAE Handbook of Fundamentals. New York: American Society of Heating, Refrigerating and Air-Conditioning Engineers, 1973.

ASHRAE Handbook and Product Directory: 1973 Systems. New York: American Society of Heating, Refrigerating and Air-Conditioning Engineers, 1973.

Atchley, Robert C. *The Social Forces in Later Life: An Introduction to Social Gerontology.* Belmont, Calif.: Wadsworth Publishing Co., 1972.
Carefully organized overview of latest research in the field.
> See especially part four, "Societal Response to the Aging," including chapters 16 on "Community" and 18 on "Primary Relationships: Family, Friends and Neighbors."

A Barrier-Free Environment for the Elderly and the Handicapped. Hearings before the Special Committee on Aging, U.S. Senate, 92nd Congress, 1st Session, Part 2, October 19, 1971. Washington, D.C.: Government Printing Office, 1972.

The Built Environment for the Elderly and the Handicapped, a Bibliography. Washington, D.C.: U.S. Department of Health, Education, and Welfare, June 1971.

Burgess, Ernest W., ed. *Aging in Western Societies.* Chicago: University of Chicago Press, 1960.

Encyclopedia review of model programs and services for the elderly in European countries.
> See especially chapter V, "Housing and Community Services," by Wilma Donahue.

Byerts, Thomas, and Conway, Donald, eds. "Behavioral Requirements for Housing for the Elderly." Report of conference held by American Institute of Architects, Association for the Study of Man-Environmental Relations, Gerontological Society, and National Tenants Association, June 1972, Washington, D.C.

Carson, Daniel H., and Pastalan, Leon A. *Spatial Behavior of Older People.* Ann Arbor: University of Michigan Press, 1970.

Day, Suzanne. *Directory of Retirement Homes and Nursing Homes.* Newark, Delaware: University of Delaware, June 1972.

Donahue, Wilma, ed. *Housing the Aged.* Ann Arbor: University of Michigan Press, 1954.

ElSamahy, Catherine M. *Population Characteristics of Delaware's Elderly.* Newark, Delaware: University of Delaware, June 1972.

Goldsmith, Selwyn. *Designing for the Disabled.* 2nd ed., rev. New York: McGraw-Hill Book Co., 1968.

Guide Criteria for the Design and Evaluation of Operation Breakthrough Housing Systems, vol. 2, "Multifamily Low Rise." Washington, D.C.: U.S. Department of Commerce, National Bureau of Standards, September 1970.

Guide to Elderly Housing and Related Facilities. Washington, D.C.: U.S. Department of Health, Education, and Welfare, October 1971.

Hochschild, Arlie Russel. *The Unexpected Community.* Englewood Cliffs, N.J.: Prentice-Hall, 1973.
Detailed study of social aspects of retirement housing in a San Francisco project.

"Homing in on Housing." *Architectural Forum,* November 1972, p. 42.

Housing the Elderly: Design of the Unit. Ottawa: Central Mortgage and Housing Corp., 1970.

Jacobs, Jane. "Housing for the Independent Ages." *Architectural Forum,* August 1958, p. 86.

Larsson, Nils. *Housing the Elderly.* 2nd ed. Ottawa: Central Mortgage and Housing Corp., 1972.

Lawton, M. Powell. *Public Behavior of Older People in Congregate Housing.* Philadelphia: Philadelphia Geriatric Center, n.d.

Lewis, Jerome R., dir. *Housing Delaware's Elderly: Findings and Recommendations.* Newark, Delaware: University of Delaware, June 1972.

———. *Programs to Aid Housing for the Elderly.* Newark, Delaware: University of Delaware, June 1972.

Liebman, Theodore; Brown, Joseph E.; and Wolf, A. Edwin. "Housing Design Criteria." New York: New York State Urban Development Corp., unpublished paper.

Locational Criteria for Housing for the Elderly. Philadelphia: City Planning Commission, December 1968.

Loether, Herman J. *Problems of Aging: Sociological and Social Psychological Perspectives.* Encino, Calif.: Dickenson Publishing Co., 1967.
Short, concise summary of basic elements in social gerontology.
See chapter 4, "Housing."

McGuire, Marie C. *Design of Housing for the Elderly: A Checklist.* Washington, D.C.: National Association of Housing and Redevelopment Officials, October 1972.

———. "Social Concepts in Retirement Housing." Paper presented at International Apartment Conference, National Association of Housing and Redevelopment Officials, October 7, 1970, Washington, D.C.

Macsai, John, AIA. *High Rise Apartment Buildings, A Design Primer.* Chicago: Published by the author, 1972.

Maxwell, Jean. *Center for Older People.* Washington, D.C.: National Council on the Aging, 1962.

Minimum Property Standards, Housing for the Elderly with Special Consideration for the Handicapped, HUD PG 46, Washington, D.C.: U.S. Department of Housing and Urban Development, Federal Housing Administration, 1971.

Minimum Property Standards for Multifamily Housing. Washington, D.C.: U.S. Department of Housing and Urban Development, Federal Housing Administration, 1971.

Mission, Noverre, and Heisinkveld, Helen. *Buildings for the Elderly.* New York: Reinhold Publishing Corp., 1963.

Neugarten, Bernice L., ed. *Middle Age and Aging: A Reader in Social Psychology.* Chicago: University of Chicago Press, 1968.
Excellent collection of articles with an emphasis on contributions from the social-psychological perspective.
See especially part VII, "The Immediate Social Environment"; chapter 42, "Housing and Local Ties of the Aged," by Irving Rosow; chapter 45, "Effects of Improved Housing on the Lives of Older People," by Frances M. Carp.

"New Life in Retirement Communities." *Business Week,* July 8, 1972, p.70.

Newman, Oscar. *Defensible Space: Crime Prevention Through Urban Design.* New York: Macmillan Co., 1972.

Pastalan, L., and Carson, D., eds. *Spatial Behavior of Older People.* Ann Arbor: The University of Michigan Press, 1970.

"Provisions for Housing for the Elderly." New York: New York State Urban Development Corp., unpublished paper.

Rich, Thomas A., and Gilmore, Alden S. *Basic Concepts of Aging: A Programmed Manual.* Washington, D.C.: U.S. Department of Health, Education, and Welfare, 1972.
Programmed learning approach to cover basic information in gerontology.
    See especially chapter 9 on "Housing."

Robbins, Ira S. *Housing the Elderly: 1971 White House Conference on Aging.* Washington, D.C.: Government Printing Office, 1971.

Schulz, David A. *A Survey of Delaware's Elderly Living in Public Housing for the Elderly.* Newark, Delaware: University of Delaware, June 1972.

Scott, Frances C., ed. *Perspectives in Aging: Operational Focus.* Continuing Education Publications, 1971.
Useful articles on the practical aspects of social programs for the elderly.
    See especially part VI, "Special Problems of the Urban Elderly"; chapter C, "The Aged in Cities," by James E. Birren; chapter E, "How Trained Managers Can Add Life to Retirement Facilities," by Marie McGuire.

Section Recommendations on Housing: 1971 White House Conference on Aging. Washington, D.C.: Government Printing Office, 1971.

The Seventh Age: A Bibliography of Canadian Sources in Gerontology and Geriatrics, 1964-1972. Ottawa: Central Mortgage and Housing Corp., 1972.
    This present volume is a classified, partially annotated, indexed bibliography drawing together 1,217 references in the field of aging.

Staats, Elmer B. *Comparison of Costs under Sections 202 and 236 for Housing Projects for the Elderly.* Washington, D.C.: General Accounting Office, 1972.

Tibbitts, Clark, ed. *Handbook of Social Gerontology: Societal Aspects of Aging.* Chicago: University of Chicago Press, 1960.
Comprehensive review and classification of housing approaches for the elderly in the United States.
    See especially part Three, "Aging and the Reorganization of Society"; chapter XVI, "Housing and Community Settings for Older People," by Walter K. Vivrett.

Toward a National Policy on Aging, 1971: A Report on Michigan's Preparations for the White House Conference on Aging. Lansing: Michigan Commission on Aging, Department of Social Services, 1971.

U.S. Department of Health, Education and Welfare. *Population, Housing and Income, and Federal Housing Programs: 1971 White House Conference on Aging.* Washington, D.C.: Government Printing Office, 1971.

Weiss, Joseph Douglas. *Better Buildings for the Aged.* New York: Hopkinson and Blake, 1969.

Working with Older People, vol. 2. Washington, D.C.: U.S. Department of Health, Education, and Welfare.

Zeisel, John. "Symbolic Meaning of Space and the Physical Dimension of Social Relations Paper presented to American Sociological Association, Annual Meeting, September 1, 1969.

RELEVANT ORGANIZATIONS and EDUCATIONAL CENTERS

NATIONAL ORGANIZATIONS

American Association of Homes for the Aging
374 National Press Building
14th & F Streets, N.W.
Washington, D.C. 20004

American Nursing Home Association
1200 15th Street, N.W.
Washington, D.C. 20005

Gerontological Society
Suite 520, 1 Dupont Circle
Washington, D.C. 20036

International Center for Social Gerontology
425 13th Street, N.W.
Washington, D.C. 20004

National Council of Senior Citizens
1511 - K Street, N.W.
Washington, D.C. 20005

National Council on the Aging
1828 - L Street, Suite 501
Washington, D.C. 20036

National Retired Teachers Association
American Association of Retired Persons
1225 Connecticut Avenue, N.W.
Washington, D.C. 20036

EDUCATION CENTERS

All University Gerontology Center*
Syracuse University
926 South Crouse Avenue
Syracuse, New York 13210

Center for Studies in Aging
North Texas State University
Denton, Texas 76203

Commission on Human Development
University of Chicago
Chicago, Illinois 60637

Florence Heller Graduate School
Brandeis University
Waltham, Massachusetts 02154

Gerontology Center*
University of Southern California
University Park
Los Angeles, California 90007

Institute on Aging
Portland State University
P.O. Box 751
Portland, Oregon 97207

Institute of Gerontology*
University of Michigan—Wayne State University
Ann Arbor, Michigan 48104

Rocky Mountain Gerontology Program
Social and Behavioral Science Building
Salt Lake City, Utah 84112

Gerontology Program
School of Public Affairs and Community Service
University of Nebraska
Omaha, Nebraska 68101

Aging Studies Program
College of Social and Behavioral Sciences
University of South Florida
Tampa, Florida 33620

Center for the Study on Aging and Human Development
Duke University Medical Center
Durham, North Carolina 27706

Program in Gerontology
Teachers College
Columbia University
New York, New York 10032

Adult Development and Aging
College of Human Development
The Pennsylvania State University
University Park, Pennsylvania 16802

* Programs with emphasis on both aging and environment.

INDEX

Acoustic control
    technical standards for, 144-45

Activity areas
    definition of, 7
    minimum requirements of, 22-23
    organization of, design examples, 90

Air conditioning
    electric provisions for, 162
    requirement of, 27
    technical standards for, 158-59

Amenities
    discussion of, 27

Ancillary facilities
    illustration of, 57
    maximum space allowed for, 20, 24
    minimum requirements of, 23-24

Architectural terms
    definition of, 6-9

Arrival court
    parking spaces required in, 53
    requirements of, 51, 53

Balconies, common
    design requirements of, 68
    requirement of, 23-24
    space requirements for, 23

Balconies, private
    design requirements of, 71, 87-88
    minimum sizes of, 20
    percentage of units containing, 20
    space calculated in activity area, 7

Bathroom, *see* Personal hygiene area

Bedroom, *see* Sleeping/dressing area

Building
    circulation, technical standards for, 138-42
    entry/exit, design requirements of, 57, 58-60, 130
    maintenance, design requirements of, 57, 63
    service, design requirements of, 51, 54, 63

Building types
    high-rise
        advantages of, 113
        limitations of, 113
    low-rise
        advantages of, 114
        limitations of, 114
    medium-rise
        advantages of, 113
        limitations of, 113

townhouses
    advantages of, 115
    limitations of, 115

Carpeting
    requirement of, 27

Carports
    as suggested amenity, 27

Ceilings
    height, technical standards for, 146
    surface, technical standards for, 147

Central food service
    design requirements of, 57, 63-64
    spatial requirements of, 24

Common facilities
    average space allotted for, 20
    coordination to community, 25-26
    design requirements of, 57, 66-67
    illustration of, 57
    locational requirements of, 66
    minimum requirements of, 26
    purpose of, 25
    spatial requirements of, 26

Common outdoor, *see* Outdoor common area

Community/region
    definition of, 30
    planning conditions for, 32
    services, clustering of, 31

Corridors
    design requirements of, 105-6
    technical standards for, 138-39

Design
    determinants
        categories of, 111-12
        site types, 110-12
    of development, criteria for, 109
    expression
        building massing and character, 116-19
        criteria for, 116, 118, 119
        illustration of, 117-18, 119

Development density
    density ratio, definition of, 6
    livability, function of, 43
    open space, area comparisons of, 16, 17

Development size
    maximum number of units, 14
    minimum number of units, 14
    outsized one-bedroom units, percentage of, 14
    two-bedroom units, percentage of, 14

Development team
    functions of, 2
    participants in, 2

171

Dining area, dwelling unit
  design requirements of, 71, 76-77

Dwelling unit area
  definition of, 7
  design organization of, 90
  percentage of larger than standard units allowed, 14
  size ranges of, 18-20

Dwelling unit mix
  determined individually, 14

Efficiency ratios
  building, 127
  dwelling unit, 127

Elderly needs
  examination of, 10-13
  human needs, as related to aging process, 46-49
  site, as related to, 29

Electrical outlets
  requirements for, 161-62

Electrical system
  technical standards for, 160

Elevators
  requirement of, 141
  technical standards for, 141

Emergency systems
  technical standards for, 154

Entry/exit
  building, design requirements of, 57, 58-60, 130
  development, design requirements of, 52-53
  dwelling unit, design requirements of, 71, 72
  service facilities, requirements of, 54, 57, 63
  site, technical standards for, 130

Fire alarm equipment
  technical standards for, 162

Fire protection
  technical standards for, 156

Floor surfaces
  technical standards for, 147

Food preparation area
  design requirements of, 71, 73-75
  equipment, 74
    minimum standards for, 148-49
    optimum standards for, 150

Furniture, outdoor
  design requirements of, 53, 126
  technical standards for, 133

General living area
  design requirements of, 71, 78-81

Grading
  advantages of, 123-24
  illustration of, 124
  technical standards for, 130

Health care, see Medical facilities

Heating
  technical standards for, 156-57

Housekeeping assistance
  design requirements of, 57, 65
  minimum requirements for, 24

Housing types, definitions
  dependent elderly, 13
  independent/dependent mixed, 13
  independent elderly, 12
  independent elderly/family mixed, 12-13

Indoor communal activities zone
  definition of, 92
  design organization of, 101-4
  functions of, 101
  illustration of, 92, 101, 102, 103, 104

Indoor/outdoor contact zone
  definition of, 92
  design organization of, 99-100
  illustration of, 92, 99, 100

Intercom system
  requirements for, 162

Kitchen, see Food preparation area

Landscape development, 120-26

Laundry
  design requirements of, 57, 61
  minimum requirements of, 23, 24
  spatial requirements of, 23, 24

Lighting
  indoor
    emergency requirements for, 161
    minimum requirements for, 160
  outdoor
    advantageous uses of, 125
    illustration of, 125
    technical requirements for, 133

Living room, see General living area

Lounge area, building
  design requirements of, 58-60

Mail and package delivery facilities
  design requirements of, 57, 62
  mailboxes, technical standards for, 153
  minimum space requirements for, 23

Management office
  design requirements of, 57, 60

minimum space requirements for, 23

Manager's apartment
    minimum requirements for, 23

Master key, dwelling units
    requirement of, 142

Measurement standards
    definition of, 6-9

Medical facilities
    off-site
        required availability of, 32
    outpatient, on-site
        design requirements of, 57, 65
        spatial requirements of, 24

Natural light and ventilation
    technical standards for, 143
        windows, 143
        draperies, 143

Neighborhood
    definition of, 30
    small town, 33, 37
    suburban, 33, 36
    urban, 33, 34

Neighborhood/development contact zone
    definition of, 91
    design organization of, 94
    functions of, 94
    illustration of, 91, 94

Outdoor area, private
    design requirements of, 87-88;
    also see Balconies, private

Outdoor common area
    definition of, 6, 91
    design organization of, 96-98
    design requirements of, 57, 68
    functions of, 95, 126
    illustration of, 91, 95, 96, 97, 98
    minimum spatial requirement of, 15

Parking
    area requirements of, 51, 54
    arrival court, spaces required in, 53
    minimum spatial requirements of, 15
    ratios, required to dwelling units, 15
    security lighting for, 54, 133
    technical requirements for, 132

Patios
    design requirements of, 87-88

Paving
    technical standards for, 131-32

Personal hygiene area
    design requirements of, 71, 85-86

equipment, 85
    minimum standards for, 151-53

Planting, site
    advantages of, 120, 123, 126
    height classifications of, 120
    illustrations of, 120-23
    limitations of, 120
    maintenance of, 121
    technical standards for, 132

Plumbing
    technical standards for, 155

Ramps
    technical standards for, 140

Recreation facilities, indoor, *see* Common facilities

Recreation facilities, outdoor; *also see* Furniture, outdoor
    design requirements of, 51, 55
    required provision of, 51, 55
    technical standards for, 133

Refrigerator, frost free
    as suggested amenity, 27

Residential zone
    definition of, 93
    design organization of, 105-7
    function of, 105
    illustration of, 93, 105, 106, 107

Room area, *see* Activity area

Service area
    requirements of, 51, 54

Signs
    building exit, requirements of, 136
    criteria for use of, 135
    indoor, technical standards for, 137
    outdoor
        advantageous uses of, 126
        technical standards for, 136

Site
    adjacent land uses
        restrictions on, 32, 44
        visual impact of, 44
    availability of services
        desirable services defined, 40
        mandatory services defined, 40
        neighborhood topography, requirements of, 38, 39
        proximity requirements of, 38-40
        walking distances defined, 40
        walkway system defined, 38, 39
    barrier-free, requirement of, 126
    configuration, desirable, 43

cultural facilities, proximity requirement of, 32
definition of, 30
density, 16, 17
distribution of elderly housing, limitations on, 41
ecology, illustration of, 43
frontage, requirements of, 42
location of, restrictions on, 44
open space, area comparisons of, 16-17
small town, definition of, 33, 37
spatial requirements of, criteria for, 15
suburban, definition of, 33, 36
topography, slope requirements of, 43
urban, definition of, 33, 34
walkways, technical standards for, 132

Site entry/exit
requirements of, 51, 52

Site types
external, 110, 112
internal, 111, 112

Sleeping/dressing area
design requirements of, 71, 82-84

Slopes
illustration of, 39, 43
percentage requirement of, 39, 43, 130

Social service facilities
design requirements of, 57, 65
spatial requirements of, 24

Stairs
technical standards for, 140

Storage, tenant
design requirements of, 71, 89
minimum space requirements for, 23

Stove
self-cleaning oven, as suggested amenity, 27

Structural systems
technical standards for, 163-65

Supportive public services
design requirements for, 57, 65

Telephones, public
special adaptation of, 65

Toilets, public
minimum space requirements for, 23

Townhouse Development Process, 87, 93, 101, 131

Trash disposal and service
design requirements for, 57, 63
technical standards for, 134

Ventilation
technical standards for, 157-58

Walkways
illustration of, 39
technical standards for, 132

Wall surfaces
technical standards for, 147

Windows, *see* Natural light and ventilation

A Blueprint for Action

Preparing for Aging in Holland

REPORT CARD TO THE COMMUNITY

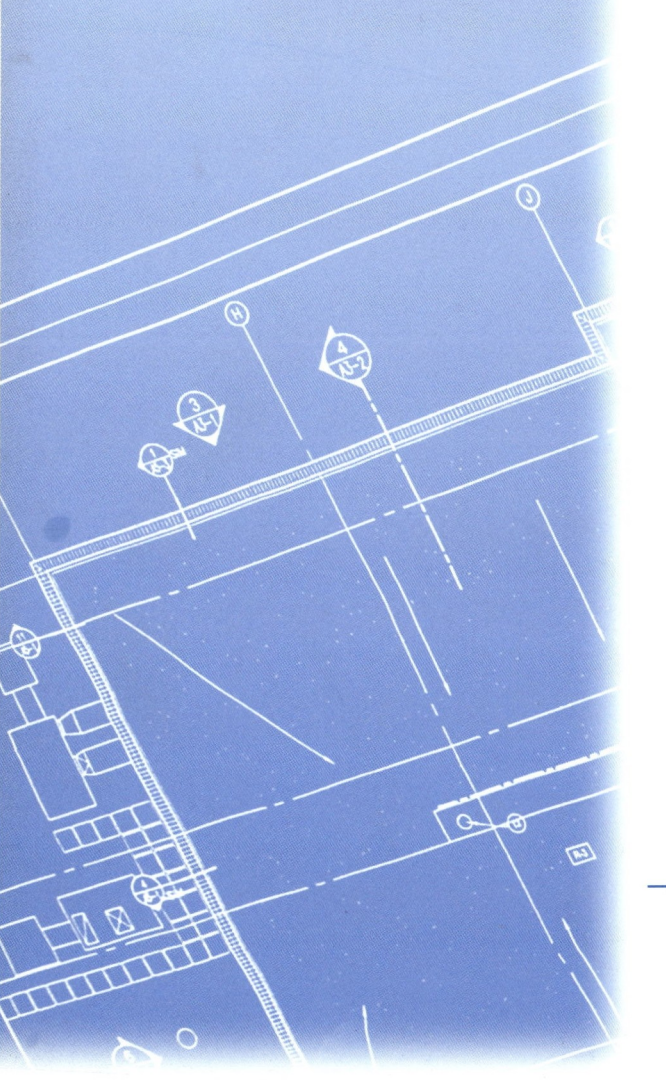

OUR MISSION
To assess Holland's readiness for a growing older adult population and present to the community a blueprint for collaborative action.

OUR VISION
Holland is an accessible and affordable community where ALL older adults live fully and are:
- Safe and comfortable.
- Engaged in a continuum of lifelong opportunities for community engagement and leisure activities.
- Supported by a caring community network which addresses basic needs, mental and physical well-being, and encourages independence.
- Empowered to make their own decisions.

Presented by the
Blueprint for Action Steering Committee
June 2009

ABOUT THE PROCESS

Communities across the nation have begun assessing their readiness for the rapidly growing older adult population. Resthaven Care Community and Evergreen Commons wanted to guarantee that Holland remained on the leading edge of services to older adults.

In the spring of 2008 Resthaven applied to the Community Foundation of the Holland/Zeeland Area for a grant to complete an assessment of the City of Holland. A Steering Committee was formed and selected a Michigan-based model for its assessment tool. Hundreds of questions were divided into five focus areas for study. Volunteers were recruited to lead and participate in workgroups that answered the questions in each focus area. The results were analyzed, summarized, prioritized and are contained within this Report Card.

The goal of the Report Card is to report back to the community a summary of findings and to present recommendations, with the anticipation that other groups will flesh out these recommendations and move them forward. Listed below are the community assests and pressing issues identified by the workgroups during the process. Two overarching recommendations were identified by the workgroups: The need for inclusion and the need for expanded coordination. Recommendations about those issues appear on page 3. Recommendations from the individual workgroups are summarized on pages 4 through 6.

ASSETS

In 2006, *Money Magazine* identified Holland as one of the top five small cities in which to retire...and we agree. Holland has an incredible structure for supporting older adults in retirement. We can credit city leaders and community members who have gone before us for making decisions which created the supportive community in which we live. Committee members cited the many parks, bikeways and walkways which allow us to enjoy the natural beauty of the area. Many community amenities such as the library, Aquatic Center, museums, symphony and the many festivals are amazing resources for a community the size of Holland. Senior-focused resources such as Evergreen Commons, Hope Academy of Senior Professionals, and many senior living options enrich the lives of many older adults. Community attributes such as increasing diversity, the philanthropic and volunteer nature of the community, a faith-based willingness to come together to solve community problems, and the capacity of social service agencies to work collaboratively, all make the City an attractive community. The City itself was the recipient of much praise during our process. The current Mayor is visible in the community and an unfailing advocate for the community. City staff is viewed as accessible and willing to problem-solve. Neighborhood services and community policing are seen as assets, as is the ability to generate social capital toward resolving community issues.

PRESSING ISSUES

Pressing issues were identified during the assessment and form the basis for the project's recommendations. The process was conducted during the most severe economic downturn since the depression. Many have lost a considerable part of their financial safety net. For seniors the significant loss of the dollars saved for retirement is huge. The economic crisis, while severe, is considered transitory and beyond the scope of this report. It is clear though, that in receiving services as an older adult, money matters. We must work to assure more equitable opportunities at all economic levels.

RECOMMENDATIONS
- ### Inclusion

Founded by Dutch immigrants with a strong work ethic and a commitment to faith, Holland has attracted families of various backgrounds who have been drawn to the community by its lifestyle, work ethic, community values and job opportunities. Even though the diversity of our community has increased, much work needs to be done for our community to be fully inclusive.

1. Develop, adopt and implement a proactive and intentional plan to integrate persons of various faiths, colors, national origins, languages, ages, and abilities into the fabric of the community.
2. Prepare for the continuing shift in demographics to a less Caucasian community.
3. Cultivate diverse individuals for decision making and leadership positions throughout the community.
4. Develop cultural competency within our senior-serving agencies. Agencies must deliver services that are desired by various cultures, and must provide access that is culturally sensitive.
5. Benchmark best practices from other communities which are truly inclusive.

- ### Coordination / Communication / Clearinghouse

In all of the workgroups, two issues became apparent: There are many things happening in Holland that could benefit older adults (and others), but many people do not know about these options and there is no single point to learn about these options. Activities available in the community are often listed by the organization but not found on a "community calendar". The community has a wonderful array of services for seniors, but knowing where to obtain information and how to select between available services or providers can be challenging for seniors and their family members. The concept of having a single point to access information and/or community activities would help consumers identify the resources available in the community.

1. Develop a "senior focus" within the City of Holland and include the needs of seniors in the City's Master Plan.
2. Create a "Senior Council" to facilitate/increase coordination among senior-focused service providers.
3. Identify and promote a gateway (or several) to access senior services, and assure the agency(ies) serving in this role is able to expand to meet the increased demand for service.
4. Coordinate access to community volunteer opportunities.
5. Foster county-wide cooperation to develop and support an array of services for older adults.
6. Develop better strategies for communicating with seniors that can be inclusive of levels of technological sophistication as well as cultural and language differences.
7. Create a central communication port for activities in the community.

HEALTHY, ACTIVE AND ENGAGED AGING

It is critical both to the community and the individual that older adults continue to be engaged in the community and to remain active in their older years. It is critical that older adults remain disease free and active for as long as possible, and to have the supports they need to both engage in their community and to have access to a supportive health care system. The community benefits when older adults continue to contribute to their community.

Recommendations

1. Develop strategies to assist individuals to plan for the aging process beginning at as young an age as possible.
2. Develop resources to assist older adults in planning for their future, including all aspects of their life, not just financial planning. How does one want to age?
3. Assist the senior-serving community in using technology to its fullest in serving older adults; and assist older adults in gaining competency using technology. Encourage community-wide use of electronic health delivery systems to better support older adults and others.
4. Increase community supports for those struggling with Alzheimer's and dementia, both patients and their caregivers.
5. Develop/expand systems that provide patient advocacy and assist older adults in navigating such systems.
6. Assure adequate, accessible, and affordable mental health and substance abuse services for older adults.
7. Sustain and invest in opportunities and assets for active lifestyles.
8. Expand opportunities for older adults to serve on community boards.

HOUSING

Having appropriate housing for each stage of life is important to the well-being of older adults. While there is a growing trend toward "aging in place" this concept is only successful when there are adequate and reliable services that can be maintained over time to support older adults in their own home. Currently there are numerous services to help the older adult remain at home, however, services most widely available are those which the older adult pays for in full. Considerably more difficult is accessing those services which are free or reduced in price. It was clear during the Blueprint process that, with money, all things are possible. Without financial resources older adults could well find themselves living in isolation without access to the most basic needs. Many older adults have chosen to move to retirement communities that provide a range of living options that can support them as needs change. Still others would prefer to live in proximity to a family member but may be prohibited from occupying a "granny flat" that could provide them this proximity to a relative.

Recommendations

1. Conduct a thorough study of current housing options and the anticipated need for those options given the increasing number of older adults in the community. Consider cultural preferences which might well dictate preferences in living arrangements.
2. The City of Holland should examine current zoning ordinances and restrictions through the lens of supporting seniors as they age in place, or as they choose to live with a loved one.
3. Develop a thorough understanding of the resources needed to keep persons safely and happily living on their own as they age. Identify gaps in the needs for accessible and affordable in-home services.
4. Identify the financial resources necessary to provide the services needed to assist older adults to live safely in their own homes as they age. Services must be affordable to the older adult using them, must be sustainable over time, and must be expandable to meet the growing need in the community.
5. Develop affordable places to live with proper assistance when people cannot live in their own homes.

PUBLIC/COMMUNITY INFRASTRUCTURE

The public/community infrastructure is all of those things available in the public sector which enhances the quality of our lives. These supports are often taken for granted but are necessary for people of all ages to live successfully in the community. We are fortunate in our community to have many of the basics needed for seniors to thrive: a community with parks, a thriving downtown, a walkable community.

Recommendations

1. Transportation
   a. Expand the MAX bus services to better support older adults, including providing off-hour service to community events.
   b. Develop transportation services to meet the needs of older adults—such as a person needing assistance at a destination.
   c. Develop more parking that is accessible to community events; perhaps remote parking with shuttle services to the center of the activity.
2. Planning
   a. Encourage special emphasis on the needs of seniors in public/commercial design.
   b. Encourage a review of zoning requirements with sensitivity to senior housing needs, considering interest in accessory buildings or "granny flats" to assist families in caring for older family members.
   c. Develop a non-motorized plan for the city.
3. Commerce
   a. Encourage businesses that will provide in-neighborhood resources (grocery stores, etc.)
   b. Encourage commercial developments to be aware of senior needs.
4. Safety
   a. Utilize various methods to communicate safety alerts and other community notices in order to reach seniors who may not use newer technology.
   b. Develop a coordinated system for identifying/monitoring seniors living alone.
   c. Encourage programs to educate seniors and their families about personal safety and security.
   d. Promote programs such as "mail carrier alert" and utility shut off notification programs to enhance security for older adults.

NEXT STEPS

To reach our vision we are inviting interested parties to join a Senior Council/Strategy Coalition led by Resthaven and Evergreen Commons. This Council will be charged with continuing the work of the Blueprint for Action project. Specific early action items include:

- Develop a collaborative effort to encourage individual planning for the "third age".
- Maintain heightened community awareness of both the needs and assets of the community's older adults and how to both engage and support them.
- Develop sustainable funding streams for services for older adults through grants and philanthropic endeavors.
- Develop an intentional inclusion plan for the community and assist service providers in increasing cultural competency.
- Encourage the marketing of the livability of our community for older adults.
- Increase awareness of the many assets in our community and the need to support those assets.

To join this effort contact:
Charlie Vander Broek at Resthaven
Phone: (616) 796-3500, Email: charlie.vanderbroek@resthaven.org
Larry Erlandson at Evergreen Commons
Phone: (616) 355-5152 , Email lmerlandson@evergreencommons.org
Copies of this report are located at www.resthaven.org/about.html, www.evergreencommons.org, or www.ottawaunitedway.org

Blueprint for Action

APPRECIATION

Thank you to those who contributed time and effort to this project!

Financial or In-Kind Contributors

John Canfield
Darell and Mary Schregardus

- community foundation Holland/Zeeland Area
- Evergreen Commons
- RAYMOND JAMES & ASSOCIATES, INC. Member New York Stock Exchange/SIPC
- PriorityHealth
- Resthaven

The Steering Committee

Charlie Vander Broek, Co-Chair • Resthaven
Larry Erlandson, Co-Chair • Evergreen Commons
Donna Cornwell, Project Coordinator
Mark de Roo • Resthaven
Norma Killilea • Community Volunteer
Tom Ludwig • Hope College
Phil Meyer • City of Holland
Jinnifer Ortquist • MSU Extension
Celia Serrano de Martinez • Community Volunteer
Selden Smith • Community Volunteer
Peg VanGrouw • Community Volunteer

Committee Members

Abby Reeg	Gray Gogolin	Leroy Hernandez	Sandy Keirnan
Amy Alderink	Greg Holcombe	Linda Falstad	Selden Smith
Annette Vandenheuvel	Greg McCoy	Linda Felder	Sharon Rocker
Barb Burmeister	Greg Robinson	Linda Jacobs	Steve Stickel
Barb VerCande	Haans Mulder	Lisa Stefanovsky	Susan DeJong
Bart Jonker	Herb Weller	Liz Vanderby	Susan Lassa
Becky Israels	Ilse Saewert	Loren Snippe	Tamra Bouman
Beth Hunt	Jack Hyde	Lorma Freestone	Theresa Westerlund
Bill Raymond	Jackie Kleinheksel	Lou Hallacy	Thun Champassak
Bill Vanderbilt Sr.	Jerry Tonini	Lupita Reyes	Tim Hemingway
Bin Lim	Jim Bussis	Lyn Raymond	Tom Wolterink
Bob Krueger	Jo Ver Beek	Lynne Bonnette	Torrey Husmann
Carla Masselink	Jodi Castillo	Marcia Westrate	Tricia Cranmer
Cathy Blackburn	Jodi Syens	Mark de Roo	Vern Boersma
Charles Vander Broek	Jody Gogolin	Mark Kornelis	Walter Thome
Charles Veldhoff	Joe Silva	MaryAnn Knowles	Will Ehmann
Chris Hofland	Joel Dye	Matt Messer	
Christiana Getz	John Buttrey	Michael Bochs	
Curt Bush	John Nordstrom	Michael Zywicki	Thank you to the older adults
Dave Ellens	John Vega	Micki Janssen	who participated in focus groups
David Beattie	Judy Parr	N. Linnea Freriks	at Evergreen Commons.
Deb Salguero	Karen Draeger	Nancy Fazio	
Deb Wilson	Kathleen Lord	Nancy Frens	
Denise Stancill	Kay Hubbard	Nancy Rock	
Domingo Hernandez	Kay Walvoord	Norma Killilea	
Eileen Nordstom	Kelli Perkins	Peg VanGrouw	
Ella L. Weymon	Lamont Dirkse	Phil Meyer	
Fennetta Raymond	Larry Erlandson	Poema Weller	
Fronse Smith	Larry Johnson	Rob Pocock	
Gene Welch	Laurie Miedema	Roberto "Bert" Jara	
George Zuidema	Len Fazio	Ruth Dirkse